A   TRAILS BO

WISCONSIN
Gardens &
Landscapes

To Helen —
Don't forget to stop
and smell the roses!
Mary Lou Santovec
with
Rick S.

MARY LOU SANTOVEC
with RICK SANTOVEC

TRAILS BOOKS
Madison, Wisconsin

Library of Congress Control Number: 2008900648
ISBN: 978-1-931599-89-4

Editor: Mark Knickelbine
Cover and interior design: Rebecca Finkel
Photos: All photos by Rick Santovec unless noted
Cover Photo: Joe DeMaio

Printed in China through World Print LTD

13   12   11   10   09   08   6   5   4   3   2   1

TRAILS BOOKS
a division of Big Earth Publishing
923 Williamson Street • Madison, WI 53703
(800) 258-5830 • www.trailsbooks.com

Dedication

TO PAT,
for the meals, e-mails, and conversations
that have kept body, mind, and soul together.

TO MARY DEE,
for taking a chance on a novice writer several decades ago
and continuing to have faith in my skills.

TO DORIS,
for her patience, cheerleading,
and guiding hand in helping me hone my craft.

TO STEVE,
for his words of wisdom, encouragement,
and moral support throughout life's challenges.

TO MARYALICE KOEHNE,
whose initial idea sparked this book.

TO MY MUSE AND MY ANGELS
by believing in me you gave me my voice.

AND TO RICK,
for his unconditional love and support.
Without his photographic talents, keen insights,
and superb driving skills, this book would not be what it is.

Table of Contents

Wisconsin

Southeast Wisconsin

Acknowledgments

As with any guidebook, I would be remiss if I didn't acknowledge the many individuals who have contributed to this project. It would not be what it is without their help. I would like to thank the following people for their time, assistance and above all, their willingness to share their knowledge with me.

Brenda Abendschein, Durham Hill; Jeff Adams, Riverside Park; Betty Adelman, Heritage Flower Farm; Diana Alfuth, UWEX Pierce County; Amber Anderson, Spooner Agricultural Research Station; Karen Anderson, Rice Lake International Friendship Association; Constance Arzigian, UW-La Crosse; Nancy Ashby, Prairie du Chien Chamber of Commerce; Lisa Ashley, Read's Creek Nursery; Gina Bailey, Kenosha Parks Department; Thomas J. Bare, West Foundation; Nancy Barker, Smith Park; Dave Barrett, Angel of Hope Garden; Lucy Basler, Sacred Grove; Judy Bausch, Yerkes Observatory; Mary Bauschelt, UW Botany Greenhouses; Jim Beard, Fox Valley Technical College; Jeff Becker, Wildwood Park and Zoo; Bill Beckman, State Capitol; Michael Beeck, John Michael Kohler Arts Center; Pete Bemis, UW-La Crosse; Nancy Benninghouse, Firefly Garden Design; Eva Berry, Villa Terrace; Kasey Benson, Sacred Heart Hospital; Liz Beyler, UW Communications; Kathy Blake, Curiosities; Tara Blazer, Black Point Historic Preserve; Liz Beyer, UW-Communications; Pat Blakely, Leigh Yawkey Woodson Art Museum; Kathy Blankenburg, Gardening Angel; Kelly Boeldt, Kohler Company; Ron Boley, House on the Rock; Pat Borcherding, Iowa County Master Gardeners; Phyllis Both, UWEX-Sauk County; Cheryl Bowen, Troha Gardens; Mary Braunreiter, Boerner Botanical Gardens; LeeAnn Briese, Salem Community Library; Laura Briskie, Menominee Park; Kim Bro, Northland College; Christine Brown, Tomahawk Regional Chamber of Commerce; Phil Brown, South Wood County Historical Corporation; Sara Bryan, Phoenix Park; Dennis Buettner, Dennis Buettner and Associates; Dave Burke, The Florian Gardens; Rudy Bushcott, City of Fort Atkinson; Barb Canne, Down to Earth Garden Center; Ruth Carlson, The Angel Museum; Keith/Laura Carlson, Blue Vista Farm; Sarah Carlson, St. Mary's Hospital; Marcia Carmichael, Old World Wisconsin; Susan Carpenter, Wisconsin Native Plant Garden; Joyce Cielecki, UWEX LaCrosse County; Christopher Clark, Village of Howard; Jerry Clark, UWEX Chippewa County; Kitty Clark, DeKoven Center; Greg Cleerman, Marinette Land and Water Conservation; Kathleen Cloyd, DeKoven Center; Susan Connor, The Flying Pig; Mary Helen Conroy, researcher extraordinare; Christopher Cook, Hudson Hospital; Kyle Corbett, Dickeyville Grotto; Helen Corbett, Chippewa Falls Lily Garden; Mike Counter, St. Norbert College; Scott Craven, Kemp Natural Resources Center; Jim Crothers, Grand Geneva Resort; Aliesha Crowe, UWEX Rusk County; Zannah Crowe, Monches Farm; Marilyn Cunningham, The Crossroads at Big Creek; Sharon Cybart, Olbrich Botanical Garden; Loris Damerow, Riverside Park; Mary Daniel, Hawks Inn; Carla David, Ministry Health Care; Randi Danner, Dr. Kate Hospice; Chriss Daubner, Door County Master Gardeners; Michael Davis, Montesian Gardens; Michael Day, Aurora Medical Center; Virginia Dell, UW-Green Bay; Len Demert, Grant County Master Gardeners; Wouterina "Riana" De Raad, Riana's Garden; Debbie DeGroot, Plymouth Chamber of Commerce; Mary Devitt, Cross Plains Garden Club; Roy Diblick, Northwind Perennial Farm; Rosemary Divock, Horticultural Hall; Shirley Dommer, Boerner Botanical Garden; Sarie Doverspike, Prairie Nursery; Carolyn Dressler, Kneeland-Walker House; LeeAnne Dukes, Ten Chimneys; Audrienne Eder, Bradley Sculpture Garden; Jill Edwards, Southeast Wisconsin Master Gardeners; Jennifer Enko, Partners Health; Laurie Engen, Christ the Servant Lutheran Church; Mohammed Fayyaz, UW Botanical Garden; Cheryl Fink, Miner Park; Frances Finley, Aurora Medical Center; Joe Fonk, Hawthorn Hollow; Eric Frydenlund, Crawford County Tourism; Janet Garrett, Holy Family Memorial Hospital; Celine Gedmin, Waushara County Master Gardeners; Rhonda Gildersleeve, UWEX Iowa County; Linda Ginkel, Lawler Park; Andy and Sharon Gleisner, Arbor View Gardens; Lisa Golda, John Michael Kohler Arts Center; Allyson Gommer,

Chippewa Falls Chamber of Commerce; Cathy Hoke Gonzales, Peninsula Art School and Gallery; Dick Granchalek, La Crosse Chamber of Commerce; Pat Greathead, Madison Herb Society; Jeff Griffiths, Monona Terrace; Kristi Gruenhagen, LandWorks; Shelly Haberman, Agnesian HealthCare; Ann Hackbarth, Milwaukee County Zoo; Carolyn Haglund, Union United Church of Christ; Jackie and Justine Hansen, Winfield Inn and Gardens; Chuck Hanson, Riverside International Friendship Gardens; Matt Hanson, UWEX Dodge County; Beatrice Harris; Fred Hardt, Wild Ones; Doug Hartman, Pamperin Park; Edward Hasselkus, Longenecker Horticultural Gardens; The Hausers, Superior View Farm; Scott Hegrenes, Carthage College; Connie Glatz Helms, Delavan Rotary Garden; Don Hendricks, Green Bay Botanical Gardens; Barb Herreid, Wood County Master Gardeners; Jayne Herring, Gateway Technical College; Cary Heyer, UW-La Crosse; Vicki Heymann, Executive Residence; Mike Hibbard, Mosquito Hill Nature Center; Steve Hirby, Lawrence University; Diane Holzschuh, Kemper Center; Carole Hopp, Wisconsin Federation of Garden Clubs; John Howard, Harold S. Vincent High School; Neil Howk, Apostle Islands National Lakeshore; Kathy Howlett-Despot, Hollyhock House; William Hoyt, Allen Centennial Gardens; Noah Huber, Milwaukee County Zoo; Margaret Ingraham, Taliesin; Ron Irwin, Aurora Health Care; Steve Jacobson, Watertown High School; Erika Jensen, Gottlieb Arboretum; Phil Johnson, Phoenix Park; Jackie Johnson, Northeast Wisconsin Unit of the Herb Society of America; Ruth Johnson, Good Earth Gardens; Wendel Johnson, UW-Marinette; Mary Jorgensen, Villa Louis; Linda Kaehler, Havenwoods State Forest; Tom Kalb, UWEX-Eau Claire; Fr. Keith, Monte Alverno; Janet Kelly, Madison Area Technical College; Deborah Kern, Garden Room; Patrick Kernan, Bradley Sculpture Garden; Wen-D Kersten, Grand Geneva Resort; John Kiefer, City of Fond du Lac; Mark Kinders, UW-River Falls; Dave Klefstad, Sheboygan County Master Gardeners; Ron Klein, Hanchett-Bartlett Homestead; Terrill Knaack, Wayland Academy; Arlene Knops, Bruce Garden Club; Marian Kobow, Green Lake Center Peace Garden; Mary Kohrell, UWEX Calumet County; Lynn Koonz, St. John in the Wilderness Episcopal Church; Wendy Koss, Hollyhock House; Charles Kostichka, Hancock Agricultural Research Station; Donna Krebsbach, Mississippi Valley Partnership; Joe Kresl, Hawks Nursery; Diane Krisman, Reiman Visitor's Center; Thomas Kursel, Forest Home Cemetery; Judith Laimon-Smith, Southeast Wisconsin Master Gardeners; Melissa Lake, UW-Marshfield; Chris Landowski, Pink Ribbon Garden; Barbara Lang, UW-Barron County; Kate Langner, Outagamie County Master Gardeners; Patricia Lawson, Upland Hills Health; Jane Leischer, Taylor County Master Gardeners; Cherie Le Jeune, American Club; Warren Lensmire, Lensmire's Village Gardens; Daniel Liedtke, Heritage Hill State Historic Park; Lynette Liepert, Fond du Lac Master Gardeners; Darlene Lochbihler, The Cottager Ltd.; Leonore Look, Wood County Master Gardeners; Patrice Luer, Sauk Prairie Memorial Hospital; Edward Lyon, Rotary Garden; Richard MacDonald, Baraboo Public Library; Tracey MacGregor, Cedar Community; Dr. Susan E. Rice Mahr, Master Gardener Program Coordinator; Dave Majerus, Landmark Landscapes; Sean Malone, Ten Chimneys Foundation; Mary Marshall, Horticultural Hall; Michele Matucheski, Mercy Medical Center; Mark Mayer, UWEX Green County; Jessica McCarty, Pilch & Barnet; Liz McClellan, Community Memorial Hospital; Christine McGinnis, Hudson Hospital; Marie McGinnis, Eble Garden; Michael McKinley, GEM Gardens; Mary Jo McBrearty, St. Nicholas Hospital; Prudence McFarland, St. Joseph's Retreat Center; Brett Meach, Wisconsin Innkeepers Association; Fr. Olivier Meney, St. Mary's Roman Catholic Oratory; Jean-Margret Merrell-Beech, Lafayette County Master Gardeners; Dave Micek, Wilson Place; Jeff Miller, UW-Communications; Cindy Mineau, Herbs in Thyme; Don Mischo, ABC Supply Co.; Martha Mitchell, VisitBeloit; Renae Mitchell, The Prairie Enthusiasts; Peter Moersch, Stonewall Nursery; Becky Moffitt, Friends of Riverside; Nancy Mosel, Fanny Hill; Sharon Morrisey, UWEX-Milwaukee County; Linda Mossman, Oak Park Inn; Dough Mrotek, Silver Lake College; Robyn Mulhaney, The Flying Pig; Ann Munson, UWEX, Dane County; Mary Narges, Free Spirit Equine Center; Nancy Nedveck, The Flower Factory; Charlotte Nelson, Alpine Gardens; Thomas and Cathie Nelson, St. Feriole Island Memorial Gardens; Frances Nemtin,

Taliesin; Lori Nero, Thistledown Greenhouses; Karen Newbern, The Ridges; Ron Nief, Beloit College; Lori Norman, UW-Richland; Mary O'Connor, Aztalan Fields; B. G. O'Reilly, Horticultural Hall; Beth O'Reilly, Destination Kohler; Keri Olson, St. Clare Health Care; Fr. Woody Pace; St. Mary's Catholic Church; Mary Kay Palmer, City of Waukesha, Parks, Recreation and Forestry Department; Edith Pederson, Pederson's Gardens, Little Café, and Landscape; Jim Perry, UW-Fox Valley; Sue Pierman, Aurora Health Care; Julia Peyton, DeKoven Center; Jackie Pickett, Pink Ribbon Cancer Survivors Garden; Susan Placzek, SentryWorld; Harvey Plansky, NEW Master Gardeners; Kathleen Polich, Platteville Area Chamber of Commerce; Nick Polizzi, Beloit College; Jennifer Pratt, Creamery Café; Thomas Ptak, Upham House; Fran Puleo, Monona Terrace; Wouterina de Raad, Riana's Garden; Becky Raasch, Wisconsin Bed & Breakfast Association; Tim Raimer, City of Portage; Marilyn Rebarchek, Riverside International Friendship Gardens; Elysia Borowy-Reeder, Milwaukee Art Museum; Judy Reninger, The Wild Ones; Scott Reuss, UWEX-Marinette; Gerard Rewolinski, Arnold and O'Sheridan Landscape Architects; Al Ritchey, Al's Auto Body & Arboretum; Louise Roach, Fanny Hill; Barbara Robertson, Labyrinth Garden Earth Sculpture; Patrick Robinson and Karen Koehler Robinson, Two Fish Gallery; Nancy Rodman, The Highground; Lois Roen, Hanchett-Bartlett Homestead; Judith Reith-Rozelle, West Madison Agricultural Research Station; James Rosenthal, City of Fond du Lac; Melissa Rowley, Kenosha Area Chamber of Commerce; Marilyn Saffert, Barron County Master Gardeners; Liz Sanders, Milwaukee Hilton City Center; Cathy Schafman, Hanchett-Bartlett Homestead; Craig Saxe, UWEX Juneau County; Erika Schendel, Hudson Hospital; Gene Schindler, Chippewa Falls Rose Garden; Mark and Alice Schoebel, Storybook Gardens; Traci Schoonover, Luther Midelfort Hospital; Vicki Schorse, Mercy Health Foundation; Lynne Schreinhart, Reiman Visitor's Center; Sue Schuetz, Taliesin; Linda and Stephen Schulte, Foxfire Gardens; Linnea Seume, Burnett Medical Center; Sister Christa Marie, Our Lady of Guadalupe Shrine; Sister Dolores, LeRoyer Memorial Walk; Sister Sarah, Sinsinawa; Dawn Sheffer, Southwest Health Center; Scott Sieckman, Monches Farm; Susan Silver, Charles A. Wustum Museum; Ann Sitrick, Beloit Memorial Hospital; Jeffrey Shilts, Fire and Ice; Nancy Acker-Skolaski, Orchids by the Ackers; Dave Smith, Smith Brothers Landing; Theresa Smith, Boulder Junction Chamber of Commerce; John Sorenson, Frame Park; Keith Staebler, Frosty's Frozen Custard; Sarah Starmer, Beloit Memorial Hospital; Art Steadman, Lowell Damon Home; Julie Steiner, Vernon Memorial Health Care; Marion Strauss, St. Joseph Parish, Grafton; Cheri Stephan, Door County Master Gardeners; Cyril Suing, West of the Lake Gardens; George Tanko, SentryWorld; Donna Teynor, St. Feriole Island; Marcia Theel, Leigh Yawkey Woodson Art Museum; Rick Thiesse, Franciscan Skemp Healthcare; Shan Thomas, Little Norway; Dorothy Thompson, UW-Richland; Alan Tollefson, Schreiner Memorial Library; Lorraine Toman, Spooner Ag Research Station; Peter Traczek, Frame Park; Lisa Traughber, Dodge County Master Gardeners; Norine Trewyn, Southe East Wisconsin Master Gardeners; Brian Tungate, Smith Park; Kris Ullmer, Wisconsin Bed & Breakfast Association; Rolf Utegaard, WIGMA Master Gardeners; Donna VanBuecken, Wild Ones; Bonnie Vastag, Brown County Master Gardeners; Kathy Voigt, Fox Cities Chamber of Commerce; Nancy Verstrate, Chamber Main Street Program, Sheboygan Falls; Sue and Scott Wald, Big Brook Greenhouse; Sr. Mary David Walgenbach, Holy Wisdom Monastery; Linda Warren, UWEX Marinette County; Rev. Terrence A. Welty III, Nashotah House; Jim Werlein, Executive Residence; June Wessa, St. John Neumann Parish; Ann Wescott, Cave of the Mounds; Emajean Westphal, Sisson's Peony Gardens; Paul Whitaker, Monk Botanical Gardens; Tim Wick, Burnett Medical Center; Ann Wied, UWEX Waukesha County; Daniel Williams, Wisconsin Chapter of American Society of Landscape Architects; Rochelle Williams, Grant Regional Health Center; Jim Wilson, Winter Greenhouse; Tim Wood, Lancaster Agricultural Research Station; Jack Woodland, Kohler Company; Bill Wright, UWEX Brown County; Stephen Wuerger, Affinity Health; JoAnn Youngman, Bradley Sculpture Gardens; Pat Zellmer, University of Wisconsin-Stevens Point; Mike Zierke, Creekside Landscaping and Nursery; Randy Zogbaum, UWEX Calumet County.

Introduction

Public gardens are a community treasure. Unlike the restaurant, hotel, and retail chains that have left their heavy footprints in communities large and small, public gardens offer a welcome respite from the stale sameness. That's because no two public gardens are alike. Even if two communities were to plant the exact same plants in exactly the same design, the microclimates (soil, sun, wind, and rain) at the individual sites would eliminate the chance of growing "identical" gardens.

Public gardens are also a way of building community. When you're up to your elbows in dirt, it doesn't matter if the gardener next to you, attempting to plant a rose bush or a new variety of hosta, is a bank president or a stay-at-home mother.

Public gardens contribute to a community's quality of life in a way no other entity can. They are the common denominator that levels the playing field between the rich and the poor, the young and the old, the genius and the average Joe or Jane. Everyone, no matter what his or her status in life or life conditions, can view and enjoy a little bit of heaven in a public garden. And this book is a tribute as well as a guide to these special gems.

Truthfully, I'm an "accidental" gardener. Although there were a few agriculturally oriented relatives in my family tree, including two county agents, I'll admit I was not born with dirt under my fingernails like many of the gardeners I've met. I am in awe of those individuals whose thumbs are a vibrant shade of green, who can make a silk purse out of a sow's ear—or, in gardening terms, a patch of floral paradise from a plot of invasive weeds. And gardeners, no matter what their skill level, are some of the nicest, most generous and optimistic people I've ever met.

As you can tell by its title, this book is a guide to the public gardens and landscapes around the Badger State. As with any guidebook, especially one focusing on the natural world, things change from the time the research begins until the book appears at your local bookstore. I have, as best as possible, tried to locate and record the majority of significant public (and even a few not-so-public) gardens in Wisconsin. While the gardens were in existence when I saw them, money, commitment, Mother Nature, and a host of other situations may cause them to change—for better and for worse—by the time you see them.

This book features more than one hundred twenty five of Wisconsin's most striking spots. These are supplemented with additional sites you won't want to miss if you're in the area. The book also contains lists of garden clubs; Master Gardener associations; garden artists; arboretums; outdoor labyrinths; as well as some butterfly and healthcare gardens that I hope will be valuable to the reader.

After thousands of miles driven and some three hundred fifty gardens viewed, I'll admit it was difficult choosing only one hundred twenty five to focus on. In some instances I've taken the liberty of combining several in the same area into one site. There are the bones of a potentially wonderful botanical garden being installed on St. Feriole Island just west of Prairie du Chien and another one under construction in Wausau. Although neither of them are finished as of late 2007, stop by and see how they're progressing. While you're visiting Prairie du Chien, don't forget to visit historic Villa Louis and its heirloom gardens, the Mississippi Valley Sculpture Garden, and the Lawlor Park octagon bed, all located on the same small strip of land. Ditto for the sites near the Monk Botanical Garden in Wausau.

There are several private gardens included in the book. Although they are privately owned and maintained, they are open to the public either during a certain portion of the year or by appointment. A word of caution: If the owner requests an appointment, please honor the request. Do not drop in unexpectedly.

I've also included descriptions of several hospital gardens among the selected sites. Healing or therapeutic gardens are the newest type of public gardens. But be cautious when you visit one. The Health Insurance Portability and Accountability Act (HIPAA) ensures that all patients have their privacy protected.

Like the Sears Roebuck catalogs of old, this book is a wish book. No garden is ever truly complete, so use this book to find ideas for your own garden.

May all your garden dreams come true!
—MARY LOU SANTOVEC

You can't stop and smell the roses unless you know where to find them.
—RICK SANTOVEC

Northwest Wisconsin

Photo by Wouterina deRaad

Angel of Hope Memorial Garden

EAU CLAIRE

PEOPLE GRIEVE IN DIFFERENT WAYS. Some prefer privacy; others want a public place to go and remember. The Angel of Hope Memorial Garden provides that kind of space for a very intense grief, that of losing a child.

Inspired by the memorial garden in Richard Paul Evans' story, *The Christmas Box*, David Barrett, his wife, and eighteen other parents created this Eau Claire garden that was dedicated on Sept. 21, 2003. One of eighty-four similar sites around the world, it is located in Buffington Heights, next to Lakeview Cemetery.

The garden is shaped like a horseshoe around a center of stone. The mixture of bulbs, annuals, and perennials provides three-season color. Tulips and daffodils bring spring hope. Other flowers bloom from early summer through fall. There are junipers and shrubs for texture and height. A bronze sculpture of the *Angel of Hope* sits on a granite base in the middle of the flowers with the engraved memorial square pavers at its base. The angel has outstretched wings and an upturned face just like the other sculptures based on Evans' book do.

Currently, there are ninety-one engraved stones representing one hundred forty two children, including the Barretts' own fifteen-year-old daughter, in the cemetery. Several teakwood benches provide a place for contemplation. Two large stone pots are filled with annuals and plans call for two more to be added.

Another Angel of Hope can be found in a memorial and healing garden connected with St. Agnes Hospital in Fond du Lac. This recessed garden was designed to descend into a private space for individuals and families to reflect and heal. A walking path connects this garden to the remainder of the site's healing and meditation gardens. There is also a sculpture located at St. Joseph's Hospital in Milwaukee in the Sister Jeanne Gengler Community Park at 50th and Burleigh streets.

COUNTY	Eau Claire
ADDRESS	On the south end of Lakeview Cemetery, Eau Claire
PHONE	715/832-3626
EMAIL	david_barrett@valpak.com
DIRECTIONS	From I-94, exit 70 (Eau Claire/Chippewa Falls) to U.S. Highway 53 toward Eau Claire. Go approximately two miles and take exit 87 (Clairemont Avenue) onto East Clairemont Avenue (also known as U.S. Highway 12). Go five miles. Turn right on Crestview Drive and drive approximately one block. Turn right on Leonard Drive and drive about four blocks. Turn right on to Buffington Drive. There's a small entrance off of Buffington Drive near the intersection of Leonard Drive.
ADMISSION	Free
HOURS	Daily, dawn to dusk.
AMENITIES	Parking along the drive into the cemetery.

Bayfield
BAYFIELD

SITUATED ALMOST AT THE TIP OF THE STATE, Bayfield's northern climate provides some interesting challenges to local gardeners. If it isn't Lake Superior's cold breezes wreaking havoc on the plants, drought conditions have plagued gardeners' best efforts over the past few years.

But those northern residents are hardy. Designated the Berry Capital of Wisconsin, the area is home to many commercial flower farms, berry farms, and orchards open to the public.

A view from Winfield Inn and Gardens

Justin Hansen

Winfield Inn and Gardens, 225 East Lynde Avenue, 715/779-3252, 715/779-5180, winfieldinn@centurytel.net, winfieldinn.com

When Jackie Hansen and her husband bought the Winfield Inn in 1994, there were no gardens. The Gardens portion of the business's name was only added later after the sloping lawn in front of the motel was turned into a set of terraced beds.

Four acres of gardens and ponds now cover the property, which includes condos as well as the motel rooms. Most of the plants are perennials including a whole row of perennial hibiscus with the dinner-plate size flowers. Annuals are planted in the

> ## *Bayfield in Bloom* is a month-long
> celebration of spring floral exuberance. Each year, between May 18 and June 17, the community is blanketed with over 14,000 daffodils. Lupine and other wildflowers bloom along trails and county roads. The Society of American Travel Writers rated the celebration as one of the top 10 festivals in North America. Visit www.bayfield.org/visitor/bayfieldbloom.asp for more information.

terrace's top two beds. Look for the pink Shirley poppy among them. You'll also find rose campion with its silver gray leaves and magenta flowers, one of Hansen's favorites. One of the beds contains a water garden complete with a waterfall, aquatic plants, and koi.

A garden overlooking Lake Superior contains astilbe and hostas with hops claiming one trellis and roses covering another. The center is anchored with a fountain that connects the eye to the lake. The Hansens also operate a gift shop nearby that includes garden art for sale.

Blue Vista Farm, 34045 South County Highway J, 715/779-5400, bluevistafarm.com

The view is compelling but so are the gardens at Blue Vista Farm. Set on a working fruit and flower farm, the Touchy Feely garden is a popular one for children, filled with selections to eat and smell. Sawdust mulch paths lead through a space filled with annuals and perennials. A clump of daylilies claims the middle of

Tulips line the garden path at Winfield Inn and Gardens

Justin Hansen

the bed. Blue salvia, dahlias, and natives fill in the spaces. Fragrance is added with roses and catmint, while the fuzzy lamb's ear tickles little fingers. There are also butterfly-attracting plants here. A vine-covered pergola frames a gorgeous view of the rolling hills. Anchoring the opposite end is a metal sculpture crafted from stair railings. One of the farm's many apple trees shades hollyhocks and foxglove under its branches. Keith and Laura Carlson grow three hundred varieties of annuals and perennials mostly for design work for weddings and business décor. They also sell bulk flowers. The rows of monarda attract hummingbirds during their migration. The farm has earned the state's Travel Green certification for its environmentally friendly practices.

Good Earth Gardens, 87185 County Road J, 715/779-5564, goodearth@cheqnet.net

The annual growing season and the vivid color in many gardens ends with the first frost. But Curtis and Ruth Johnson's dried flowers add floral hues throughout the coldest months. The Johnsons grow many natives such as yarrow, goldenrod, and monarda to dry, but have also added nigella with its balloon-shaped seedpods of pale green and maroon stripes as well as mixed grasses to their list of dried material. The typical strawflowers and statice are available, but look for the white, starlike flowers of ammobium or the small-tufted orange balls of carthamus. Flowers are sold by the bunch or in specially prepared bouquets. Good Earth has also earned the state's Travel Green certification for its environmentally friendly practices.

Hauser's Superior View Farm, 86565 County Highway J, 715/779-5404, superiorviewfarm.com

In 1908, the first members of the Hauser family settled in Bayfield and started their horticultural career growing strawberries and potatoes. But the 1912 seed embargo closed the pipeline to European varieties and caused the family to switch to growing perennials and strawflowers.

As one of the largest producers of northern field-grown perennials, the Hausers open their doors each May for their annual Red Barn Plant Sale. Customers can choose their favorite perennials from freshly dug rootstock. All of the plants are wintered outside so they're hardy in Zones 3 and 4. If your taste runs to balloon flowers, sweet William, or valerian, the Hausers have it. If you miss the sale, the Hausers will mail plants. The Farm, once featured in *House Beautiful* magazine, also sells fruit trees, ornamental and flowering shrubs, annuals, bulbs, roses, and clematis. The red barn was built with plans purchased from a Sears catalog.

Raspberry Island Lighthouse

The Raspberry Island Lighthouse is one of the six lighthouse stations among the Apostle Islands. Lighthouse keepers and their families lived on Raspberry Island from 1863 to 1947. An extensive renovation project has restored the structures to the 1920s time period and the Park Service recently installed a series of flowerbeds reminiscent of the ones found then.

Most of the ten or so flowerbeds are round although several are rectangular. All are edged with boulders. There are flowers planted along the base of the lighthouse running parallel to its foundation. Plant selections include a mix of annuals and perennials. Zinnias are bordered with petunias, dianthus, or pansies. Pansies also ring a dianthus bed. There are nasturtiums and astilbe, dahlias and daylilies here.

Big Brook Greenhouse

CABLE

WHAT DO MARTHA STEWART and Cable, Wisconsin have in common? The answer is Big Brook Greenhouse. The lifestyle diva has featured one of Sue Wald's living succulent wreaths in an episode of her show.

Wald and her husband, Scott, own both Big Brook Greenhouse and the Web site SimplySucculents.com. While the greenhouse features the requisite annuals and perennials, it's the succulents that steal the show. Some can be found planted in gravel with hardscapes of driftwood, planters, and limestone paths in a desertlike rock garden to the north of the property.

The shade garden at Big Brook Greenhouse

The Walds grow more than three hundred varieties of succulents, eighty-five of which are available for sale with thirty more in the pipeline. Sue, the artist, places various sedums, sempervivums, jovibarbars, and aracnoidiums onto moss wreaths, where they root and grow. The Walds sell the wreaths, as well as succulent-trimmed moss turtles, to the public.

For those who prefer other perennials, a display garden contains a gazebo with open slats in the roof. It provides the shade for the hostas, ferns, astilbe, Solomon's seal, and lily of the valley that prefer the "dark side." Look for a handmade birch log chair with a mossy seat. A waterfall and pond are trimmed with perennials and garden art.

COUNTY	Bayfield
ADDRES	43785 U.S. Highways 63, Cable
PHONE	715/798-3191, 715/798-3091
EMAIL	simplysucculents@cheqnet.net
WEBSITE	www.simplysucculents.com
DIRECTIONS	Big Brook is located on Highway 63 about one mile north of Cable.
ADMISSION	Free
HOURS	May 1 to mid-July. Call or check the Web site for hours.
AMENITIES	Parking. Toilets and water inside the gift shop.

Dahlka Gardens

RIVER FALLS

WHEN THEY MAKE A LARGE DONATION TO THEIR ALMA MATER, most alumni want a building named after them in return. The late Dennis Dahlka, a 1977 alumnus of the University of Wisconsin-River Falls, had other ideas.

Dahlka, who studied art and agriculture at River Falls, endowed a garden located between the Kleinpell Fine Arts Building and Centennial Science Hall on the university campus. With perennials such as sedums, roses, and lilies, ornamental grasses and prairie flowers, native shrubs, and a nice selection of dwarf conifers, the Zen-inspired Dahlka garden provides a lush green animat-

ed artwork against the backdrop of the red bricks of the Fine Arts Building.

Designed by Earthworks, an area landscape company, the gardens include hardscapes of six cedar benches, concrete walking paths, and limestone slabs that weigh two tons apiece. Imperial Honey Locust trees shade each of the benches located in concrete segues off the main path. There are dwarf Siberian, Norway, and 'North Star' spruces as well as a Japanese white pine. Look for wild qui-nine, Indian and other ornamental grass-es as well as blazing star. A square con-crete sculpture of a reclining woman set on top of a granite base is placed between the doors to the building and the garden. A metal sculpture of flames contained within a circle also has a home in the gar-

Bi-color foeteda and Macfarlane lilac

den. On the north side of the Fine Arts Building is the Swenson Sundial, the largest vertical sundial on the North American continent.

Along with the Dahlka Garden, UW-RF students can also spend some time at the smaller Wall Memorial Garden located in the quad between Hagestad, (the former Student Center), and South Hall. The Wall Garden fea-tures a contemporary water feature, a trio of cement columns set in an angu-lar concrete pond. Three sets of cedar table/chair combinations set on stone pavers complete the hardscape. Perennials, shrubs, and evergreens represent the softscapes. There are also two perennial beds flanking the concrete sidewalk leading to the Wyman Education Building, and a herbaceous perennial plant identification and teaching plot located south of the Melvin Wall Amphi-theater. The plot is open to the public in September and October.

COUNTY	Pierce
ADDRESS	University of Wisconsin-River Falls, Cascade Avenue, River Falls
PHONE	715/425-3771
DIRECTIONS	From I-94 East, take exit 3 south on State Highway 35 seven miles to River Falls. Go past the first River Falls exit ramp and drive 1.5 miles to the first stoplight at the junction of State Highway 29. Take a right on Cascade Avenue and go 1.5 miles to the center of campus. Kleinpell will be on your left. From I-94 West, take River Falls/New Richmond exit (exit 10). Drive south on State Highways 65/95 for nine miles. Turn left on to the Highway 65 River Falls bypass. Take a right at the first stoplight at junction Highway 29 (which becomes Cascade Avenue).
ADMISSION	Free
HOURS	Seasonal. Daily, dawn to dusk.
AMENITIES	Parking in the visitor's lot or on the street. Toilets, food and water inside the buildings.

Fairlawn Mansion

SUPERIOR

OVERLOOKING BOTH BARKER'S ISLAND AND SUPERIOR BAY is the historic Fairlawn Mansion. Completed in 1891 by Martin Pattison, a wealthy lumber and

Fairlawn Mansion

mining baron and the city's second mayor, the 42-room Queen Anne Victorian and grounds now belong to the Superior Public Museums organization.

Although Pattison did not have gardens on his property while he lived in the house, he did have a now-defunct conservatory, the outline of which you can see during a tour of the home. After the Pattison family moved away, the house became a children's orphanage. When the orphanage closed its doors after forty-two years, the city bought the house and undertook a massive renovation project.

Recently, two period gardens were installed on the front lawn to complement the Victorian architecture. The one on the north end of the property is dedicated to Captain Alexander McDougall, designer of the whaleback freighter. From this garden you can see across the road to Barker's Island where the S.S. Meteor, the last surviving whaleback ship is permanently docked.

McDougall's garden is a shade garden with two benches placed on a circular brick patio. A gray gravel path forms a keyhole shape that links the patio to the lawn. The focal point is a ship's anchor. Plant selections include cranesbill, ornamental grasses, shrubs, arborvitae, junipers, coral bells, and irises. Towering mature trees provide ample shade.

The John T. Murphy garden on the south end of the front lawn is dedicated to the owner of the *Superior Evening Telegram* newspaper. A larger keyhole shape can be found in this garden, this time constructed out of grass. The grass path separates the garden into two distinct sections. Shrubs and junipers, perennials and natives are some of the choices in this sun-loving garden.

Edith Pederson of Pederson's Gardens and Landscapes designed the two major gardens. In the McDougall garden, she took her cue from the captain's irascible personality and tried to capture his crankiness through her plant selections. Heavy with roses and lilacs, Murphy's garden resembles one on the Murphy family estate.

A third garden, an annual-filled circular bed anchored by a statue, was planted near the walkway to the front door. Future plans call for a total of eleven gardens to be installed on the property including a children's garden that will be located at the entry.

COUNTY	Douglas
ADDRESS	906 East Second Street, Superior
PHONE	715/394-5712
WEBSITE	www.superiorpublicmuseums.org
DIRECTIONS	From U.S. Highway 53, exit U.S. Highway 2, which is also East Second Street.
ADMISSION	Admission to the gardens is free. Admission to the home is $8 for adults, $6.50 for seniors/students age 6 to 18 or with a valid school ID. Children 5 and under are admitted free.
HOURS	Summer hours are 9 a.m. to 5 p.m. Monday through Saturday and 11 a.m. to 5 p.m. Sundays. Winter hours are 10 a.m. to 4 p.m. Thursday through Saturday and noon to 4 p.m. on Sundays.
AMENITIES	Parking lot. Toilets inside the historic home. Water available in the gift shop.

 Gardens under construction:

While all gardens are ephemeral in nature there are some that were under construction or renovation during the researching of this book that are likely finished at publishing time.

Monk Botanical Garden, Wausau

St. Feriole Island Botanical Garden, Prairie du Chien

Cyrus Yawkey House, Wausau

Shake Rag Alley, Mineral Point

Rooftop Garden at Columbia St. Mary's new hospital, Milwaukee

Healing Garden at Luther Midelfort Hospital, Eau Claire

Healing Garden at St. Mary's Hospital, Madison

Rooftop Healing Garden at Marshfield Clinic's satellite hospital in Rice Lake

Healing Garden at Columbus Community Hospital, Columbus

Heritage Park and Gardens, Mount Horeb

Gateway Technical College landscape, Kenosha

Plainfield Community Garden, Plainfield

Holy Family Catholic Church, Woodruff

Black Point Nature Preserve, Lake Geneva

Racine Zoological Gardens, Racine

House on the Rock, Spring Green

Gardens on the Canal, Portage

Veteran's Memorial at Armory Park, Whitefish Bay

100 Miles of Gardens, along Highway 35, the Great River Road

Fanny Hill Victorian Inn, Restaurant, and Dinner Theater

EAU CLAIRE

THE VICTORIAN AGE seems to be alive and well at Fanny Hill, located on the outskirts of Eau Claire. While the bed and breakfast is noted for its dinners and live theater, it's worth a trip just to see the gardens at this very pink destination.

The resoundingly pink buildings with their white shutters form a lively setting for the site's six gardens. Approximately three-quarters of an acre is devoted to plants on this three-acre property.

A white picket fence forms the backdrop for the English Rose Garden with two large blue spruces anchoring each end. Mature trees are part of the overall landscape. The Rose Garden includes three species of roses: Red 'Grootendorsts' line the back of the bed while 'Nearly Wild' pink ones fill the middle and red shrub roses claim the front.

Red gravel paths lead through the English formal garden. Here, metal strips edge the space, which is filled with a mass of annuals and perennials. White geraniums, blue salvia, and red roses might seem a bit Fourth of July, but they're only part of the show. Daisies, irises, coral bells, yarrow, and sedums add some contemporary color to the garden's formalized structure, which is really cottage style with very formal corners.

The garden is laid out in a cardinal grid. Two similar white statues of female figures seem to mirror each other at the north and south ends of the garden. White benches are placed in front of them and at the west end.

The very pink entrance to Fanny Hill

Courtesy of Fanny Hill

Across from the English garden, interrupted by an expanse of lawn, is the Lily Garden, another formal structure designed with clipped spireas in a parterre style and filled with irises and lilies.

The Heart Garden at Fanny Hill

Courtesy of Fanny Hill

A similar pattern of path and lawn is carried around to the back. Use the stepping-stones to find your way through the cottage-style plants in the Riverside Garden. This garden competes for your attention with the stunning view of the Chippewa River valley, but only for a moment. The dining room overlooks the purple yarrow, irises, sedums, monarda, lilies, and peonies in this garden.

Astilbe, hosta, and Siberian iris all surround a small pond with a fountain in the Pond Garden. A dry streambed with some ornamental grasses leads from the pond along the length of the property.

Striped hostas border a perennial bed that's called the Heart Garden. It's a secret little space between the pond and a pergola hidden among large evergreens. There are red astible surrounding the stone statue of a woman in the center of this formal bed. 'Palace Purple' coral bells are planted in the shape of a heart.

The gardens contain some unusual surprises. When the three angel trumpets bloom, the fragrance captures your attention. Two are found in the English formal garden and one in a pot near the Riverside Garden.

Fanny Hill utilizes sixty pots as part of its design scheme. There's a corner of calla lilies and some instances of elephant ears and hyacinth bean vines dotting the beds. When all of the gardens are in bloom, describing the outcome as lush is an understatement.

COUNTY	Eau Claire
ADDRESS	3919 Crescent Avenue, Eau Claire
PHONE	Phone: 715/836-8184
EMAIL	office@fannyhill.com
WEBSITE	www.fannyhill.com
DIRECTIONS	From I-94 East, exit 59. Turn right on U.S. Highway 12 (east). Turn right on North Town Hall Road/County EE. At the third stop sign, turn left. Continue to follow County Road EE/Crescent Avenue for one mile. From I-94 West, exit State Highway 37 N (exit 65). Go half a mile and turn left at Short Street/Hamilton Avenue. Go one mile and turn left on Ferry Street. Go one block and turn right on Crescent Avenue. Follow Crescent for one-and-one-half miles. From U.S. Highway 53 North, exit Highway 124 south to the North Crossing. Exit Highway 12 (Clairemont Avenue) and turn left. Go 2.8 miles to Menomonie Street and turn right. Go three blocks and turn left on Ferry Street. Go an additional four blocks and turn right on Crescent Avenue. Continue on Crescent for one-and-one-half miles. You'll know you're at the right place when you see the letters "F" and "H" spelled out in hostas at the entrance.
ADMISSION	Free
HOURS	Seasonal. Daily, dawn to dusk.
AMENITIES	Parking lot. Toilets, food, and water inside the restaurant.

The Florian Gardens

EAU CLAIRE

THREE DIFFERENT GARDENS, three different wedding possibilities. Brides who dream of an outdoor wedding can choose between the Indigo Garden, the Rock Cress Garden, or the Rosemary Garden at the Florian Gardens in Eau Claire.

Open to the public when there are no events scheduled, the contemporary blue spruce topiaries at the entrance signify that this commercial site is no ordinary reception hall. Starting in spring with flowering bulbs and continuing on through early summer, late summer, and fall, there are always enough blooms to satisfy any bride or garden lover.

A continuous earth berm creates a natural amphitheater and frames the back of each of the gardens. The berm continues around the exterior side of the Indigo and Rosemary gardens. Blue spruce trees, three hundred eighty four to be exact, were planted on top of the berm. When the spruces mature, they will form a natural barrier against the wind and noise from the nearby highway. Two large berms of plants that carve out the center Rock Cress Garden provide privacy and beauty for all three sites.

The gardens are a continual work in progress, with plants changed out frequently to ensure continuous color. Roses, lilies, peonies, and coral bells are some of the perennials showing off their blooms. Annuals include dianthus, petunias, marigolds, and salvia. Other plantings are intended to attract hummingbirds and butterflies. Junipers and spirea help define the spaces. Hostas huddle under mature trees.

Concrete steps lead from the reception facility's patio to the boulder fountain ringed with arborvitae and set in gray stone. From the fountain focal point, separate serpentine paths lead to the cedar pergolas in each of the gardens. Shepherds crooks display baskets of flowering plants. An Asian sculpture called *Double Happiness* is mounted on a limestone boulder in the Rosemary Garden.

One of the wedding location possibilities at the Florian Gardens

While you're in the area, stop and see the University of Wisconsin Extension Demonstration Gardens located at the Eau Claire Expo Center on Lorch Avenue. Here, Tom Kalb, the UWEX horticulturist, is spearheading the site's conversion into a series of inspirational and teaching gardens. There's a rain garden, a wildflower forbs and native grasses demonstration bed, a prairie planting demonstration bed, a boulevard/tree line demonstration area, an orchard, an ideas garden, and an adaptive garden for the disabled and elderly. The beds contain annuals, perennials, trees, shrubs, and grasses. Hardscapes include gravel paths, a bridge, and decorative boulders.

COUNTY	Eau Claire
ADDRESS	2340 Lorch Avenue, Eau Claire
PHONE	715/832-8836
EMAIL	info@thefloriangardens.com
WEBSITE	www.thefloriangardens.com
DIRECTIONS	From I-94, take the Eleva/Eau Claire exit (exit 68), which is also State Highway 93. Go south on Highway 93 and turn west on to Lorch Avenue. You'll see the Extension display gardens first.
ADMISSION	Free
HOURS	The facility has booked weddings on Fridays, Saturdays, and Sundays. It also hosts business meetings, reunions, parties, and dances during the week. Call for availability. If the gate on the white fence is open, the public is invited to enjoy the gardens.
AMENITIES	Parking lot. Toilets and water available in the reception facility.

 ## Foxfire Botanical Gardens

MARSHFIELD

In 1985, East met West in a garden just outside of Marshfield and the result was spectacular. Stephen and Linda Schulte have created a true sanctuary on their property with the development of Foxfire Botanical Gardens. The Schultes bought the fifteen-acre property in 1978 and have turned a former reforestation effort into an Asian-influenced botanical garden that they generously share with the public.

These "philosophic" gardens exhibit European formality, Chinese simplicity, and even Japanese austerity and symbolism. Foxfire, or will-o-the-wisp, is a light often seen over marshes and low-lying areas and is thought to be the result of methane from decaying plants.

To create the gardens, the couple started by doing a little clearing, getting rid of many of the property's dead and overcrowded white spruce trees. They filled in some of the space with a three-acre pond that's bordered by rhododendrons and flowering shrubs. There are perennials like lilacs, irises, weigela, and lilies scattered around. Part of the space includes the Annette G. Hofmann Violet Garden. But it's the more than 1,000 varieties of hostas that Foxfire is known for.

Finding tranquility at Foxfire Botanical Gardens

Protected under a canopy of trees, exceptional hostas are identified with a blue reflector stake. The majority of them have identification signs.

The site also features seven acres of Oriental gardens starting with the minimalist So Garden. This garden, with its white stone, large boulders, and golden sedum groundcover, is usually seen adjacent to a monastery or temple. In the Schultes' case, it's located next to their Japanese teahouse, where stone dragons watchfully wait. The So garden was modeled after the Royanji Temple meditation garden in Kyoto, Japan.

> *On East Veterans Parkway* (also Highway 13 North) entering Marshfield are two "otherworldly" sculptures from Jurustic Park. Both the huge dragon and turtle are placed in round beds filled with perennials, conifers, and ornamental grasses.

The Shin Garden features stone bridges and a large waterfall. This full-scale, formal "Imperial" garden replicates one you'd find in ancient China. The bridges help link the Shin Garden with the main portion of the site. The Gyo Garden, developed in Korea and Japan and located in front of the teahouse, is not as minimalist as the So Garden, but still leaves something to the imagination.

The site includes a Scholar Meditation Garden with quiet meditation areas along the large pond. In this type of garden, problems are identified in the east. The questioner seeks the positive and negative results of the choice in the south. Then the questioner heads to the west for information on how the solution will influence others and makes the decision in the north.

"Samurai Warriors," a collection of exposed tree roots that protect the spirit of the garden, form the backdrop for some of the hosta beds surrounding the Torii Gate, an entrance to the future Japanese gardens. These gardens will feature Wisconsin ferns, a strolling path and sitting area, and an extensive moss garden.

There's a collection of ferns adjacent to a waterfall that tumbles into a hidden pond, a miniature hosta display garden, and a sandcastle sculpture on the grounds.

The Schultes kept many of the pines left from the reforestation efforts and with a little creative trimming shaped them in a bonsai style. Some denote *sabi,* a rustic, country esthetic; others embody *wabi,* a tranquility found in the weathering of age. You're encouraged to look up and under the trees to see the arms and necks of dragons.

With its Buddhist style, the wood and metal Moon Gate marks the property's entrance and "enhances the spirit of the garden." A Japanese teahouse with two large stained glass windows is another of the wonderful hardscape features. Stephen Schulte created the windows: the colored Genesis, an electronic microscopic view of the DNA molecule when viewed end to end; and the clear, leaded glass window called Karma. Installed in the east wall of the teahouse, Genesis is the symbol of Foxfire and, in Eastern cultures, east signifies renewal and spring. On the north wall, Karma, shown as the symbols of yin and yang, refers to the chain that merges action with results. The large metal planters

A canopy of trees shades this water feature at Foxfire

scattered around the grounds are actually liners from cone rock crushers made by Metso Minerals. The Schultes found them discarded in quarries.

In preparation for what you'll see in the gardens, the path from the gravel parking lot progresses from hard granite stones to the Moon Gate, softer wood chips through the covered pergola tunnel, to flexible, crushed recycled asphalt. The calming progression of materials causes the voice to lower and the body to relax.

One of the latest additions to the site is the lower-level Walter Hoover Hosta Garden. Selections from hosta associations from around the Midwest are represented here.

COUNTY	Marathon
ADDRESS	M220 Sugarbush Lane, Marshfield
PHONE	715/387-3050
EMAIL	foxfire@tznet.com
WEBSITE	www.foxfiregardens.com
DIRECTIONS	Take State Highway 97 four miles north of Marshfield. Turn onto County Highway E at the Wal-Mart stoplight. Go north, past Menards for 3 miles to Sugarbush Lane. Turn left on Sugarbush Lane. The gardens are located one-half mile on the left.
ADMISSION	Free
HOURS	10 a.m. to 4:30 p.m. daily, May 1 through October 1. Group tours by appointment.
AMENITIES	Parking lot. Toilets and water available.

GEM Gardens

EAU CLAIRE

MICHAEL McKINLEY HAS BUILT his own "field of dreams" on twenty-five acres just south of Eau Claire. GEM Gardens—a "jewel" of a place—contains thirty-seven different gardens. You'll find everything from a pond with a waterfall and an extended streambed to an evergreen maze. McKinley, along with three employees, mows fifteen of the twenty-five acres, the rest is gardens.

Both McKinley and his late wife, Nancy, had professional careers in public speaking and speech pathology. But when they moved to this location in 1980, they decided to indulge in their love of landscaping and gardening.

That evergreen maze? It contains five hundred and thirty evergreens trimmed to five feet high. The entrance is framed with an allee of willows. In the center is a wooden lookout tower to help the confused find the exit.

That pond with the waterfall and extended streambed? There are six more water features on the property including one located in the woods.

You can't help but follow the stone paver paths to see where they lead. The paths vary in color, shape, and size, sometimes within the same stretch. A large pergola is also part of the hardscape as is a bridge that connects the waterfall

An old wagon wheel frame makes a nice piece of garden art at GEM Gardens

pond near the raspberries to the stream bed. McKinley has built a gazebo and added a bronze sculpture of children playing near his house.

Raspberries are GEM Gardens' claim to local fame. Not content with planting soldierlike rows of bushes, McKinley decided to plant the latest five hundred raspberry bushes in the shape of a chain, which frames a portion of the maze. He intends to sell rhubarb, asparagus, and Asiatic lily bulbs in future seasons.

But let's get back to the gardens. Shrub-filled circular beds are planted in formal designs; one features a pyramid-shaped trellis and four pots. Clumps of catmint have found a home in a figure-eight shaped bed filled with tiny gray gravel.

Flowering bushes and trees comprise a portion of Nancy's Garden, a bermed bed that features irises, sedums, daylilies, and some annuals. A red granite path with flagstone pavers leads through the space. A wishing well will be added as part of the hardscape.

The "rock" garden takes its name literally. A double row of trees is planted in individual beds filled with various colors of gravel. There's a terraced bed complimented with aging farm implements and wagon wheels. More farm implements and an old, half-buried canoe are hidden in a bed filled with multiple species of evergreens.

McKinley has converted an old granary into a garden shop that sells whimsical art and accessories. He's working on adding a shade garden in back of the gift shop.

COUNTY	Eau Claire
ADDRESS	7021 Lowes Creek Road, Eau Claire
PHONE	715/579-9759
DIRECTIONS	From I-94, take exit 68 (Eleva/Eau Claire), which is State Highway 93. Go south on Highway 93 for two miles. Turn west onto County Road II (Deerfield Road) for three miles. Turn south onto County Road F for half a mile.
ADMISSION	Free
HOURS	Seasonal. Daily, dawn to dusk.
AMENITIES	Some onsite parking. Portable toilet located behind the gift shop.

The Highground Veterans Memorial Park
NEILLSVILLE

SET HIGH ON A RIDGE OUTSIDE OF NEILLSVILLE, the Highground Veterans Memorial Park represents a tangible way of creating order out of the chaos of war. Constructed both to heal and to educate, the site honors veterans and their service in all of the twentieth century's wars.

A portion of the one hundred and forty-acre spot is filled with nine tributes, most of which include bronze sculptures. The two that do not are the Earthen Dove Effigy Mound and the Gold Star. The dove, measuring one hundred feet from beak to tail with a one hundred and forty-foot wingspan, was dedicated to Prisoners of War (POWs) and those Missing in Action (MIAs). The soil used to form the dove came from all of Wisconsin's seventy-two counties as well as various places around the United States.

The Gold Star flowerbed, which measures one hundred and twenty-five feet from point to point, is filled with shrubs and annuals. It honors the Gold Star Mothers, those women who have lost children in war. Like the effigy mound, the soil was contributed from families' yards, gardens, or locations where they last saw their loved ones alive.

The incredible view from the plaza spans a half million acres—and then there are the Highground's gardens. One is located around the Women Air Force Service Pilots (WASP) tribute. Stella d'oro lilies, roses, and shrubs are some of the plant selections found in this garden.

The newest one is the four-room Meditation Garden located to the west of the World War II and WASP tributes. Installed in 2007, hardscapes break the space into four rooms. There's a family arbor, a meditation shelter with a floor of memorial stones, the Prayer Stone, and the Falling Tears Fountain. The *Ascension of Doves* sculpture sits at the center of the garden's four quadrants.

When completed, the Falling Tears Fountain will include two sculptures. A soldier who carries the dog tags of his friend and fellow soldier will be placed at the head of the fountain. The wife and child of the fallen soldier will be seated at the rim of the pond that collects the water from the fountain.

A sculpture placed in a fountain is part of the Korean Tribute. Other sculptures honor Native American Vietnam veterans, nurses who served in the wars, and the fallen in Vietnam. A large globe marks the site's entrance.

While you're in Neillsville, visit the gardens at St. Mary's Catholic Church located at 1813 Black River Road. Volunteers there are working to transform a former farm field into a significant grouping of gardens. A metal arbor marks the entrance to a completed series of beds. There's a path being cut through a wooded portion of the acreage for the Stations of the Cross. A portion of the field will be left for wildflowers.

COUNTY	Clark
ADDRRESS	W7031 Ridge Road, Neillsville
PHONE	715/743-4224
FAX	715/743-4228
EMAIL	highgrnd@tds.net
WEBSITE	www.thehighground.org
DIRECTIONS	The Highground is located four miles west of Neillsville on U.S. Highway 10.
ADMISSION	Free
HOURS	The grounds are open 24 hours a day, seven days a week. The Timberframe Information and Gift Shop is open 10 a.m. to 5 p.m. seven days a week.
AMENITIES	Parking lot. Toilets in separate structure. Water available in the information center.

 Hudson Hospital

HUDSON

WHEN THE COMMUNITY OF HUDSON built its new hospital in 2003, board members made sure that the final design emphasized "an environment of care." The landscape architect and members of the building committee took that mandate and incorporated it into a series of gardens and a unique labyrinth that will provide hope and serenity for years to come.

The Jayne Bachman Linger Longer Labyrinth, located on the hospital's east side, melds flowers and rocks with gravel paths. The Circle of Peace design features red gravel and grey stone pavers, with weathered teak chairs in its center. Small beds installed at various stops along the paths contain irises, prairie smoke, lilies, spirea, and peonies as well as fieldstone boulders. A grass path encircles the labyrinth's exterior.

Besides the flowers in and around the labyrinth, gardens are tucked into every nook and cranny of the hospital's exterior, beginning at the main entrance. A concrete sidewalk splits the entry garden into two sections. One section contains a dry streamed with ornamental grasses, spirea, hostas, and astilbe; the other includes a water feature with a bronze statue of a little girl and her dog perched on a limestone boulder. Helping tie both sides together are similar plant selections, a continuation of the dry riverbed, and a serpentine path of red gravel. A water feature with an original painting of a St. Croix landscape and three life-sized bronze sculptures set among rocks found inside the entry doors continues the exterior theme indoors.

Curving, asymmetrical borders filled with perennials and shrubs flow from the entry gardens around the building. Funky mosaic bird feeders are placed outside of the patient rooms. The curvilinear form is continued on the building's west side, where two covered swings overlook a wild natural area. The grass between the hardscapes and the natural area is mowed in a similar curving pattern.

Plants were chosen for three-season color, texture, and interest. The palette is cool blues, pinks, and yellows. A limited list of perennials comprises most of the plant selections, along with trees and shrubs. Spruces, lilacs, lilies, ornamental grasses, catmint, peonies, and turtleheads can be seen in most of the beds. Clumps of spirea replace barberry as a living hedge.

Located between the Emergency entrance and patient rooms, the only garden in a protected area contains some roses and ninebark shrubs. Even the Emergency entrance gets its own unique garden—a dry streambed with a bird feeder in the shape of an ambulance, and some interesting shrubs.

Located on the Mississippi just east of the Twin Cities, the growing season in Hudson is short. So the hospital installed a "winter garden," a Scandinavian concept that allows pateints and their families to enjoy the gardens even in the coldest weather. A room with hardwood floors, a fireplace, and comfortable furniture invites visitors to enjoy the indoor planter filled with begonias.

COUNTY	St. Croix
ADDRESS	405 Stageline Road, Hudson
PHONE	715/531-6000
EMAIL	info@hudsonhospital.org
WEBSITE	www.hudsonhospital.org
DIRECTIONS	From I-94, exit Carmichael Road (exit 2). Turn south on Carmichael for about half a mile and turn east on to Stageline Road.
ADMISSION	Free
HOURS	Daily, dawn to dusk
AMENITIES	Parking. Toilets, food, and water inside the hospital.

Marshall Park

CHIPPEWA FALLS

A DISPLAY GARDEN gives a garden club instant credibility. For the Chippewa Valley Rose Society the rose and lily gardens located at Marshall Park in Chippewa Falls have done just that.

The Society first met in 1982. Since most rose societies have a local display garden, members decided to install a rose garden at the park in 1986. The space features some five hundred fifty roses of all varieties. There are the hybrid teas and the grandifloras, climbers and old garden roses, mini-floras and the miniature roses. And because of the hardiness of the Canadian varieties, the group installed one hundred fifty of the William Baffins, John Cabotts, and similar cultivars last year. An early spring brings blooms around May 20, which last until the roses are put to bed for the winter.

The enormous rock fountain bisects the two gardens. Local Jaycees commissioned the water feature in memory of a deceased member long before the gardens were installed. An allee of conifers flanking a concrete walk leads to the fountain.

The lily garden was installed on the west side of the fountain. Members of the Wisconsin Regional Lily Society dedicated the garden in 1993 to introduce the community to the many lily varieties available. Several hundred lilies including Asiatic, Oriental, trumpets, and a hybrid of a trumpet and an Oriental called an "oreopet" can be found there. Since these lilies only bloom for about two weeks during the season, perennials were planted for additional interest. Sedums, hostas, peonies, poppies, and liatris are just some of the plants sharing space in the six lily beds.

COUNTY	Chippewa
ADDRESS	Bridgewater Avenue, Chippewa Falls
PHONE	715/723-9089
DIRECTIONS	Located on the corner of State Highway 124 and Bridgewater across the street from the Leinenkugel Visitor's Center.
ADMISSION	Free
HOURS	Open May to October. Daily, dawn to dusk.
AMENITIES	Street parking.

 ## Octagon House Museum
HUDSON

THE VICTORIANS KNEW ALL ABOUT LUSHNESS when it came to gardens, and the staff at Hudson's Octagon House Museum have tried to recreate that experience for visitors.

Gazebo at the Octagon House

Built in 1854 for Judge John Shaw Moffat, his wife, Nancy Bennet Moffat, and their daughter, Mary, the eight-sided house was a popular architectural style during the Victorian period. The family and its descendants lived on the property for one hundred and two years, long enough for the tiny maple trees planted by the Moffat's grandson to become mature and cause plant selections to be switched from sun to shade.

Starting in the frontyard, shrub roses have nearly taken over the sign. A birdbath and a white oversize planter basket are tucked in among the lawn's floral and shrub borders. Annuals such as ageratum, zinnias, and alyssum are planted throughout the borders for summer color.

Garden beds are full of blooming perennials and bulbs. Daffodils and tulips add color in the spring, and a clematis takes over an octagonal shaped white pergola that mimics the angles of the house. Juniper balls surround the base. A white Victorian tea table and chairs is placed on flagstones edged with grass. A row of trimmed arborvitae and lilies backs a similar bench and tables.

You've heard of beer gardens, but *Chateau St. Croix Winery and Vineyard* in St. Croix Falls has installed a formal garden in its front entrance. White statues and a fountain, sculptured evergreens, and shrubs are juxtaposed against the backdrop of rolling farmland and the gray stone, castlelike winery.

Hydrangeas, lilies (tigers and stella d'oros), and twisted trunk lilac trees pop up along the home's exterior. Lining the sidewalk that leads back to the carriage house, hostas and ferns add texture to the landscape while peonies offer height, blooms, and fragrance.

A rose garden features varieties of New Zealand hybrid teas, 'Full Sail' and 'Queen Elizabeth.' Roses are planted in the center of yew parterres in two small garden rooms. A wall of conifers stands along the black wrought iron fence dividing the property from the neighbors.

COUNTY	St. Croix
ADDRESS	1004 Third Street, Hudson
PHONE	715/386-2654
EMAIL	octagonhousemuseum@juno.com
WEBSITE	www.pressenter.com/~octagon
DIRECTIONS	From I-94, exit State Highway 35 (exit 1). Go north on Highway 35 (also known as Second Street). Two blocks after the third stoplight, turn right onto Myrtle Street. The house is located on the northeast corner of Myrtle and Third streets.
ADMISSION	$7 for adults; $3 for students ages 13 to 18; $2 for children ages 6 to 12; children younger than five are free with an adult.
HOURS	May through September, noon to 4:30 p.m., Wednesday through Saturday; 2 p.m. to 4:30 p.m. Sundays.
AMENITIES	Street parking.

Pederson's Gardens and Landscapes

SUPERIOR

AFTER RETIRING FROM PROFESSIONAL CAREERS, Edith Pederson and her husband opened up Pederson's Gardens and Landscapes in 1999 in the town of Oakland, about a thirty-minute drive south of Superior. Finding this "garden center in the woods" is like following a treasure map. Directions and signage are a necessity to get here.

The site features nine demonstration gardens, although Pederson had not factored demonstration gardens into her plans until she saw the piles of dirt that were pushed into small hills while grading the land for the greenhouse building. Never one to ignore an opportunity, Pederson decided to invite her master gardener friends over to help her develop the gardens.

A rock garden welcomes visitors to the site. The butterfly garden, an extension of the rock garden, quickly serves up a dash of color. A professional birder designed the bird garden, which provides examples of the groundcovers that are appropriate for the northern climate. An apothecary garden features medicinal plants and herbs.

A perennial garden includes a section of flowers for cutting and eating —think of spicy nasturtium leaves. There's also space for the plants that were named "Perennial of the Year." The quiet woodland or shade garden is ringed with mature evergreens. A rose garden features hardy Canadian species and hardscapes such as a shade pergola, a fountain, and a split-rail fence. The iris and peony garden is separated from the rose garden only by small bridges and arbors.

Look for the giant frog perched alongside the pond in the secret garden. The bog garden includes a mini forest of dwarf Alberta spruce. In the works are an Oriental garden that will lead from the shade garden and a conifer garden.

COUNTY	Douglas
ADDRESS	5575 South Eastman Road, Superior
PHONE	715/399-0840 or 715/399-0839
EMAIL	ae@pedersongardens.com
WEBSITE	www.pedersongardens.com
DIRECTIONS	From U.S. Highway 53, go west on B to Eastman Road. Go north on Eastman Road 1.5 miles. (Eastman Road is a gravel road). From State Highway 35 South, go north to Highway B. Go east on B four miles to Eastman Road. Go north on Eastman Road. From the north, go south on Highway 35 1.5 miles outside of Superior to the cemetery. Go east and then south on Highway C (Highway C becomes Highway A) for nine miles to Thunderhill Road. Follow signs.
ADMISSION	Free
HOURS	April through October.
AMENITIES	Gravel parking lot. Toilets, food, and water available in the café.

 Phoenix Park

EAU CLAIRE

IT'S FITTING THAT PHOENIX PARK is named after the mythical bird that rises from the ashes. It's the only name that would fit this redeveloped former brownfield.

This lovely public space, located at the junction of the Chippewa and Eau Claire rivers in downtown Eau Claire, was once an old industrial property owned, interestingly enough, by Phoenix Steel Company; previously, a coal plant stood here. It took $1.5 million to restore the site to make it usable for anything besides a junkyard.

Phoenix Park is atypical for an urban park. It features a brick labyrinth, an amphitheater, and walking trails, as well as native plants and wildflowers. About a half mile of the nine-acre park is river frontage. An old trestle bridge, now exclusively for pedestrians, is part of the hardscape.

In designing the park, Phil Johnson, superintendent of parks, and his staff imagined a vine with the plant's trunk as the main path and the sprigs of leaves becoming the trails off of it. With the convergence of the two rivers, Johnson wanted a soft edge to the design. The riprap along the shore was covered with dirt and seeded with plants.

Beds of natives are interspersed with areas of mown grass in a series of soft terraces that lead down to the waterfront. Large boulders placed at various

Phoenix Park on Eau Claire's riverfront features hardscapes befitting its name

City of Eau Claire Parks Department

Boulders and black-eyed Susans at Phoenix Park

spots along the hillside offer a place to sit. Want something a little more comfortable? There are also black metal memorial benches and rectangular stone ones scattered about.

One of the "sprigs," the Confluence Plaza Path, has eight-inch brick pavers set in unique patterns. Four other plazas use a combination of natives, which are underplanted with annuals, to set them off. The objective was to use plants to separate the walkers from the bikers.

A total of six stone planters decorate the trestle bridge and one of the sides of the Royal Credit Union building. These large planters feature a mix of annuals, perennials, and ornamental grasses in all shapes, sizes, textures, and colors.

The black metal found in the memorial benches is carried through in the unusual streetlights, which have an etched design of a phoenix as a decorative accent. Boulders represent a significant portion of the hardscape. Rolled dice from the game of Yahtzee was the inspiration for the boulder grouping near the labyrinth and amphitheater.

> *Ashland's Northland College* uses northern native plants in its sustainable landscape design. The entry road to the campus features more naturalistic landscaping representative of northern meadows and wetlands. The entrances to the Ponzio Campus Center offer the formality of traditional gardens.

COUNTY	Eau Claire
ADDRESS	Riverfront Terrace, Eau Claire
PHONE	715/839-4738
DIRECTIONS	The park is located at Riverfront Terrace, Barstow, and Madison streets in downtown Eau Claire. From I-94 West exit 70 (Eau Claire/Chippewa Falls) onto U.S. Highway 53 North. Bear right onto Highway 53 North to Brackett Avenue. Turn left. Follow Brackett as it turns into Harding Avenue and Washington Street. About a block after Washington Street, turn right onto South Farwell Street. Go half a mile to Eau Claire Street and turn left. Go one block on Eau Claire Street to South Barstow Street and turn right. Go another block and turn left onto Riverfront Terrace.
ADMISSION	Free
HOURS	Daily, dawn to dusk.
AMENITIES	Street parking. Toilets.

Pink Ribbon Garden

MARSHFIELD CLINIC, WISCONSIN RAPIDS

WHEN JACKIE PICKETT WAS FIRST DIAGNOSED with breast cancer in 1998, she decided that if she got well, she would do something to ease the journey for other breast cancer patients. Pickett, a master gardener, approached the Marshfield Clinic and asked if it would help support a Pink Ribbon garden for breast cancer patients at its Wisconsin Rapids satellite location. The clinic agreed, even donating $15,000 to the cause and conducting a fund-raising campaign throughout Central Wisconsin.

Pickett and members of the River Cities Evening Garden Club, planted the 5,200-square-foot healing garden, which was dedicated in June 2007. Its intent is to be a place of hope, serenity, and peace for patients, family members and caregivers, clinic staff, and even the public.

As its name implies, the garden's centerpiece is a pink concrete path in the shape of a breast cancer ribbon pin. The six-foot wide path is large enough to allow two wheelchairs to utilize it at the same time. Other hardscapes include two water features: a copper wall of water with a vine of copper leaves that's located in the eye of the ribbon and a gazing ball on top of a pillar. Garden club members and the husbands of three club members crafted the water features. Pickett's husband, who is blind, hammered the finish on the copper sculpture.

There are also solid teak benches and several inspirational plaques. A large bronze angel with her arms raised, looks toward the heavens and symbolizes peace and hope.

Plant selection was based on year-round interest and varieties that would attract hummingbirds and butterflies. There are spring bulbs, flowering trees, fall grasses, and evergreens that add winter interest among the 1,100 plants. Peonies and hibiscus are just some of the perennial selections. There are also Wisconsin natives including penstemon, white coneflowers, miniature pink monarda, and prairie smoke. All of the plants are in comforting colors—shades of pinks, blues, purples, and whites. There are no oranges, yellows, or reds. The spring daffodils blossom in pink and white. The garden is visible from the Clinic's second floor windows where patients undergo chemotherapy.

COUNTY	Wood
ADDRESS	Marshfield Clinic, 220 24th Street South, Wisconsin Rapids
PHONE	715/424-8600
DIRECTIONS	From State Highway 13, turn onto 8th Street, which is also State Highway 54. Turn right on to Chestnut Street and travel about a mile. Turn left onto Plover Road for two blocks and take a right onto Peach Street for a block. Turn left onto 24th Street.
ADMISSION	Free
HOURS	Daily, dawn to dusk.
AMENITIES	Parking in the lot. Toilets, food, and water inside the clinic.

Riana's Garden

BELDENVILLE

STEPPING INTO THE GARDENS of Wouterina de Raad is like stepping into a fairy tale. Except that the otherworldly sculptures placed deliberately around her yard resemble nothing like those in the Brothers Grimm stories.

Since Riana (as she likes to be called) created her first mosaic sculpture eighteen years ago, she has continued to follow her muse just like several other Wisconsin artists whose work has been preserved as sculpture gardens. But unlike artists whose structures comprise the whole "garden," de Raad's works are functional pieces set among a lushness of her floral fantasy. One garden is full sun; the remainder are tucked under the canopy of mature trees that adds a fantastical feeling to the experience.

The fairy tale that's at Riana's Garden

Located on two acres of former farmland, the gardens have so far claimed about one acre. A mosaic arch beckons you to the "great lawn." On either side of the arch, a handmade fence of discarded branches sets the stage for the visual daydream. In designing her gardens, de Raad has crafted many entrances and exits. The phrase "garden room" could have been coined here.

A perennial border parallels the fence that hugs the property's east side. It's interrupted by a fanciful chicken coop and run topped with weathered birdhouses. Trees anchor other perennial borders with various species of hostas thriving in the shade. On the footprint of an old granary, handmade green cement benches are placed in front of a fire pit ringed with limestone and encircled again with perennials and dwarf conifers.

All of de Raad's sixty sculptures are functional. Some act as birdhouses, others hold old railroad torches for light. A crown-holding mermaid contains a small pond. Two oversized caterpillars anchor long benches used for outdoor dining. Test out the concrete chair—it's actually very comfortable. Look for Jack, the "husband" of Millie, the first sculpture to greet visitors at the entrance.

Jack, who has a birdhouse in his heart, is tucked into a wild space that will remain natural located on the west side of the 1878 house.

Besides her sculptures, de Raad has created some interesting hardscapes. Garden arches are crafted from rebar, the metal used to reinforce concrete, and clematis have eagerly adapted to it. Tree branches get new life as fences. Recycled blades from an old farm windmill make a vain attempt to keep the animals out of the vegetable/flower bed. Sculptures of humans and a bird decorate the clothesline.

Wherever you look, color is there in the form of pink poppies, blue delphiniums, yellow globe thistles, orange lilies, and purple alliums. That's no surprise; de Raad grew up on a coffee and rubber plantation in the Dutch East Indies and lived in Holland for ten years. Bright tropical colors make her feel at home.

Color and whimsy can be found in Riana's Garden

COUNTY	Pierce
ADDRESS	N7652 650th Street, Beldenville
PHONE	715/273-5959
WEBSITE	www.concretemosaicsculpture.com
DIRECTIONS	From I-94, exit U.S. Highway 63 at Baldwin and go south. Turn west on State Highway 29. Continue on Highway 29 for three miles. Look for 650th Street (there will be a sign for an apple orchard) and turn south. Go several miles and look for a dirt road. The entrance is the first left following the dirt road.
ADMISSION	$5 donation
HOURS	By appointment only. June through September.
AMENITIES	Gravel parking lot. Outdoor toilet.

Rudolph Grotto Gardens and Wonder Cave

RUDOLPH

AS A YOUNG SEMINARIAN studying in Europe, Father Philip Wagner became ill. Traveling to Lourdes for healing, he promised that if he recovered he would build a shrine that included gardens and statues. In 1917 he was appointed the pastor of St. Philip's Catholic Church in Rudolph, where he began work on his labor of love.

Completing the first of the shrines, the Lourdes Grotto, in 1928, Wagner and the pastors that followed him went on to complete some thirty more. The last project was finished in 1983.

The five-acre grounds are planted with a variety of bulbs, perennials, annuals, flowering shrubs, and mature trees. The tree canopy gives the site a woodland garden feel. Some thirty-five pickup truckloads of annuals are planted each year, along with thirty baskets of bulbs.

Beds filled with delphiniums, bleeding hearts, peonies, and sedum are tucked into the woods. For color, annuals like begonias, marigolds, and petunias are added. And spring welcomes the onset of honeysuckle and lilac blooms. A hosta bed showcases varieties such as 'Sea Octopus', 'Invincible', 'Great Expectations', and 'Sun Power.' Ferns are ever present. The thorn tree, a type of swamp locust, sprouted and grew on its own.

Large boulders edge the beds, which are placed near and around small shrines and structures. The Wonder Cave features a one-fifth mile trail through a structure intended to resemble the Roman catacombs.

Entrance to the Wonder Cave at Rudolph Grotto Gardens

Like Mathias Wernerus at Dickeyville, Wagner employed a variety of materials to construct his hardscapes. Bricks from abandoned kilns, bits of colored glass from old windows, and fallen timber from local wood lots were woven together to support the plantings. Most of the distinctive rock, called "gossan," came from within a fifteen- to twenty-mile radius of Rudolph. Unless otherwise noted on the signs, all of the religious statues, murals, and Catholic iconography were carved from Carrara marble imported from Italy.

There are more contemporary inclusions to the gardens, such as a wagon wheel and the Soldier's Memorial Monument dedicated to the fallen in World War I. Gravel paths snake from shrine to shrine. The sunken garden includes a fish pond, waterfall, water wheel, and lighthouse. While the gardens at the Dickeyville Grotto emphasize formality, the Rudolph Grotto Gardens are more informal.

COUNTY	Wood
ADDRESS	6975 Grotto Avenue, Rudolph
PHONE	715/435-3120 or 715/435-3456
WEBSITE	www.mnmuseumofthems.org/Grotto/Wonder1.html
DIRECTIONS	The grotto gardens are located on the grounds of St. Philip's Church at the corner of Second Street and Grotto Avenue.
ADMISSION	Free; donations accepted.
HOURS	Memorial Day through Labor Day or by appointment. Daily, dawn to dusk.
AMENITIES	Parking lot. Toilets and water inside of the church.

✒ Types of Public Gardens:

The American Public Gardens Association defines public gardens in the following way:

Arboreta – these are typically parks which grow woody trees and shrubs for educational and scientific purposes.

Botanical gardens – these contain collections of plants that have a scientific order to them.

College and university gardens – gardens maintained by educational institutions for public display and research.

Conservatories – a collection of plants displayed under glass.

Display gardens – in these gardens plants are chosen and maintained for their aesthetic value.

Entertainment gardens – these gardens are expected to enhance the experience of visitors at golf courses, theme parks, water parks, etc.

Historical landscapes and sites – also intended to enhance the experience of visitors to a particular historic site, these gardens generally reflect the type of plants of a specific historical period. You'll find these in churches, cemeteries, historic homes, and museums to name a few places.

Nature gardens – the intent of these gardens is to connect visitors with nature and illustrate how humans, animals, and flora are all intertwined.

Specialized collections – these gardens are "focused on the propagation, growth, and development of specific plant species."

Zoos – the objective of zoo gardens is to protect and enhance the habitat for the animal species as well as represent the plants that the animals experience in their native habitat.

Sentry World Golf Course

STEVENS POINT

GOLFERS FACE MORE than the usual share of surprises when they attempt to play the 16th hole at Stevens Point's SentryWorld golf course. Each year the course's signature hole, better known as the "flower hole," is planted with some 51,000 annuals.

Blame the extra challenge on golf course architect, Robert Trent Jones, Jr., who added the distinctive one hundred and seventy three-yard, short par-3 hole to this "classic" course. Although it was Jones' idea, SentryWorld staff are responsible for changing the frame of flowers around the cusp of the hole each year. Along with the frame design, flower and color selections also vary depending upon maintenance issues, resistance to disease and insects, and what the deer seem to avoid.

Planting flowers in such large masses calls for solid colors for impact and lots of one type of plant. This can be tricky because one sick flower or an unexpected insect invasion can wipe out a significant portion of the beauty. So SentryWorld's landscape designer and groundskeepers try to rotate the variety every year. It takes between ten and twenty people almost ten early mornings to fill the beds for the season.

Flower favorites include marigolds, fibrous begonias, and ageratums. There are other brilliant color varieties that would make a similar impact, but they can present problems when planted in large quantities. Deadheading thousands of geraniums is a high maintenance task. A heavy rain will flatten out petunias for a week. But with researchers developing new varieties at a fast pace, don't rule these selections out for the future.

The hole used to require the planting of more than 70,000 annuals for every new design, but over the past few years, some of the 25,000 square feet around the hole's cusp has been planted with perennials, resulting in color from early spring to late fall. No matter when the golfer wants to play, there's always something special blooming on hole 16.

COUNTY	Portage
ADDRESS	601 North Michigan Avenue, Stevens Point
PHONE	715/345-1600
WEBSITE	www.sentryworld.com
DIRECTIONS	From I-39 south, exit Business 51 and continue north on Northpoint Drive. Turn right on Michigan Avenue. From I-39 north, exit Business 51 and continue south on Northpoint Drive. Turn left onto Michigan Avenue. Follow the signs for the golf course.
ADMISSION	Free
HOURS	Call 866/479-6753 for appointment.
AMENITIES	Parking lot. Toilets, full-service restaurant, water, pro shop, available in the clubhouse.

South Wood County Historical Museum

WISCONSIN RAPIDS

THE IMPOSING NEO-CLASSICAL REVIVAL STYLE MANSION overlooking the Wisconsin River was once the home of Isaac Witter, a Wisconsin Rapids banker with ties to both the Mead papermaking family and one of the founders of the former Dean Witter Reynolds financial company. Its previous life included a stint as the local library before becoming the home of the South Wood County Historical Museum.

The museum's board wants both the mansion and its gardens to be a destination spot, so members of the Wood County Master Gardeners have free reign on this property, which is the size of eight city blocks. Their enthusiasm has yielded some delightful results.

Flowers line the Museum sidewalk

The gardens around the 1907 brick mansion, called Shadow Lawn, soften the structure's imposing façade. The sidewalk to the front entrance is flanked with a cheery mixture of perennials and annuals. Red barberry shrubs accent the Russian sage, liatris, Oriental poppies, fairy candles, and campanula that perk up the space. This is just one of the thirteen beds you'll see on the property.

Flowering shrubs give a bit of vertical lift to a hosta border that runs along the property's south side. Astilbe and tiger lilies add shots of color to the hostas' variegated greens, creams, and yellows.

A large shade garden tucked under several mature black walnut trees proves that the trees' reputation for killing off anything nearby can be overcome with the right plant selections. Ferns, hostas, and daylilies are thriving despite the juglone-filled soil. The shade garden overlooks Second Street and the river. It's appropriately placed to break up the large expanse of lawn leading down from the back of the house. Originally the grounds included a fountain and flower gardens that extended to the river's banks. A portion of an old stone wall from the original landscaping remains.

On the north side of the house, a large border is anchored at one end with a clump of hydrangeas and at the other end with astilbe. The center portion consists of a strip of sedums and peonies that's cut in half with a grass path. A row of mature arborvitae separates the museum from its northern neighbors.

Clematis covers a large, unique trellis built by students at Nekoosa High School. The students also crafted a Victorian-style tree bench for the property. A set of concrete steps leads down from the house, and streetlights are replicated in a style from that era.

The trees get special attention from the students in the forestry program at Mid-State Technical College. College instructors use the site as a hands-on lesson in pruning well-established trees.

Two spots to check out while you're in the area are the grounds of the Central Wisconsin State Fair Park (www.centralwisconsinstatefair.com) with its enormous round barn. The Wood County Master Gardeners have installed a demonstration garden around a gazebo on the grounds. Drive a little farther to Vesper and see where the master gardeners are renovating a former prairie garden at the Park and Sports Facility. Little garden paths are being installed to form a butterfly garden. A scent garden is being considered. Tulips and daffodils announce the arrival of spring. A large oak is the perfect spot for hostas and some astilbe, and a covered bridge traverses a streambed. Members of the area's Amish community put up the gazebo. An herb garden borders part of the gazebo; a walking path leads past raspberry and blueberry plants.

COUNTY	Wood
ADDRESS	540 Third Street South, Wisconsin Rapids
PHONE	715/423-1580 or 715/423-6369
EMAIL	museum@wctc.net
WEBSITE	www.swch-museum.com
DIRECTIONS	From State Highway 13, follow it into Wisconsin Rapids. Continue on 8th Street, which is also State Highway 54. Turn left onto East Riverview Expressway (also Highway 13 North) and go about a block. Turn right on Lincoln Street and go about two blocks. Turn left on Witter Street and go another two blocks. Turn left on South Third Street.
ADMISSION	Free
HOURS	The museum is open from 1 p.m. to 4 p.m. Tuesdays, Thursdays, and Sundays, Memorial Day to Labor Day.
AMENITIES	Parking lot. Toilets and water inside the building.

Spooner Agricultural Research Station
SPOONER

THE FIFTY-FOOT BY SIXTY-FOOT DEMONSTRATION GARDEN at the Spooner Agriculture Research Station provides a welcome burst of color set amidst the station's large crop fields. The eight perennial beds, set off with boulders, are a relatively new addition to the site. The space where the heirloom tomato trials are currently being conducted was previously used as a rose trial bed, an optimistic endeavor given the area's average one hundred and twenty-day growing season and light sandy soil. A particularly severe winter during the three-year trial killed all but four of the original one hundred and twenty roses.

Yet roses are still undeniably evident in the perennial beds. You'll find 'Therese Bugnet,' 'John Franklin,' 'Mrs. Dorene Pike,'

> Both the *Hotel Mead* and the *McMillan Public Library* in Wisconsin Rapids have nice plantings and they're located across the street from one another. Look for the spiral topiaries near the front entrance to the hotel and the water feature at the library.

The gardens at the Spooner Agricultural Research Station

and 'Knockout' varieties interspersed with perennials such as butterfly weed, bleeding hearts, and 'Heavy Metal' switchgrass. Lilacs, hydrangeas, and azaleas provide backdrop height, as do the Nankin cherry and Russian cypress trees. There's even the very twisted Harry Lauder's Walking Stick helping to anchor one of the beds.

A split-rail fence bisects one bed that includes two benches as hardscapes. Delphiniums and daisies use the fence for support. Tucked under a shade arbor covered with 'William Baffin' roses and clematis is another bench offering a bit of respite.

The University of Wisconsin sponsors the Spooner station, one of twelve agricultural research stations around the state. Sheep and heirloom tomatoes are two of this station's main research specialties. The garden is one of the state's seven All-America Selections designated display gardens.

COUNTY	Washburn
ADDRESS	W6646 Highway 70, Spooner
PHONE	715/635-3506 or 800/528-1914
FAX	715/635-6741
DIRECTIONS	The station is located on the east side of Spooner on State Highway 70.
ADMISSION	Free
HOURS	Seasonal. Daily, dawn to dusk.
AMENITIES	None

Upham Mansion

MARSHFIELD

TO PARAPHRASE MAMA ROSE in the play, *Gypsy*, "everything's coming up roses" at Marshfield's Upham Mansion. The restored 1883 Victorian home of former Wisconsin Governor William Henry Upham boasts a formal heritage rose garden in the backyard.

The thirty varieties of roses are among the oldest varieties in the world. From the 'Cardinal Richelieu' gallica variety that blooms only once a growing season to the Salet moss rose that's a repeat bloomer, the beauties and their fragrances are certain to delight the senses. A 1530 'Charles de Mills' crimson red gallica is one of the oldest on the property although there are a few that date back to the year 200 at the time of the Roman Empire.

Planted in nine raised beds, rose varieties run the gamut from damask, polyanthus, portland, vine, alba, rugosa, foetida as well as the 'R. foeteda' variety, centifolia species, and hybrids perpetual and spinosissima. An attempt at growing hybrid teas ended in failure, so the choice was made to plant varieties that are ageless and that would reflect what might have been there during the time that Governor Upham and his family lived there. Of the thirty varieties planted, half only flower once during the season; the rest are repeat bloomers.

A virtual rainbow of colors appears in mid-June when the plants are in bloom. From the

Upham Mansion

'Madam Hardy' rose; peony; iris

Tom Ptak

Pergola on the garden path at Upham Mansion

pinks, crimsons, and purples to the orange-yellows and whites, it's hard to pick a favorite. A wooden pergola with bower seating along the walkways frames the scene, providing both an architectural as well as a historical perspective.

Although the garden was put in over a three-year period in the 1990s, it isn't out of character for the site. Turn-of-the-century photos from the 1900s revealed that the Upham family did have a rose garden in their backyard. So, in keeping with tradition, the North Wood County Historical Society, whose headquarters are located in the mansion, decided to reinstall one. The organization hired Stephen and Linda Schulte of Foxfire Gardens to design the site. The mansion also has beds of perennials such as hostas, lilacs, irises, and peonies, but it's the roses that stop the show.

COUNTY	Wood
ADDRESS	212 West Third Street, Marshfield
EMAIL	uphammansion@verizon.net
WEBSITE	www.uphammansion.com
DIRECTIONS	From State Highway 13, turn west onto Third Street.
ADMISSION	Free
HOURS	1:30 p.m. to 4 p.m. Sundays and Wednesdays, June through September. Guided group tours by appointment.
AMENITIES	Street parking. Toilets and water inside the mansion.

Wildwood Park and Zoo

MARSHFIELD

THERE ARE NO AFRICAN LIONS OR TIGERS at the sixty-acre Wildwood Park and Zoo, but there is a grizzly bear. Gardeners won't miss the felines but they shouldn't miss the two sensory gardens on the park property connected to the zoo.

Designed to appeal to four out of the five senses (taste was not factored into the design), the Asian-inspired gardens exude a sense of peace and calm. Thanks to Stephen Schulte of the nearby Foxfire Gardens who was on the board of the Zoological Society during the design stage, the gardens adhere to basic standards of Japanese design and follow the "less is more" principle.

Rocks are the basic foundation for a Japanese garden, and they're abundant in this site. The large boulders were positioned before anything else was installed. In Japanese design, the boulders represent unchanging permanence.

Unlike Western gardens where color and flowers predominate, plants play a secondary role in a Japanese garden, so you won't find many flowers here. The emphasis is on structure and plants. Junipers, arborvitae, hostas, and ornamental grasses are accentuated with the occasional azalea for color. Plantings convey a sense of impermanence in contrast to the rocks.

The sight and sound of water is to remind visitors of the passage of time. The gardens' ponds are bordered with small rocks and then ringed with bark mulch and plantings. A wooden bridge, which denotes a journey, crosses one of the ponds.

Japanese touches accent the garden at Wildwood Park and Zoo

Enclosure is another component that's key in designing a Japanese garden. Generally accomplished with a fence or a gate, at the zoo a series of wooden benches set on a patio are "enclosed" with a small, triangular-shaped wooden fence. While not practical for keeping things in or out, it gives the viewer a sense of retreat from the outside world. A road bisects the two gardens, yet there's an interconnectedness between the two spaces. One appears more minimalist than the other, but they are both cut from the same cloth.

Outside the education building, the zoo has installed a native plant garden. Woodland plants are growing on the building's east side while the west side contains prairie plants.

COUNTY	608 West 17th Street, Marshfield
PHONE	715/486-2056
FAX	715/384-2799
WEBSITE	http://ci.marshfield.wi.us/pr/Zoo
DIRECTIONS	From State Highway 13, turn left on to Wildwood Park, go one block. Turn right on South Central Avenue for one block. Turn left on to West 17th Street.
ADMISSION	Free
HOURS	Wildwood Park is open from 6 a.m. to 10:30 p.m. daily. The Zoo is open from 7:30 a.m. to 7:30 p.m. daily from the end of April to mid-September.
AMENITIES	Parking lot. Toilets and water available.

Winter Greenhouse

WINTER

WITH A GOOD MAP, you can find almost any buried treasure. While Winter Greenhouse isn't exactly buried, it is in the middle of a grove of trees, smack dab on the outskirts of the Chequamegon-Nicolet National Forest. Mature evergreens edge the serpentine gravel drive into the property. Nothing is revealed until the absolute last minute.

Opened in 1984, the greenhouse grows more than 1,000 perennial varieties, proving that the cold weather and sandy soil of the north woods is no barrier to a lovely garden. The greenhouse also carries a full selection of annuals and hanging baskets as large as thirty-six inches in diameter. Several large display gardens (one full shade, one partial shade, and one full sun) as well as a border with multiple gardens, are the journey's treasures.

The established full-shade garden features the requisite hostas and ferns underplanted beneath mature trees. Pachysandra, lamium, and astilbe are used for groundcover. Tree peonies, foxglove, and snakeroot are scattered about. The partial shade garden wasn't on the drawing board until a large storm hit and took out several of the oaks and maples. What remains of one of the downed trees is now a natural support for a clematis.

The full sun garden at the Winter Greenhouse

The owners, Jim and Kelly Wilson, try to push the envelope with their plants, testing varieties to see what will survive the northern climate. Technically located in Zone 3, there are Zone 5 recommended plants that seem to do well here. The Wilsons have found a hardy hibiscus that doesn't shy away from the cold.

A small waterfall tumbling into a stream leading to a pond acts as a focal point for the full sun garden. A wooden bridge goes over the stream. Cannas and angel trumpets anchor the annual beds. Two rattan arbors support roses and clematis. Paths made from river stone encircle the sun garden and help with the transition between the circular bed and the border.

Frederick Law Olmsted did the landscaping for the historic Wilson Place in Menomonie. The mansion, built for the founder of the city of Menomonie, was enlarged and remodeled when the estate passed into the hands of the heirs, the founder of the University of Wisconsin-Stout and his wife. Many of the trees and shrubs along the riverbank are original to Olmsted's plan. A small circular garden with a fountain is located in the backyard.

The border features herb, rock, shade, and sun beds. There's a bog bed and a buffalo bed, named for the large rock that resembles a buffalo. The Wilsons are in the process of installing a garden that will be hidden in the woods. Inside one of the hoop houses is a pond with aquatic plants. A series of raised beds between the hoop houses is attractively filled with plant material.

COUNTY	Sawyer
ADDRESS	W7041 Olmstead Road, Winter
PHONE	715/266-4963 or 715/266-5502
EMAIL	mail@wintergreenhouse.com
WEBSITE	www.wintergreenhouse.com
DIRECTIONS	Two miles north of Winter on Highway W.
ADMISSION	Free
HOURS	Seasonal. 8:30 a.m. to 5:30 p.m. daily, April 19 to July 4. 8:30 a.m. to 5 p.m. July 5 to Oct. 15. Fridays in May open till 7 p.m.
AMENITIES	Parking lot. Toilets available. Water and soda available under the pergola that's used as a garden center.

"Yuujou Niwa" Friendship Garden
RICE LAKE

GARDENS CAN BE USED TO BRIDGE FRIENDSHIPS across the world; evidence of that can be found in Rice Lake. In 1998, on the tenth anniversary of the sister city relationship between the cities of Rice Lake and Miharu-Machi, Japan, the Rice Lake International Friendship Association undertook the task of building an authentic Japanese garden. The garden is located on the south side of the campus library at the University of Wisconsin-Barron County. With the help of three master gardeners from Miharu, volunteers from Rice Lake turned the space from lawn to rock garden in three weeks.

Surrounded by a unique bamboo fence lashed together with black cord, the garden features some four hundred plants and trees in a space that's thirty-five feet by forty

Water feature at the Friendship Garden

feet. Selected plants include junipers, lilacs, Siberian iris, spirea, lilies, and hostas. Rocks and plants are placed to resemble a mountain range and waterfall.

A red-brick paver path entices the curious. Stepping stones set in fine gravel begin just inside the entrance gate and lead to a covered meditation bench.

There are three small lanterns. The Yukimi lantern placed along the water symbolizes snow. The Kasuga lantern hidden in the garden's far west side represents modesty. And the Oribe lantern, located near the garden exit, is one similar to those used in a Japanese tea ceremony and was named for a Japanese warlord who designed it specifically for garden use.

The water feature can be found on the garden's south end. Four Japanese characters are etched in a water basin at

Knapp Stout City Garden in Rice Lake includes a gazebo with a perennial garden, a raised annual garden, and a tree and shrub border. The Rice Lake Garden Club maintains this garden as well as the perennial garden found in Rice Lake City Park.

12 o'clock (ourselves), 3 o'clock (only), 6 o'clock (enough), and at 9 o'clock (realize/know). When the water feature is on, visitors are invited to wash their hands in the basin before resting at the meditation bench.

Yukimi lantern at the Friendship Garden in Rice Lake

A rectangular bed, an extension of the garden, continues along the south wall of the library. Trees and shrubs anchor large boulders on a bed of white stone. A shorter bamboo fence defines the garden's edge from the building's red brick. The fence's design is mirrored in the roof of the meditation bench. Black cord was also used to assemble a vertical twig fence that backs the bench. Other hardscapes include a granite bridge and a dry streambed.

COUNTY	Barron
ADDRESS	Campus Library, 1800 College Drive, Rice Lake
DIRECTIONS	From U.S. Highway 53, exit Highway O. Go east and turn north on Main Street. Turn west on West South Street to College Drive. Take College Drive north to UW-Barron County and follow the signs for the friendship garden.
ADMISSION	Free
HOURS	Seasonal. Daily, dawn to dusk.
AMENITIES	Parking lot. Toilets, food, and water inside the buildings.

Northeast
Wisconsin

Arbor View Gardens

CLINTONVILLE

IF YOU GIVE A HORTICULTURIST A PLANT, there's a chance he or she will try to expand it into a public garden. That's roughly what happened to Andy and Sharon Gleisner of Clintonville. Their Arbor View Gardens blossomed as the result of a hobby that got a little out of hand.

It all began back in 1975 when Andy, a horticultural graduate from the University of Wisconsin-Madison, and Sharon began collecting trees, shrubs, and flowers. What was once a hobby appears to have turned into an obsession, really gaining steam in 1999. The result is a twenty-acre public garden and arboretum filled with over a thousand varieties of woody plants and perennials.

Driving the gravel road into the property you'll first encounter a large, carved peace pipe. This "friendship pipe," honoring the local Menominee and other woodland tribes, depicts the Gleisners' belief that friendship should be extended to "peoples of all races who take the stewardship of the earth's environment seriously." The pipe, set in what is called the History Circle, is part of a display representing the "owners" of this particular piece of land. Tumbled glacial rocks signify the land's glacial period. The peace pipe represents the Native Americans. The fences and heirloom plants recall the settlement period when the land was homesteaded and the farm wife would bring lilacs and hollyhocks to plant in her new garden.

The Fairies' garden with its tiny Cotswold cottage at Thistledown Greenhouses

This interactive display symbolizes what author Joseph Beuys calls the three miracles of the universe. Planted between the glacial rocks are three trees, a yellow birch from the United States, a European linden from Europe, and a ginkgo from Asia. The three rocks represent basic existence; the trees signify life; and the person viewing the display as having the capability of conscious thought.

Behind the barn, which acts as a visitor's center, is Sharon's "playpen." The courtyard features a series of beds ringed with stones containing a mixture of annuals and perennials as well as garden art. There's a stone vulture that keeps watch in the cactus bed.

Just outside of the playpen, stones border a koi pond with a waterfall and aquatic plants. On the west side of the property, a rock garden helps blend a silo's stone base into the landscape. An overlook built on top of the silo base offers expansive views. Around the corner mature trees shade an angel garden. Engraved stones and wood benches provide the hardscape for hostas and other shade plants.

Two of the most interesting gardens here are the sand garden and the Green and Gold garden. Andy, who regularly heard complaints about the sandy soil in Central Wisconsin, decided to show that a variety of plants could grow there. He dug out two feet of soil and filled the bed with quarry sand. What's planted there is left on its own to survive.

The Green and Gold garden is a tribute to Packers fans everywhere. All of the plants have golden blooms or foliage. There are Chicago Sunrise lilies, Chinese and Mother Lode junipers, golden forsythia, Bonanza Gold barberry, and Tiger eye staghorn sumac. Two Asian-inspired lattices seem to resemble the teams' Eoal posts. A metal frame of the Super Bowl trophy will eventually be covered with Star Showers Virginia creeper.

A Japanese garden, a moss garden, and a massive stone bridge are under construction. The water from a fountain in the Japanese garden will morph into a stream that travels under the bridge to keep the moss garden moist.

Grass walking paths are carved throughout the prairie on the south side of the property. One path leads to a teahouse overlooking a pond and a marsh. The structure's double overhang roof and square floor plan are oriented to the four directions. The arcing design of the window mullions represents an Oriental moon bridge, and Chinese characters placed above the front entrance signify long life, happiness, tranquility, and wealth. The teahouse design and siting follows feng shui principles.

The Gleisners' land is divided into various arboretums including one honoring Edward Hasselkus, the emeritus curator of the Longenecker Horticultural Gardens at the University of Wisconsin-Madison Arboretum and Andy's mentor.

While you're in the area, visit Thistledown Greenhouses (www.thistledown.us) outside of Bonduel. John and Lori Nero have created a magical fairyland that's full of miniature plants. An eight-foot by eight-foot Fairies' Garden contains a tiny Cotswold Cottage, a waterfall, bridge, and even a moat. Fairies enjoy the miniature conifers, groundcovers, and mosses of their English estate. The greenhouses also carry a selection of unusual plants such as Australian cushion bush, fern leaf tansy, purple- and white-striped verbena, and abutilon.

COUNTY	Waupaca
ADDRESS	E10540 County Road C, Clintonville
PHONE	715/823-2763
EMAIL	arborvw@frontiernet.net
DIRECTIONS	Go east on State Highway 156 on the north side of Clintonville to the Embarrass River Bridge. Right after the river, go south on County Road Y. Go two miles on Highway Y until it connects with Highway C. Turn west and go about half a mile. A deer fence surrounds the gardens.
ADMISSION	Freewill offering
HOURS	10 a.m. to 4 p.m. Wednesday through Sunday. Closed Monday and Tuesday.
AMENITIES	Gravel parking lot. Toilets on the grounds.

The Clearing/The Ridges Sanctuary
ELLISON BAY/BAILEYS HARBOR

IN 1935, Jens Jensen, a Danish-born landscape architect who was superintendent of the Chicago Parks Department, wanted a place where people could go to "breathe and feel kinship with the earth." His idea of paradise became the Clearing, now a folk school for adults, located near the tip of the Door County peninsula.

Jensen's vision was to offer hands-on learning experiences to young landscape architects. After they finished their formal schooling and received their degrees, Jensen would bring the newly minted graduates to his one hundred and twenty eight-acre property on Ellison Bay where they could apply their knowledge to real-world situations.

Jensen, the founder of the "prairie style," showed many young landscape architects how to take their lead from the soil. Components of the prairie style include open spaces and paths, the use of native plants and materials, and an emphasis on wandering rather than on straight lines. Jensen named his school the Clearing because its intent was "to clear away all debris of overstuffed learning steeped in form and tradition and to get to the source of all wisdom ... the soil."

The property includes forests, meadows, rustic stone and log buildings, as well as fences and stair railings made from tree branches. Many of the stones for the buildings came from the property itself. The school is set on the Niagara Escarpment, a limestone cliff running along Door County's western edge. There are no formal "gardens" as such on the property, but trails lead you to wildflowers and meadow plants that Jensen would have used for inspiration.

While you're in the area, stop in at The Ridges Sanctuary in Baileys Harbor that Jensen helped establish. While some five hundred species of vascular plants can be found among the boreal forest and wetlands on this 1,500-acre site, the most sought after are the orchids. Here you'll find more than twenty-five species of native orchids, including the pink moccasin flower, the grass pink orchid, the showy lady's-slipper, and the ram's head lady's-slipper. Other wildflowers of note are the early blooming trailing arbutus, the season-long bloom of the Indian paintbrush, and the later blooming fringed gentian.

COUNTY	Door
ADDRESS	**The Clearing:** 12171 Garrett Bay Road, Ellison Bay **The Ridges:** County Highway Q, Baileys Harbor
PHONE	**The Clearing:** 877/854-3225; **The Ridges:** 920/839-2802
EMAIL	www.theclearing.org or www.ridgesanctuary.org
DIRECTIONS	**The Clearing:** From State Highway 42, turn left at Garrett Bay Road. **The Ridges:** Turn on Highway Q off of State Highway 57.
ADMISSION	Free for the Clearing; $3 for adults and free for children at the Ridges.
HOURS	The Clearing is only open to the public from noon to 4 p.m. Saturdays and Sundays from May to October. The rest of the time it is a "closed campus" for the use of the students enrolled in the classes. The Nature Center at The Ridges Sanctuary is open from mid-May to mid-October.
AMENITIES	Gravel parking lot. Toilets in the visitor's center.

Door County
DOOR COUNTY

WITH DOOR COUNTY'S NATURAL BEAUTY, it's hard to improve on Mother Nature. But many of the communities along State Highways 42/57 have taken it upon themselves to dress Mother up.

It's probably best to start the fashion show in Sturgeon Bay, where the two highways are one. Highlights to see are the Master Gardeners' dream display garden, The Garden Door, located behind the Peninsular Agricultural Research Station just north of the city; and Crossroads at Big Creek Historical and Environmental Learning Preserve (www.crossroadsatbigcreek.org). The preserve features an extensive heritage garden that's a part of the Historic Village. Annual, perennial, and vegetable selections in this garden are based upon Rudy and Joy Faveretti's book, *For Every House a Garden*, and JoAnn Gardner's book, *Heirloom Flower Gardens*, according to Marilyn Cunningham, a Master Gardener and member of the Sturgeon Bay Home and Garden Club. Plants are further verified against lists from the Brooklyn Botanic Garden. While still in Sturgeon Bay, stop by Jefferson Street (www.jeffersonstreetshops.com) for interesting gardens tucked among the whimsical shops found there.

Veer off on Highway 57 toward Institute. The colorful palette outside of Shear Style includes perennials, ornamental grasses, bulbs, and reseeding annuals. It won the Best Commercial Garden in the 2007 Door County Advocate Gardening Contest.

Heading north to Baileys Harbor will bring you to the Ridges Sanctuary (www.ridgesanctuary.org), the oldest private nature preserve in the state. The sanctuary is also designated as a State Natural Area and a National Natural Landmark. Also in Baileys Harbor are the display gardens at Bridenhagen Tree and Landscape (2199 Lime Kiln Road). The Door County Master Gardeners designated the site a Garden of Distinction for 2007 as part of the self-guided garden tour for the annual Festival of Blossoms.

Bjorklunden, a seminar site for Lawrence University with an ancient Norwegian stave church on the property, welcomes visitors between 1 p.m. and 4 p.m. Monday and Wednesdays from mid-June through August. Door Shakespeare performs in the grove next to a woodland garden with an ancient stone fence. Decorate your own garden with art from Nita's Garden Gate (8081 Highway 57).

Connect up with Highway 42 in Sister Bay and head north to Ellison Bay and Gills Rock, where various businesses have added plantings to their landscapes. In Ellison Bay, don't miss the Clearing (www.theclearing.org), Jens Jensen's school and retreat. From the tip of the peninsula, retrace your route down Highway 42 to Sister Bay.

It's probably safe to say that the first "green" roof in the state was located in Sister Bay at Al Johnson's Swedish Restaurant. But unlike the current green roofs that are planted with sedums, this one is covered with grass for the goats. Yup, four goats make their home on the roof and keep the grass nice and tidy. Shop in a garden at Country Walk Shops (www.countrywalkshops.com).

From Sister Bay, head south just a few miles to Ephraim. One place you won't want to miss here is Fine Line Designs Gallery (www.finelinedesigns-gallery.com). The display garden in the frontyard is filled with funky garden sculptures and all kinds of native and perennial plantings including hollyhocks, lilies, and Queen Anne's lace. Limestone boulders add structure to the garden. There's also a pond and garden located behind the City Farmer.

From Ephraim, continue south to Fish Creek. It seems there's a bit of colorful competition between Fish Creek and Egg Harbor; both communities have planted a row of colorful annuals along the curb that borders Highway 42 (Fish Creek chose marigolds, while Egg Harbor installed petunias). One of the Gardens of Distinction, the Gilbraltar Town Hall, can be found in Fish Creek. Flowers have taken over the tree line in front of the town hall with lilies, roses, alliums, black-eyed Susans, and purple coneflowers usurping the lawn. Two large blue spruces flank the front door.

Don't forget to stop and see the grounds of the Peninsula Art School and Gallery (www.peninsulaartschool.com), also in Fish Creek. Art students don't need to look far for floral inspiration with the gardens here. Copper sprinklers from artist David Cain can be found at the Rusty Rabbit Shop (www.rusty rabbitshop.com).

Egg Harbor is the last stop on Highway 42 before it merges again with Highway 57. The Cupola House Shops (www.cupolahouse.com) are housed in an 1871 Gothic Revival home and the gardens around it supplement the beauty inside. There's art and sprinklers tucked into the gardens in front of Dovetail Gallery/Studio and Egg Art Museum.

This is just a smattering of the color you'll see. There are many more shops, restaurants, and businesses that have beautified their sites with flowers, trees, and shrubs, accenting Mother Nature's own loveliness.

COUNTY	Door
DIRECTIONS	Follow State Highways 42 and 57 around the peninsula.
ADMISSION	Free
HOURS	Daily, dawn to dusk
AMENITIES	Parking lot. Toilets, food, and water inside the restaurants.

The Flying Pig Gallery and Greenspace
ALGOMA

YOU EXPECT A BIT OF WHIMSY when pigs fly, and the Flying Pig Gallery and Greenspace, located just south of Algoma on State Highway 42, does not disappoint.

Realizing the futility of competing with big box stores on flora and mass produced garden art, owners Susan Connor and Robyn Mulhaney have decided to go all out—actually, way out—in stocking their greenhouse with unique plant materials and artisan-crafted sculpture and landscape art.

Coming from the south, the first thing that catches the eye is actually an eye, an ever-green topiary in the shape of the organ of sight. Next are a series of evergreen topiaries that spell out "Believe." A flying pig topiary completes the message. These living sculptures are just a few found around the grounds.

Plant selections lean toward the fanci-ful: miniature cattails, Harry Lauder Walking Sticks, whirly girl shrubs, espaliered trees. The vine-covered rock gar-den features wooden elf carvings. Pots of herbs, dwarf conifers, and sedums are

The spitting fish fountain at The Flying Pig

tucked in and around the rocks. Back in the grove of cedars there's an execu-tive chair that's used as a base for sedums and mosses. A metal frame from a

Whimsical touches at Flying Pig

baby grand piano is the backdrop for pots of blue lyme grass. Hanging pots are actually conical rather than the traditional bowl shape.

Without a doubt, the hardscapes are truly one of a kind. The water feature is a moat with rock falls and a stream. The moat includes two metal spitting fish fountains. A wooden "royal" bridge leads to an overgrown sandbox that overlooks the moat. An oversized dragonfly appears to have landed in the stream-fed wetland pond.

The sandbox includes toys for kids and Adirondack chairs for tired shoppers or their patient spouses. There's a full-size metal harp, a giant shiny-black cockroach, and several types of glass art a la Dale Chihuly. A wonderfully funky pergola, made from weathered logs and topped with a metal cupola, is not to be missed. Who says garden structures have to be geometric? Several cabins painted in either red or purple are used for storage or as a demonstration stage for visiting artists.

Connor and Mulhaney opened the store in July 2003. The fifteen acres is mostly conserved wetlands. The flying pig for whom the shop is named is a bright red one with purple wings. It appears to fly off of the second story of a three-story corrugated metal building that resembles an old feed mill. Interior beams came from a farmer's field in Luxemburg. In designing the space, the architecture utilized both passive solar and geothermal energies. Plans are being considered for a wind energy system.

The store stocks garden art and cards, serves as a gallery for artists, and hosts Music in the Garden events.

COUNTY	Kewaunee
ADDRESS	N6975 State Highway 42, Algoma
PHONE	920/487-9902
WEBSITE	www.theflyingpig.biz
DIRECTIONS	Located 2 miles south of Algoma on Highway 42.
ADMISSION	Free
HOURS	Open 9 a.m. to 6 p.m. daily, May through October. Open Friday, Saturday, Sunday, and Monday from November to April.
AMENITIES	Gravel parking lot. Toilets, food, and water inside the shop.

Multiple garden beds dot the 5,000-foot-long *LeRoyer Memorial Walkway at Langlade Medical Center in Antigo.* Built as a memorial for hospice patients, the walk includes a labyrinth and a geranium bed that's replanted every Memorial Day.

Fox Valley Technical College

APPLETON

FROM DRIVEWAY TO DAZZLING DISPLAY. That describes the transformation that's occurred at Fox Valley Technical College's Appleton campus. Landscape architect James Beard's redesign of the school's grounds started with moving the parking lots and driveways away from the buildings. His decision left a lot of space to be filled.

After the plan was approved, Beard joined the college as a faculty member in the horticultural department. Enlisting the help of his students to fill the open space, they've transformed what was a rather nondescript campus into one that's been included on community garden walks. And the conversion continues.

Architecturally, the campus buildings are pretty angular and straight-forward, with few architectural embellishments. To soften the look, Beard and his students set about installing trees, shrubs, perennials, and annuals around all of the buildings. Some of the plant selections include cranes-bill, butterfly plant, impatiens, geraniums, Siberian iris, even a new variety called a heucharella developed from a cross between coral bells (heuchera) and foam flower (tiarella). Plantings are installed in various beds that run along the exterior of the build-ings; others are part of gardens found on the property.

Pond and waterfall at Entrance 10 at Fox Valley Tech

Courtesy of Fox Valley Technical College

Commercial growers have dis-covered Beard and his students. Goldsmith and Fisher Plant Breeders send cultivars for test-ing in trial gardens. Students learn how to propagate plants that will eventually be installed on campus. Each year, students plant 30,000 to 40,000 annuals.

Gardens can be found at entrance 1, between entrances 3 and 4, and at entrance 6. Students in the campus's culinary program use the herbs grown in the garden next to entrance 8. Entrance 10 boasts a pond with a waterfall, a pergola, and dwarf conifer collection. There's also a garden planted on the rock outcroppings around the sign at the college's main entrance.

More than one hundred varieties of perennials dot the campus. Tree lovers will find interesting specimens of paper bark and Japanese maples. During the summer, three dozen flowering baskets and pots, including some that are thirty-six inches in diameter, grace the grounds. Ten acres of the thirty-acre campus are devoted to native prairie. Students have installed a green roof on a small building that they've constructed at the entrance to the two miles of walking trails.

> Twenty-four rose bushes represent the sisters' legacy of caring at *St. Elizabeth's Hospital* in Appleton. The roses, benches, and cross that stood on top of the hospital's 1920 addition comprise the healing garden.

Beard and his students constructed most of the decorative hardscapes. Outside of the culinary garden, Beard built a small storage building that holds garden tools, and an eye-catching purple Adirondack chair from a 1918 plan. Pergolas and arbors are scattered throughout the grounds.

COUNTY	Outagamie
ADDRESS	1825 North Bluemound Drive, Appleton
PHONE	920/735-5600 or 920/996-2962
WEBSITE	www.fvtc.edu
DIRECTIONS	From U.S. Highway 41, exit 138 (State Highway 96 East/West Wisconsin Avenue). Turn left at North Bluemound Drive.
ADMISSION	Free
HOURS	Seasonal. Daily, dawn to dusk.
AMENITIES	Parking lot. Toilets, food, and water inside of the college.

 ## The Garden Door

STURGEON BAY

TUCKED BEHIND THE BUILDINGS of the Peninsular Agriculture Research Station just north of Sturgeon Bay, the Garden Door is a demonstration garden for the Door County Master Gardeners. More than just a series of labeled beds, this garden is a treat for the senses.

The place is aptly named; visitors enter the garden through a unique wooden arbor decorated with unusual faux doors complete with doorknobs. A sculptural planter rests on a half-circle patio made from red pavers and framed with rose bushes. Created by Door County kaleidoscope artist Robert Anderson, the planter is fitted with a "teleidoscope," a lens that allows the flowers to create the pattern as the planter is rotated. Gravel paths lead to the pond and continue through the rose garden, annual and perennial beds, a butterfly garden, and a rock garden. In the center of the pond is an "island" planted with dwarf conifers. The island divides the water stream into two, after which it merges to fill a larger pond. Mature evergreens frame two sides of the pond.

A view of the Tunnel sound garden centerpiece at the Garden Door

An espaliered fruit tree is attached to the side of a wooden shed topped with decorative gingerbread. Nearby, raised beds grow vegetables and edible flowers. Native perennial beds feature concrete leaves as garden art. Trials of echinacea varieties are being conducted in one of the beds.

The rock garden begins with a plot of pea gravel and then grows to feature large limestone slabs, ending with a limestone planter and large boulders. Lots of sedums and succulents turn the rocks into an alpine garden. Simple blue, glass bottle "trees" provide an inexpensive alternative to a Dale Chihuly piece. Near the rock garden is a weathered wood gazebo and matching fence. Hypertofa pots filled with sedums and a sumac tree can be found nearby. Purple ruffled basil marks the sections in the formal herb garden. There's even an ornamental grass display on the grounds.

Large conifers act as a backdrop to the Rock Garden

The site's centerpiece is a tunnel and sound garden that leads to a metal gazebo with a triangular-shaped wind chime and a heart clapper. Clematis varieties such as 'Niobe', 'Fireworks', and 'Snow Queen' use the sides of the tunnel for support, and five-leaf akebia makes its way up the gazebo's metal lattice sides. The water feature, a ball on a stone pillar, stands in the middle of the metal gazebo. Mosaic benches surround the fountain.

The color scheme is serene and inviting, with many blues and purples offset with splashes of yellow and white.

One of twelve agricultural research stations sponsored by the University of Wisconsin, research is conducted here on fruit trees and potatoes. The plans for this garden were developed in 1996 and the garden opened to the public in 2005.

COUNTY	Door
ADDRESS	4312 State Highway 42 North, Sturgeon Bay
PHONE	920/743-5406 or 920/743-1080
DIRECTIONS	The site is located on the grounds of the Peninsular Agriculture Research Station, located a few miles north of Sturgeon Bay on the east side of Highway 42.
ADMISSION	Free
HOURS	Seasonal. Daily, dawn to dusk.
AMENITIES	Parking lot.

 Gardens of the Fox Cities
APPLETON

THE FOUR SEASONS GARDEN and the Veteran's Dry Stream Memorial warmly welcome visitors to the Gardens of the Fox Cities. Once known as Memorial Park Gardens and Arboretum, the name of the thirty-five acre site was changed to reflect a broadening of the garden's mission.

No matter the time of year, there is always something of interest in the Four Seasons Garden, from colorful spring bulbs to ferns, shrubs, and perennials. Set on a patio, the Dry Stream Memorial is composed of trees, stone, and light. Slate slabs form the stream bottom. Linking the two stream banks are bridges representing peace and understanding. Individually polished river stones symbolize sacrifice and lives lost while the rows of trees offer the prospect of life and growth. Lights inserted into split boulders express hope and memory.

Charles Montooth, a protégé of Frank Lloyd Wright and one of the senior architects from Taliesin, designed the Henry and Mary Scheig Learning Center, where a waterfall graces the Great Room. Located north of the Center, the Great Lawn provides a view of the gardens.

The Fragrance Garden is filled with lilacs, roses, irises, peonies, mock orange, and yarrow. Four pergolas outline this garden room. The center contains a square planter created from slabs of limestone topped with another wooden pergola. Native species are planted in the Wild Garden where a metal sun hangs from a decorative shepherd's crook.

Like a child's marble maze, the water feature zigzags from top to bottom along stone channels. A large copper sculpture of butterflies and coneflowers leaves no doubt that the space is filled with bird- and butterfly-attracting plants like New England asters, Shasta daisies, bush cinquefoil, Russian sage, and purple coneflower. A birdbath marks the center while a stone paver path is laid out in the shape of butterfly wings.

Four wood lattice arbors mark the site of the formal rose garden. Clipped hedges, square pavers, and red gravel paths ring Dallas Martin's sculpture, *Reflections of Love*, a ballerina holding a bouquet of roses. 'Modern Fireglow', 'Firecracker', 'Carefree Sunshine', and 'Flower Carpet Red' are just some of the species featured here.

The Wisconsin Garden Club Federation sponsored the Wisconsin oak savanna. Red, white, and bur oaks are set in a field of prairie grasses and wildflowers. A river birch is the focal point in the All Seasons Garden. Encircled with junipers, annuals, and perennials, a stone wall planter contains examples of weeping white and mugo pines.

In the Native Rose Garden, two triangular trellises and bench arbors are the dominant features. Nearby is an herb garden growing with creeping thyme, sage, chocolate mint, and horseradish. Hops climb up a lattice arbor.

A Garden of the Heart memorial garden borders the back of the learning center. Three stone benches provide a respite among the dwarf wild columbine, rhododendron, sweet woodruff, tamarack, viburnums, and woodland phlox.

Outlined by a green picket fence and brightly colored letters across the top of its entrance pergola, Marvin's Garden entices children to get their hands dirty. This garden is part of a summer-long program for kids ages 5 through 12. Each participant receives a small garden plot to plant with herbs, vegetables, and flowers. Behind Marvin's Garden is the Family Garden, bordered on three sides with a fence.

> According to the *All-America Rose Selections* organization, of the roses that have won the AAS title over the years the most popular are: Peace (1946), Queen Elizabeth (1955), Tropicana (1963), Mister Lincoln (1965), Angel Face, (1969), Double Delight (1977), and Bonica (1987).

The Master Plan, developed in 2005, has broadened the garden's vision. Currently on the drawing board are a Perennial Garden, a Serenity Garden, Meadow, Wet Meadow, and Bird Meadow gardens, a Winter Garden, and a prairie. An Orangery will extend the garden's interest into the cold months with a conservatory-type space filled with Mediterranean plants, forced bulbs, perennials, and other potted plants. The Children's Garden will be expanded to include a rock garden, a workshop garden, a tree house, a grocery garden, and a please-pick-the-flowers garden.

COUNTY	Outagamie
ADDRESS	1313 East Witzke Boulevard, Appleton
PHONE	920/993-1900
FAX	920/993-9492
EMAIL	info@gardensfoxcities.org
WEBSITE	www.gardensfoxcities.org
DIRECTIONS	The gardens are located in Appleton's Memorial Park. From U.S. Highway 41, take the Ballard Road exit (144) south to Capitol Drive. Turn west on Capitol. The park's entrance will be on the left (Witzke Boulevard). Turn into the park and follow the road approximately one-quarter mile until you see the sign and driveway for the gardens.
ADMISSION	Free
HOURS	Daily, dawn to dusk. The Scheig Learning Center is open from 9 a.m. to 5 p.m. Monday through Saturday from mid-April through mid-October. The Center is open from 9 a.m. to 5 p.m. Monday through Friday from mid-October through mid-April.
AMENITIES	Parking lot. Toilets and water available.

 ## Green Bay Botanical Garden

GREEN BAY

A LITTLE OVER A DECADE OLD, this upstart botanical garden is poised to become one of the premier gardens in the Midwest. Only seventeen of its forty-seven acres have been developed, leaving thirty more dreamscapes to imagine. Once an apple orchard, the gardens are actually the working gardens for the horticulture students at Northeastern Wisconsin Technical College. Students grow many of the plants that are found here.

The first garden encountered between the parking lot and the Visitor's Center is the "Cornerstone Foundation of Northeastern Wisconsin Entry: A Four Seasons Garden." The lilacs, magnolias, and crab apple trees wake up the garden in spring and then hand off their duty to the perennials that continue the color until the first frost.

> Consider the formal garden at *Pamperin Park* in Green Bay as a shelter without walls. That's because it's not open to the public and is available only for a fee. A sixteen-foot decorative round gazebo anchors 10,000 square feet of gardens bordered with a decorative metal fence. Because the Park Department has experienced a heavy demand for special event photography, it built this garden with the express purpose of funding it with user fees. For information, call 920/448-6242.

The Agnes Schneider Terrace located behind the gift shop contains an American perennial garden. Here you'll find ornamental grasses and blooming perennials. The terrace offers a great view of the Mabel Thome Fountain. Ringed with junipers, bulbs, and flowering trees, this fountain can be seen from various points around the site.

A portion of the original orchard was saved in the Larsen Orchard, just to the left off the Schneider Terrace. Hostas, ferns, coral bells, and other shade lovers are underplanted beneath the remaining apple trees. Along with uncut bluegrass, the look is pure rural Wisconsin.

If it's one thing the Green Bay Botanical Garden should be remembered for is the hardscapes. The Schierl Wellhouse is one of the lovely architectural structures you'll encounter in the gardens. This circular brick structure with a chocolate kisslike roof and round windows, hides the garden's well. But it doesn't hide the Larsen Orchard, the Wellhouse Garden, or the Marguerite Kress Oval Rose Garden.

The formal Wellhouse garden is meant to be seen from the structure. Cement edges the beds of annuals and herbs. Some are planted in the pattern of a knot garden. A circular garden set on a cardinal grid with an armillary or ring sundial in the center, sets the theme. Two other groupings of beds ring the circle with red gravel paths bisecting the two sets. The set of beds nearest the center contains parterres that frame the knot gardens. Each of the exterior beds is filled with plants representing a theme. There's the fairy garden, a butterfly garden, a medicinal herb garden, and my favorite, the chocolate garden.

A path of memorial red brick pavers leads from the Wellhouse Garden to the John and Janet Van Den Wymelenberg Color and Foliage Garden. This garden makes a statement with trees, shrubs, perennials, grasses, and vines in the colors of gray, yellow, maroon, chartreuse, and green. Even the pergola is painted the purple of an allium. Switch grasses, showy stonecrop, weigela, forsythia, ginko, and azaleas—even a moon shadow winged euonymus—can all

Ed Lyon

Brick structures such as the Schierl Wellhouse adorn Green Bay Botanical Gardens be found here. One bed contains a combination of weigela, purple alliums, red barberry, and 'Magic Carpet' Japanese sedum. Various groundcovers fill in between the boulders. A metal sculpture perched between the boulders represents birds and tall plants with berries. Concord grapes have adopted one of the metal arches for support.

From the Van Den Wymelenberg Garden, a black asphalt path splits into two. Taking the upper path leads to the Stumpf Belvedere, another one of the outstanding hardscapes. If you look skyward, you'll see that the copper structure, balanced atop six columns, is carved with the moon, stars, and outlines of clouds.

Ed Lyon

The Meredith B. Rose Cottage in the Vanderperren English Cottage Garden

Even the concrete paths join in the fun. The stark white sidewalk is tamed with the addition of random brown swirls of pigment. The walk from the belvedere features a border of roses leading to the Upper Rose Garden and the Marguerite Kress Oval Con-temporary Rose Garden. The shrub roses include 'Island Dancer', 'Garden Jubilee', and 'Lifestyle Garden Snowdrifts.' Everything's coming up roses here. The horseshoe-shaped beds hold the All-America Selection roses, such as the 'Tropicana Imperial' tea, the 'Olympiad hybrid' tea, and the 'Harison's yellow hybrid' foetida rose.

It's impossible to ignore the 'William Baffin' climbing rose that covers the arch between the Upper Rose Garden and the Marguerite Kress Oval Contemporary Rose Garden. Paths in the Upper Rose Garden lead to the copper-topped Kaftan Lusthaus (a Scandinavian four-season gazebo) or the "Sharing" Kaleidoscope. A collection of dwarf iris borders the Lusthaus. The kaleidoscope planter is filled with annuals and some foliage plants. Spin the basin and watch the plant colors morph into continually changing patterns.

A mix of hardy perennials and roses makes its home in the Marguerite Kress Oval Contemporary Rose Garden. Two white wooden arches frame the entrances to this space. A group of roses arc away from a bench directly across the oval from Dee Clements' bronze sculpture, *Serenade*. Other benches are interspersed with perennial selections like Asiatic lilies, artesmia, and pasque flowers, Flames of Passion, blue oat grass, and alliums. The oval's center is grass. An evergreen hedge encloses the entire oval and its contents.

The Meredith B. Rose Cottage located in the Vanderperren English Cottage Garden mimics the shape of the Schierl Wellhouse. A wooden, weathered fence outlines the circular garden filled with iris, peonies, and a variety of ground-covers. Phlox, shrub roses, lupine, and bleeding hearts add splashes of color. All of the garden art in this site is crafted from weathered wood or natural materials. Directly behind the cottage garden is the All-America Selections Garden.

From the Visitor's Center, the gravel path from the entry garden leads toward the Mary Hendrickson Johnson Wisconsin Woodland. The path, which is flanked on one side by boulders and plantings and on the other side by trees, drops down from the first floor of the Visitor's Center to the building's lower level. One bed located near the outside patio includes a mix of peonies, spirea, and dwarf conifers. Another bed has a horseshoe-shaped parterre framing a dogwood and several roses.

The gravel path turns into a path of wood chips and leads to a collection of magnolias. From there, the path meanders to the Memorial Grove with its stunning metal Moebius strip sculpture. The sculpture is set on grass and bordered with curving limestone slab walls.

The wood chip path connects up with a path located behind the belvedere. Several square beds represent the beginnings of a set of international culinary gardens representing Hmong, Oneida, Hispanic, Italian, and All-American cultures. The wood chip path eventually connects with the lower black asphalt path that leads out of the color and foliage garden. The lower one leads to the Gertrude B. Nielsen Children's Garden with its decorative bridges, gazebo slide, waterfalls and streams, and the Chia Pet-like lion, giraffe, and goat natural sculptures.

Besides the gardens and hardscapes, the Green Bay Botanical Garden features a number of plant collections. There are eleven species of ornamental onions, seventy-six magnolias, and several varieties of grape hyacinths.

> Seven garden plots in the *Lenfestey Family Courtyard* located in the Cofrin Center for Biodiversity at the University of Wisconsin-Green Bay represent groupings of ecologically related native plants and cultivars. You'll find a butterfly garden, a tallgrass prairie, a sand prairie, a fern garden, a woodland, heirloom vegetables, Native American herbs, and Northern barrens.

The gardens are also home to fifteen types of Purple Passion tulips. As a daylily repository, visitors can acquire the pollen from any of the gardens' one hundred eighty or so daylilies to hybridize their own flowers.

COUNTY	Brown
ADDRESS	2600 Larsen Road, Green Bay
PHONE	920/490-9457 or 877/355-GBBG
WEBSITE	www.gbbg.org
DIRECTIONS	From U.S. Highway 41, exit West Mason Street (also Highway 54). Go west to Packerland Drive. Go north on Packerland Drive to Larsen Road.
ADMISSION	$5 for adults; $2 for children 5 to 12. Members are free.
HOURS	From 9 a.m. to 8 p.m. daily, May through September; 9 a.m. to 4 p.m. Monday through Friday, October through April.
AMENITIES	Parking lot. Toilets and water located inside the Visitor's Center.

～ *Harmony Arboretum*
MARINETTE

SITUATED ON FOUR HUNDRED SIXTY ACRES just east of the city of Marinette, the Harmony Arboretum offers something for both garden and nature lovers. The site includes one hundred acres of old-growth forest (primarily maples), a restored prairie, an orchard, and gardens. The Northern Lights Master Gardeners have worked diligently at turning three acres of the site into both trial and display gardens.

The seventeen-acre prairie was once a cornfield. Some twenty-five native wildflower and grass species thrive in this exposed, dry, windy location. The largest trees in the Harmony Hardwoods Memorial Forest actually escaped the Great Peshtigo Fire of 1871. The orchard contains an abundance of species including apricot, mulberry, peach, plum, and cherry trees as well as the requisite apple. Some of the new varieties of amelanchiers are also being grown here.

A wooden fence encloses an herb garden, which concentrates on over one hundred culinary herbs and teas. Some species of herbs that historically have been utilized for dyeing are also found here. There are perennial beds and a few garden rooms that feature flowers for drying, fragrance flowers, and composting methods. Roses line a fence that separates the herb garden from the trial gardens. The trial gardens compare mostly vegetable varieties for hardiness in this location. Occasionally flowers will be tested for their performance. There are grass paths through the various gardens.

> ～ The North Central Plant Diagnostic Network will train *Master Gardeners* on techniques for identifying agricultural terrorist threats and procedures for reporting pest problems. For information, visit the Web site: www.ncpdn.org.

They say necessity is the mother of invention and in this case, necessity—in the form of wide open land with no respite from the elements—resulted in the construction of a shade pergola. The attractive weathered wood pergola not only provides shade for visitors, but also offers a focal point and a spot for shade loving plants to flourish. The more recent water feature, a waterfall with a stream, adds a soothing touch. Sit on the benches inside the pergola and relax to the sound of the water flowing over the rocks. A limestone slab serves as a bridge.

The back of the shade garden is lined with old-fashioned lilacs. Newer varieties were planted on the north side of the structure. Inside the pergola you'll find hostas and coral bells and an outstanding variegated Solomon's seal, along with other natives. Columbine and clematis also enjoy the shade.

Don't let the large fence around the property scare you. It's the deer they're trying to keep out, not the visitors.

The site hosts a wildflower walk in the spring and a prairie walk in the fall. The season ends in October with Haunted Harmony, a very scary half-mile walk on the nature trails through the hardwood forest.

COUNTY	Marinette
ADDRESS	Marinette
PHONE	715/732-5510
EMAIL	gcleereman@marinettecounty.com
DIRECTIONS	Located seven miles west of Marinette on State Highway 65 and one-half mile south on County E. Watch for the sign.
ADMISSION	Free
HOURS	Daily, dawn to dusk.
AMENITIES	Gravel road parking. Toilets.

 ## The Hollyhock House

KEWAUNEE

TUCKED AWAY in a residential part of the city of Kewaunee is a Queen Anne-style home with a surprising acre-and-a-half cottage garden. A site for retreats, meetings, and weddings, the Hollyhock House also welcomes visitors to its rose garden path, secluded shade gardens, and lots of hardscape features.

Neatly aligned hostas hug both sides of the front walk beckoning visitors to take a step back in time. Large stone urns filled with annuals are placed on either side of the driveway. 'Carefree Wonder', 'Dortmund', and 'New Dawn' climbeing roses decorate the front exterior. Lush gardens surround the house, and thousands of tulips signal the start of spring.

Approaching the back yard, a metal arch is flanked on either side by dwarf Alberta spruces. The first arbor frames a lion fountain encircled with pink 'New Dawn' climbing roses; behind the fountain is another arbor covered with red 'Henry Kelsey' climbing roses. Two sets of metal chairs and tables are found under a white wooden pergola that supports a Chinese wisteria. Nearby is a small pond formed by water that flows out of a rusty old pump handle. Sparkling bits of "garden glass" from Diggings, a local rock shop and pizza parlor, catch the sun.

Through the rose arbor that supports a 'William Baffin' climbing rose, enter a secret garden and follow the stone path built with old brick pavers and gravel. A kneeling stone angel ringed with a double circle of groundcover and hostas and accented by irises alerts visitors to one of the "angel paths." There are several angel paths winding through the overhang of trees in the garden's eastern perimeter.

Phlox, violets, tiger lilies, and the house's namesake, hollyhocks, form the bulk of the plant selections located next to the old red barn. Look for the teacup and saucer tucked in among some yellow daylilies.

Opposite the barn is a three-tiered black fountain placed among spirea, giant phlox, and hostas. There is also a small, wooden bridge found in one of the serpentine, shaded walking paths trimmed with ferns and hostas.

COUNTY	Kewaunee
ADDRESS	1408 Dodge Street, Kewaunee
PHONE	920/388-3445
EMAIL	TheHollyHock@TheGatheringCommunities.Net
DIRECTIONS	One block west of State Highway 42 at 1408 Dodge Street
ADMISSION	Free
HOURS	Daily, dawn to dusk. Call ahead.
AMENITIES	Street parking.

 Paine Art Center and Gardens

OSHKOSH

WHAT DO A HISTORIC HOME, an art museum, and a series of display gardens have in common? Plenty, as the Paine Art Center demonstrates. The Paine calls its outdoor gardens "galleries of horticulture," viewing them as an extension of the art inside.

The Tudor Revival house located in Oshkosh was built for lumber baron Nathan Paine and his wife, Jessie Kimberly Paine, beginning in 1927. Through a series of misfortunes, the Paines never actually lived in the home. Jessie oversaw the completion of the home's construction after Nathan died in 1947. Opened to the public in 1948, the gardens were most recently renovated in 1997.

Visitors will be captivated to discover the depth and breadth of garden and flora types found on this English country "estate," which features the only walled garden in the state open to the public. Over five hundred trees, mostly evergreens, were planted on what was once a cow pasture. There are twenty gardens, alternating between formal and informal, planted throughout the site.

Courtesy of the Paine Art Center and Gardens

Paine Art Center

Once through the main entrance on the Algoma Boulevard side of the property, you'll follow the concrete path to the driveway. Look for the Secret Garden with a tulip tree from George Washington's Mount Vernon estate tucked into the property's far left corner. Donal Hord's sculpture, *Winnebago Lady*, is a little farther on.

Continue past the public entrance to the five gardens located in the North Court area. The Pennau and Below Garden near what was the limousine garage identifies the entrance to the Woodland Path. Walk through the wisteria-covered pergola, past the stone urn filled with annuals. Jack-in-the-pulpit, Dutchman's breeches, wild ginger, and other Wisconsin wildflowers border the shady, winding path.

Veer off to see the Reception Garden and the Ceremony Garden. A canvas tent serves as a canopy over the circular Reception Garden. The focal point here is an elaborate black iron gate that once was used to separate Nathan's property from that of his brother, Edward. A yew hedge patterned after one at Sissinghurst Garden in England encircles the garden.

With its Tuscan columned pergola, the Ceremony Garden is aptly named. Since the garden is used for many weddings, the plantings stay within a green and white palette so as not to upstage the bride.

From the Ceremony Garden, return to the Woodland Path and continue on to the Mark L. Tremble Garden. Formerly known as the Bird Garden, the circular Tremble Garden showcases one of the site's water fea-

Courtesy of the Paine Art Center and Gardens

The large reflecting pool in the rose garden at the Paine.

tures. A three hundred-pound granite lotus birdbath basin floats atop of a central reflecting pool. The plantings and shrubs were selected specifically to attract the birds. From this garden, the annual-filled urn in the Pennau and Below Garden is visible, adding connective tissue to the design.

Leaving the Tremble Garden, the path heads east toward the U.S. Bank Contemporary Garden. A wooden arbor marks the entrance to this informal space. With an emphasis on the contemporary, the Paine expects to renovate this garden every five years. Also referred to as the Fall Garden, plant selections are chosen especially for their fall color. Look for asters, anemones, coleus, dahlias, and cleome. A metal and ceramic sculpture of a black latticework vase ringed with cream-colored ceramic nicotiana blossoms acts as this garden's focal point.

The Pergola Garden and Oshkosh Area Community Foundation Garden are next on the tour. A long wooden pergola provides a bit of shade and supports a variety of vines hardy to Wisconsin such as clematis, male kiwi, and Boston ivy. An annual-filled urn visually connects with a pair of flower-filled urns found on the Morning Terrace next to the house. Several wooden benches are tucked under the pergola's rafters.

The Oshkosh Area Community Foundation Garden, also known as the Sunken Garden, could be considered fit for a king. Designed after the sunken garden in one of Henry VIII's palaces, Hampton Court, this two-tiered symmetrical space features a plethora of cool-colored tulips in blues, silvers, and pastels on the lower tier, which are dug up after their blooms are spent and replaced with annuals. The top tier features perennials in hot colors of red, orange, yellow, and pink. A pineapple-topped fountain anchors the garden. A limestone path in front of the Pergola Garden leads down to the Sunken Garden tying the two spaces together.

Backtracking a bit, follow the path from the Pergola Garden to the Carriage House Courtyard, which is planted with an annual or vegetable border in a new theme each year. Nearby is the Herb Garden, a four-bed symmetrical design with a sundial in the center. There are over sixty species of herbs planted in this eighteenth-century reproduction. Along the wall are examples of espaliered apple and pear trees.

Retrace your steps and discover the Birch Grove with its flowering bulbs and groundcovers, and the spectacular Rose Garden with the second of the site's water features. An allee of arborvitae guides you to a large reflecting pool and fountain that bisect the parterres of red barberry bordering the roses. Two varieties of modern shrub roses, the Explorer from Canada and the Meidiland series from France, were planted here in 1992. Perennials and annuals supplement the color. Two sculptures, one of a shepherd, the other of a shepherdess, signify a transition between the Rose Garden and the Great Lawn.

The calming green carpet of the Great Lawn contrasts with the perennials, bulbs, and annuals found bordering it. Framing part of the Great Lawn is the South Path that wanders past the Shade Garden and Leo Smith's *Roman Head* sculpture. Unlike the Woodland Path with its native wildflowers, the Shade Garden emphasizes exotics and new hybrids under a canopy of mature trees.

The Morning Terrace with its flagstone patio is next. A boxwood hedge encloses the plants around the loggia. The area once housed the rose garden, which was moved to its current location in 1973 and replaced with a traditional Victorian monochromatic garden. Plants with blooms or foliage in white, silver, and gray including white bleeding hearts, star magnolias, hydrangeas, and false spirea, can be found here. Also known as a "moon garden," these plants look as magnificent in the moonlight as they do during the day. A pair of urns at the end of the gravel path connects the eye with the urn located in the Pergola Garden.

A border of blooms catches the evening sun in the Evening Terrace located at the front of the house. The Front Lawn is decorated with combinations of annuals and perennials placed along the home's balustrade. A tall grass prairie, a maple basswood forest, and an oak savanna can be found in the Prairie Woodland, located directly across Algoma Boulevard.

Just across Algoma Boulevard is the Oshkosh Public Museum. The Oshkosh Garden Club maintains several garden spaces on the property that are worth seeing.

COUNTY	Winnebago
ADDRESS	1410 Algoma Boulevard, Oshkosh
PHONE	920/235-6903
WEBSITE	www.thepaine.org
DIRECTIONS	From U.S. Highway 41 exit State Highway 21. Go east on Highway 21 to Algoma Boulevard
ADMISSION	$7 general, $6 seniors, $5 students, $4 children (5-12), family $18. Free to members. Visitors to the gardens must pay admission from May 1 through September 30.
HOURS	11 a.m. to 4 p.m. Tuesday through Sunday. Closed on Mondays and national holidays.
AMENITIES	Parking lot. Toilets and water in the museum.

Sculpture Gardens:

Some sculpture gardens are actually gardens containing folk art sculptures. Others simply focus on the sculptures themselves.

Herman Rusch's Prairie Moon Sculpture Garden and Museum, Cochrane – no plantings

Fred Smith's Concrete Park, Phillips – no plantings

Nick Engelbert's Grandview, Hollandale – some gardens

August Klatt's Buildings, Veteran's Park, North Prairie – some plantings

James Tellen Woodland Sculpture Garden, Town of Wilson (Sheboygan) – no plantings

Paul and Matilda Wegner Grotto, Cataract – some plantings

Mary Nohl Lake Cottage Environment, Fox Point – no plantings

Rev. Mathias Wernerus' Holy Ghost Park, Dickeyville – gardens

Rev. Philip Wagner's Grotto, Rudolph – gardens

Riana's Garden, Beldenville – gardens

Bradley Sculpture Garden, Brown Deer – gardens

Mississippi River Sculpture Park & Interpretive Center – Prairie du Chien, some plantings

Carl Peterson, John Michael Kohler Arts Center, Sheboygan – gardens

Leigh Yawkey Woodson Art Museum, Wausau – gardens

Madison Museum of Contemporary Art, Madison – a rooftop garden

Two Fish Gallery and Sculpture Garden, Elkhart Lake – gardens

The Highground, Neillsville – gardens

The Glacial River Bike Trail, Fort Atkinson – gardens

Peninsula Art School and Gallery, Fish Creek – gardens

Shrine of the Queen of the Holy Rosary Mediatrix of Peace, Necedah – some plantings

Arts/Industry Walk, The Botanical Gardens of Kohler – gardens

Fine Line Design Gallery, Ephraim – gardens

Fountain City Rock Garden, Fountain City – some plantings

Peninsula Art School and Gallery

FISH CREEK

ARTISTS LOOKING TO CAPTURE THE BEAUTY OF NATURE need not look any further than the grounds of the Peninsula Art School and Gallery. A series of gardens encircle part of the octagonal gallery and office building, with more in the works.

Although the school opened in 1965, the seeds for it were planted after World War I when faculty from the Art Institute of Chicago would summer in Door County to paint and teach. Now the school offers classes year-round.

A large circular perennial bed greets you as you enter the grounds of the ten-acre campus. Lamb's ear, coneflowers, roses, liatris, and ornamental grasses are just a few varieties planted beneath a large, metal, horseshoe-shaped sculpture.

Horseshoe shaped sculpture at Penninsula Art School

A perennial border flanks both sides of a red paver walkway. The walkway changes to flagstone when it reaches the gardens on the building's west side. A large, multi-colored, butterfly-like metal sculpture called *Conundrum* almost eclipses the lyre fountain placed inside a perennial bed. A few steps further and you'll find weathered Adirondack benches resting on a patio of bark mulch. Tall perennials peek up over the back of the benches like flags.

A large wooden gazebo takes up a portion of the yard in front of the office building. Vines wind their way up its support pillars. A red brick patio in the shape of double diamonds is found on the building's east side overlooking a wooded area. Under a canopy of evergreens, structures crafted from logs and branches are installed. Perennials including hydrangeas, snow-on-the-mountain, daylilies, and hostas form the beginnings of future gardens.

COUNTY	Door
ADDRESS	3900 County F, Fish Creek
PHONE	920/868-3455
FAX	920/868-9965
EMAIL	staff@peninsulaartschool.com
WEBSITE	www.peninsulaartschool.com
DIRECTIONS	From State Highway 42 turn west onto County F. The school is on the left.
ADMISSION	Free
HOURS	Office, gallery, and classroom hours: 9 a.m. to 5 p.m. Monday through Saturday. The gardens are open daily, dawn to dusk.
AMENITIES	Parking lot. Toilets, water, and food in the office building.

St. Mary's Roman Catholic Oratory of the Immaculate Conception

WAUSAU

THE STEEPLE of St. Mary's Roman Catholic Oratory of the Immaculate Conception watches over Wausau's Grand Avenue like a proud sentinel. Follow the steeple and you'll discover some luscious gardens below it.

Plantings are everywhere. Islands in the north and south parking lots are filled with a variety of trees, shrubs, and plantings. Each island is actually an individual landscape, yet blends into the whole. Many unusual varieties of junipers and spruces are planted in the self-contained beds. The dolomite rocks scattered about came from a quarry in Chilton.

The gardens surrounding the church, oratory, and parking lots are part of the church's second restoration project completed in 2003. The first occurred after a 1953 fire gutted the interior of the 1893 neo-Gothic building.

The landscape offers spaces for prayer and meditation, including a court-yard garden located off of the north parking lot that's dedicated to Our Lady of Fatima. The St. Joseph statue on the church's south side is bordered with roses, black-eyed Susans, catmint, and shrubs.

The mixed beds around the grounds contain four-season interest. Cannas, lavender, petunias, ornamental grasses, groundcovers, and shrubs are just some of the plants sharing space in the south border facing Grand Avenue.

Evergreen topiaries dot the landscape. A shade garden features hostas, ferns, astilbe, and an eye-catching combination of a blue spruce and a char-treuse barberry. Rhododendrons are tucked up against one of the red brick walls. A Mission-style fence outlines the property's north and south borders.

When asked why the church emphasized gardens in its restoration efforts, the rector, Fr. Olivier Meney, replied that the gardens provide those who see them with a glimpse of the beauty that's contained inside. "Many people are attracted to the gardens and through the beauty of the gardens [are attracted] to God," he said.

COUNTY	Marathon
ADDRESS	325 Grand Avenue, Wausau
PHONE	715/842-9995 or 715/848-5615
WEBSITE	www.institute-christ-king.org/wausau/index.html
DIRECTIONS	From U.S. Highway 51 South, exit Business 51 (185) toward Rothschild/Schofield. Head north for three miles. Turn right onto East Grand Avenue/Business 51 for 4 miles. From Highway 51 North, exit WI-29 West/WI-52 East exit (192) toward Wausau/Abbotsford. Turn east onto WI-29 East /WI-52 East for two miles. Turn right onto East Grand Avenue/Business 51 South. From State Highway 29 East, take Business 51 South exit (171) toward Rothschild/Schofield. Turn north onto East Grand Avenue/Business 51 for 4 miles. From Highway 29 West, the highway becomes WI-52 East. Follow it for 2 miles. Turn south on East Grand Avenue/Business 51 South.
ADMISSION	Free
HOURS	Daily, dawn to dusk.
AMENITIES	Parking lot. Toilets and water available when the church is open.

St. Norbert College Shakespeare Garden

DE PERE

THE BARD SECURED HIS LEGACY with his many plays. The Monday Shakespeare Club guaranteed its with a formal garden installed at St. Norbert College. Located on the quad between Austin E. Cofrin Hall, F.K. Bemis International Center, the Todd Wehr Library, and John Minahan Science Center, the Shakespeare Garden provides an elegant, quiet place to study, rest, or simply regroup.

A gift from the club to the people of Green Bay and DePere, and a revival of the club's first Shakespeare garden, this forty-foot square space features clipped boxwood hedges, flax, primrose, and tulips. Surrounded by ornamental shrubs, the garden, with its hedges set in triangular red brick planters, resembles the very formal gardens of the large English estates. Terra-cotta granite gravel paths, which separate the planters from each other, intensify the garden's geometry. A center pedestal with a sundial acts as a focal point. Teakwood benches are placed in four corners identifying the parameters of the garden rooms. The colorful annuals planted in front of the hedges, soften some of the site's rigidity.

On the north end, eight weathered teakwood benches flank a long terra-cotta granite gravel path. A wooden arbor supporting large climbing roses anchors the south end. The arbor frames a colorful geometric Plexiglas sculpture.

While on campus, look for a memorial garden at the corner of Fifth and Reid streets. The garden is tucked between Vander Zanden and Mary Minahan McCormick halls. An elaborate wooden pergola with finials and a half-moon roof looks much like a paddle wheel on a sternwheeler boat. A red gravel circular

A sundial acts as a focal point in the Shakespeare Garden at St. Norbert College

path with four wooden benches replicates the pergola's geometry. Another pergola, directly opposite the entrance, frames a statue of the Virgin Mary. Garden beds with lily of the valley, stella d'oro lilies, peonies, junipers, and ornamental grasses, flank each of the benches. Mature trees encircle this hidden space that overlooks the Fox River. A circular expanse of lawn fills the center.

COUNTY	Brown
ADDRESS	100 Grant Street, De Pere
PHONE	920/337-3181
EMAIL	mediarel@snc.edu
WEBSITE	www.snc.edu/tour/ReligiousS/shakespeare.html
DIRECTIONS	From U.S. Highway 41, exit at Main Avenue in De Pere. Veer right and take Main Avenue East through four sets of stoplights. Main Avenue will eventually turn to the right and become Reid Street. Get in the right lane. When you go through the second set of lights on Reid Street, you'll see the campus in front of you.
ADMISSION	Free
HOURS	Seasonal. Daily, dawn to dusk.
AMENITIES	Parking lot. Toilets, food, and water inside of the college.

 ## Formal Gardens at Smith Park

MENASHA

THE ANCIENT AND THE CONTEMPORARY COME TOGETHER in Menasha's Smith Park. Three ancient one-hundred-twenty-five-foot effigy mounds reside on the park's south end; it's thought that the Oneota Indians built these panther-shaped burial mounds sometime around 800 A.D.

A formal garden full of annuals gracing the park's north end represents the contemporary. Each year the city of Menasha, in conjunction with an area greenhouse, designs a new pattern for the flowerbeds.

The garden's cardinal grid design features a gazebo at the south end, a fountain in the middle, and separate garden rooms filled with cannas at the east and west points. Brick pavers, added in 1997, connect the pieces together.

The side beds are filled with stripes of color—pinks, yellows, and purples—softened with white alyssum and brown millet. Ornamental kale anchors two corner beds, with the millet doing the same for the remaining corners. One year when the petunias failed to take, coral bells were planted as replacements. Two garden regulars are Dusty Miller and cannas.

The family of Dr. A.B. Jensen donated the two-tiered "Little Boy" fountain in the center of the garden. It originally had stood in the dining room of the Hotel Menasha, where the family had resided as owners of the property.

> Look for Minnie Bergman's headstone at the former *Duck Creek Cemetery* located at the corner of Riverview and Velp Avenue in Howard. It's tucked in among the perennial beds bordering three sides of a former cemetery.

The Victorian gazebo, ringed with spirea, features a cedar shake roof. Two large planters are filled with additional annuals, while four conifers add some vertical interest.

In the northwest corner are four white, latticework arbors that border a shade garden. Sedums outline a square bed filled with hostas. A maple tree acts as the bed's focal point. Because the tree was planted on the tenth anniversary of the founding of the United Nations, it's called the United Nations Tree. Across the street from the park is the Isle of Valor, which honors two Medal of Honor recipients from Menasha.

Smith Park is located on Doty Island where the Fox River splits. Part of the river travels through Menasha and the other part through Neenah.

COUNTY	Winnebago
ADDRESS	301 Park Street, Menasha
PHONE	920/967-5106
DIRECTIONS	Located on Doty Island between Cleveland and Park streets. From U.S. Highway 41 North, exit 131 (Winneconne Avenue, also known as State Highway 114 East). Follow Highway 114 to Nicolet Boulevard. Turn right. Go approximately one block and turn left on to Ahnaip Street. Go a half mile and turn right on Keyes Street. Go approximately three blocks and turn right on Park Street.
ADMISSION	Free
HOURS	Daily, dawn to dusk.
AMENITIES	Street parking.

 Leigh Yawkey Woodson Art Museum

WAUSAU

THE FIVE GARDENS at the Leigh Yawkey Woodson Art Museum are as much a work of art as are the various pieces located in and outside the building. Housed in a 1931 English Tudor period Cotswold-style residence, the museum and grounds cover four acres on the east side of Wausau.

Originally the private residence of Leigh Yawkey Woodson, one of the daughters of a local lumber baron, many of the gardens were in place when the house was donated to the city of Wausau for use as a museum. Visitors enter the site through the Gateway Garden, an eye-shaped structure located near the entrance to the one-and-a-half-acre Margaret Woodson Fisher Sculpture Gallery. With its pergola-like top and brick pilasters, the sculpture gallery features seventeen permanent bronze and marble works situated around an expanse of lawn, dotted with various trees and shrubs. Birds and animals are the subjects of the artworks, in keeping with the Woodsons' love of birds.

Large firs frame the Sculpture Garden's parklike setting enclosed within a six-foot decorative wrought-iron style perimeter fence. Meandering red paver sidewalks usher visitors from one work of art to another. In the spring when the crab apple trees bloom, the white blossoms provide a floral juxtaposition to the manicured lawn and brick hardscape.

The four beds of the Formal English Gardens lie southeast of the Sculpture Gallery garden. Slate slab paths form the cardinal grid that leads to the bronze sculpture by Edith Barretto Parsons, *Duck Baby*. The sculpture is perched on a fountain in the middle of the four perennial beds. Kent Ullberg's *Blue Heron* is tucked in a shady niche.

From the Formal Garden, stroll east to the Woodland Pond Garden where you'll find Rosetta's bronze cougar looking for its next meal, poised on a boulder above the top of a tiny waterfall; nearby, Walter Matia's great blue heron fountain keeps an eye on the cat. Seasonal greenery acts as a backdrop for the statues.

Follow the expanse of grass from the Woodland Pond Garden to the Terrace Garden, where brightly colored annuals and vines decorate the limestone stonework.

Leigh Yawkey Woodson Art Museum

A parklike setting near the entrance to the museum offers hints of larger delights

The Secret Garden is hidden along the west side of the building facing 12th Street. Cascading water, a fountain, and flowering plants make this spot worth finding.

Because each garden has its own microclimate, plant selection is diverse. You'll find natives such as coneflowers and false indigo, perennials such as hostas, poppies, astilbe, and coral bells and annuals such as marigolds, snapdragons,

Leigh Yawkey Woodson Art Museum

The Formal English Garden with Duck Baby sculpture at the Woodson

and petunias. Some interesting selections include Northern sea oats, Irish moss, and turtleheads. Wooden benches scattered throughout the site provide restful sanctuaries to stop and stay awhile.

COUNTY	Marathon
ADDRESS	Franklin and 12th streets, Wausau
PHONE	715/845-7010
FAX	715/845-7103
EMAIL	museum@lywam.org
WEBSITE	www.lywam.org
DIRECTIONS	From Interstate 39/U.S. Highway 51, take exit 139 (Bridge Street). Turn East (right) onto Bridge Street. Continue on Bridge to 5th Street. Turn right on 5th Street to Franklin Street. Turn left on Franklin Street to 12th Street. Turn right on 12th Street.
ADMISSION	Free
HOURS	Tuesday through Thursday, 9am to 4pm; Saturday and Sunday, noon to 5pm. Closed Mondays and holidays. Open until 7:30pm weekdays during *Birds in Art*.
AMENITIES	Parking lot. Toilets and water available inside the museum.

southwest
Wisconsin

Photo by John Epping

Allen Centennial Gardens

MADISON

STUDENTS, FACULTY, AND STAFF at the University of Wisconsin-Madison don't have to go far for a natural break from stress. The Allen Centennial Gardens offer a quiet respite in the portion of campus devoted to agricultural studies.

The two-and-a-half-acre site features various types of gardening styles from around the world showcased in twenty-two gardens. Managed by the university's Department of Horticulture, the gardens are actually an outdoor classroom and laboratory for horticulture and landscape architecture students. They also act as a training ground for plant identification and nomenclature and as a place to hone techniques in site management and ecology. Because the site's mission is to demonstrate the latest and greatest in floral selections, visitors will find an ever-changing tableau of varieties, colors, and designs.

The gardens wind their way around a Victorian Gothic house that the first four of the deans of the College of Agriculture once called home. The structure currently houses the offices of the college's twelve Agricultural Research Stations.

In 1979 the original horticulture gardens were demolished to make room for an addition to the Plant Sciences Building. Five years later, the house was placed on the National Register of Historic Places and university officials decided that the site would be an appropriate place to relocate the gardens. In 1989 the gardens were named for Oscar and Ethel Allen, both UW faculty members; Oscar in bacteriology and Ethel in horticulture.

Ed Lyon

Gothic architecture anchors the garden spaces at Allen Centennial Gardens

Alumnus and landscape architect Dennis Buettner designed the 90,000 square feet of space to allow for science, but to emphasize art. The exotic shrub garden hosts species of shrubs collected from around the world. The dwarf conifers garden illustrates textures, colors, and shapes. Red and green barberry hedges interlock much like the links of a chain and form the border for the herb beds in the Muriel and Douglas Frost Herb Garden.

Don't miss the Erna and Fred Kunz French Garden, which is noted for its boxwood parterres set in gravel beds in the shape of a fleur de lis, the emblem of the French kings. The Marion Fish Carlson Iris Garden features selections of Siberian, German alpine dwarfs, Japanese, and American plants.

The water garden contains native and tropical water lilies. The bridge over the pond was modeled after the Seat Bridge found in the Governor's Palace garden at Colonial Williamsburg. A small Edible Garden, located near the home's cellar doors, is filled with vegetables.

One of the gardens' focal points is a sixty-foot cedar pergola located in the Classes of 1935 and 1937 Arbor and

Pergola overlooks the water garden   Ed Lyon

Vine Garden. It defines east and west in the gardens and separates the Burkhardt English Garden and the Whitehead Italian Garden.

The Burkhardt English Perennial Garden is frequently used for weddings and receptions. With its cream-colored Victorian pavilion and borders of color, brides won't be upstaged by its understated elegance. The Moria J. Whitehead, M.D. Italian Garden takes its cue from the Mediterranean, featuring columnar junipers and foliage plants in shades of gray.

Annuals aren't forgotten in the Allen Centennial Gardens. The James F. and Helen L. Wilson Shady Annual Garden and the Professor Paul George Fluck Sunny Annual Garden guarantee summer-long color and interest.

The largest garden is the New American Garden, which features native plants. The idea for using natives in a garden came from a Brazilian designer, Roberto Burle Marxs, who transformed gardening styles by planting natives rather than European ornamentals, said William Hoyt, Allen's head gardener. Once the idea caught on in Europe, it rose in popularity in the United States.

Other gardens include a woodland garden, terrace and hillside gardens, orchard and small fruit gardens, a wetland garden, and a daylily garden. The George and Francis Burrill Victorian Garden surrounds the house and features exotic plants from throughout the British Empire. The Orientation Garden rings the map that's adjacent to the entrance to the house.

The gardens' large tree, the Goff larch, was planted in 1899 to commemorate the birth of the son of Dean William A. Henry. Its days are numbered because of heart rot but it did rebound after a heavy snowstorm during the winter of 2007 that almost destroyed it. The Ground Cover Garden uses the larch as a shade canopy.

COUNTY	Dane
ADDRESS	620 Babcock Drive, Madison
PHONE	608/262-8406
WEBSITE	www.horticulture.wisc.edu/allencentennialgardens/
DIRECTIONS	Located at the corner of Babcock and Observatory drives across from Steenbock Library. From the east, take University Avenue and turn right on Charter. Then turn left onto Observatory Drive and right on Babcock Drive. From the west, take University Avenue to Campus Drive (which becomes East Johnson Street). Turn left on Charter Street, left again on Observatory Drive, and right on Babcock Drive. Some metered parking is available in the lot next to Steenbock Library.
ADMISSION	Free
HOURS	Daily, dawn to dusk.
AMENITIES	Parking lot or street parking. Tables and chairs. Toilets and water available in surrounding buildings.

Alpine Gardens
MONROE

WHEN CHARLOTTE NELSON moved into her Monroe home seven years ago, she decided it was time to prove a point. Someone had once told her that she would never be able to grow alpine plants in southern Wisconsin. The garden in front of her house on Smock Valley Road is Nelson's response to her doubters.

Some seven hundred feet of rock placed on a layer of plastic has replaced what was her front lawn. A variety of alpine plants are tucked into the cavities in and between the rocks. Nelson's favorite is a pink flowering prickly pear cactus, *Opuntia fragilis*. The pink color is rare; most of this variety sprouts yellow blooms. Hens and chicks, hardy sedums, yuccas, creeping thyme, and edelweiss also do well there. This garden is definitely low maintenance.

> *The University of Wisconsin Extension* has published a free publication on native plant sources. Download a copy at http://clean-water.uwex.edu/pubs and click on "Shoreland and Habitat Management."

You'll find many of the same plants a little higher up. Deciding that she wanted a roof garden, Nelson threw dirt-covered plants on the cedar roofs of two small sheds covered with chicken wire, with good results.

As the largest grower of alpine rock garden plants in the Midwest, Nelson has planted over 100,000 plants on her property including seventy varieties of sedums, native wild flowers, and seven kinds of willows. For vivid color, Nelson adds annuals, usually begonias, petunias, veronicas, pinks, and geraniums. Her partner, Willi Lehner, has built a replica of the Matterhorn in the back yard, complete with a waterfall. The chalet in the front yard is also his and attests to his Swiss heritage.

COUNTY	Green
ADDRESS	W6615 Smock Valley Road, Monroe
PHONE	608/325-1836
DIRECTIONS	One mile west of Monroe off of State Highway 11. Turn right on Smock Valley Road.
ADMISSION	Free
HOURS	By appointment only.
AMENITIES	Street parking.

Cave of the Mounds
BLUE MOUNDS

WHILE MOST TOURISTS are attracted to the below-ground treasures of the Cave of the Mounds, gardeners have a special reason for stopping by the state's most famous cave. The above-ground beauty includes a substantial rock garden, cultivated gardens, as well as a prairie and a savanna that are being restored.

Chert boulders that were removed when the Visitor's Center and Gift Shop was built were reused as the foundation for the massive, three-tiered rock garden located directly in back of the building. Crystals in the small cavities in the rocks capture and reflect the sunlight on a bright day.

Tucked in among the rocks are varieties of sedum, phlox, chrysanthemum, coral bells, and viola. Natives, including coreopsis, gayfeather, wild quinine, and bergamot border the Visitor's Center. Ornamental grasses are thrown in for a bit of spice. Thousands of iris, daffodil, tulip, and allium bulbs signal the arrival of spring.

As part of the prairie and savanna restoration project, asters, bluestem, goldenrod, purple coneflowers, and blue false indigo are interspersed among the perennials. The natives help tie in the cultivated gardens with the restoration areas as well as add color throughout

Courtesy of Cave of the Mounds

Visitor's Center at Cave of the Mounds

the growing season. Hostas ring the waterfall and sluice that are part of the Gemstone Mine and Fossil Dig exhibit.

COUNTY	Iowa
ADDRESS	2975 Cave of the Mounds Road, Blue Mounds
PHONE	608/437-3038
WEBSITE	www.caveofthemounds.com
DIRECTIONS	From U.S. Highway 18/151, head west and turn right on Cave of the Mounds Road. From the north, take State Highway 78 into Mount Horeb. At the stoplights, turn right on to County Highway ID (also called Main or Springdale). Take Highway ID five miles out of Mount Horeb and turn right onto Cave of the Mounds Road.
ADMISSION	$14 for adults; $7 for children age 4 to 12; children 3 and under are free.
HOURS	From March 15 to the Friday before Memorial Day, 10 a.m. to 4 p.m. weekdays and 9 a.m. to 5 p.m. weekends. From Memorial Day weekend through Labor Day Monday, 9 a.m. to 6 p.m. daily. From Tuesday after Labor Day to November 15, 10 a.m. to 4 p.m. weekdays and 9 a.m. to 5 p.m. on weekends. From November 16 through March 14, 10 a.m. to 4 p.m. weekends. Hours vary on weekdays. Call for tour times.
AMENITIES	Parking lot. Toilets, food, and water inside the visitor's center.

River Park Trail Flower Gardens Islands Project

DARLINGTON

THE PAVED WALKING PATH along the Pecatonica River borders the flowerbeds that make up the River Park Trail Flower Garden Islands Project in Darlington. Each has its own quirky personality. There's one with a sign that invites angels to stop by. Another, sponsored by the Blossom Buddies, became a friendship garden. The Buddies, a group of five friends who go out to eat every month, brought something from their home gardens to put in their plot.

Some twenty-five oval beds extend from the Cheese Country Bike Trail on one end across State Highway 23 to the west. Although not sophisticated in design, the beds are no less heartfelt for that. For example, the garden in memory of Amie Smith had a patriotic theme, sporting red geraniums, blue and white alyssum, and mums.

A cooperative effort between the city of Darlington, the Darlington Garden Club, and community members, each garden boasts a wooden butterfly sign that acknowledges the individual or group that takes care of it. During the fall, the beds turn seasonal with the addition of scarecrows, pumpkins, and blooming mums.

COUNTY	Lafayette
ADDRESS	Wells Street, Darlington
DIRECTIONS	From State Highway 23, also known as Main Street, go east on Alice Street and south on Wells Street.
ADMISSION	Free
HOURS	Daily, dawn to dusk.
AMENITIES	Parking lot, food, water, and toilets in Dick's Piggly Wiggly grocery store.

Dickeyville Grotto, Shrines, and Gardens

DICKEYVILLE

BEHIND THE RED BRICK HOLY GHOST CHURCH and rectory in Dickeyville lie the Dickeyville Grotto, Shrines, and Gardens. The layout behind the free-standing folk art sculptures was intentional as were the gardens that are part of the site.

Dedicated on Sept. 14, 1930, the Grotto was the vision of Fr. Mathias Wernerus, then pastor of the church. Wernerus had begun the project as a memorial to three local men who died in World War I. Volunteers from the Grotto Gardens committee keep up the gardens, which were installed from 1928 through 1930.

At Dickeyville, Wernerus sought to build a roadside tourist attraction that tied together two American ideals, "love of God and love of country." Catholic iconography can be found throughout the grounds, from statues of saints to the Fatima shrine. A few distinctly patriotic shrines, notably Abraham Lincoln and Christopher Columbus, fulfill the "love of country" ideal.

The grotto, shrines, and fences, which frame the gardens, were crafted from stone, mortar, and colored objects collected from all over the world. Look closely and you'll find bits of china teacups and plates, petrified wood, amber, even wooden balls from the top of automobile stick shifts in the mix. Although Wernerus's plan specifically called for live flowers, he did create some urns filled with flowers crafted from the unusual materials.

Mature trees form a partial backdrop to the site, although the plantings must like full sun. Decorative mosaic fences made from a combination of

Curlicues on a decorative fence at the Dickeyville Grotto

mortar, stone, glass, and shells, edge the asphalt paths. The curlicues on one particular fence resemble a fern just before it uncurls.

Inside the fences, the clipped hedge parterres enclose the flowerbeds filled with annuals and perennials. In one garden, pink begonias are planted in a cross bed, while in other gardens, the designs are less formal. Marigolds, sedums, violets, hostas, gerbera daisies, salvias, and yarrow add splashes of color against the green arborvitae and white fences.

> Back in 1964, Lawrence and Lucinda Arnes donated the *Floral Clock* in New Glarus in memory of her parents. The bronze clock hands rest on 10:55. The clock is surrounded with a small formal garden filled with annuals.

Statues of angels, children, and swans are scattered throughout the gardens. By placing an eagle on top of a large fountain, Wernerus emphasized his patriotic theme. The formality and structure of the Dickeyville gardens are in stark contrast to the Rudolph Grotto and Gardens, which has more of a woodland garden feel.

COUNTY	Grant
ADDRESS	305 West Main Street, Dickeyville
PHONE	608/568-3119
DIRECTIONS	Located at the corner of U.S. Highway 151 and State Highways 35 and 61 behind Holy Ghost Church.
ADMISSION	Free, donations appreciated.
HOURS	Tours of the site run from 11 a.m. to 4 p.m. daily, June through August. Visitors are welcome to view the gardens and folk art on their own.
AMENITIES	Parking lot. Toilets, water inside the church.

William T. Evjue Garden

MADISON

OVERLOOKING LAKE MONONA, the William T. Evjue Garden perched on the roof of the Monona Terrace Community and Convention Center is a mix of contemporary and the familiar that captures your attention without detracting from the space and the view.

Opened in 1997 after being on the drawing board for nearly sixty years, the Frank Lloyd Wright-inspired building showcases the architect's famous ingenuity. All of the circles in the building's design were put there to mimic the dome of the State Capitol, said Margaret Ingraham, a tour guide at Taliesin, Wright's principal home in Spring Green. With the lake on the south side and busy John Nolen Drive on the north side, there wasn't a great deal of space left for plantings so the decision was made to add green space on the roof.

The semi-circle garden space is named for the late publisher of Madison's Capital Times newspaper, who was a longtime friend of Wright's. Because the

Pete Olson

Evjue Garden on the rooftop of Monona Terrace

roof is frequently used for convention and community gatherings, the garden comprises only about twenty percent of the roof's 60,000 square feet, and hardscapes take up much of it—brick pavers, planters, and planter walls. Turf covers some of the square footage.

The planters hold a variety of trees and perennials, with spots of annuals and grasses for emphasis. The trees are fast-growing locust, dogwood, and flowering crab trees. There are also lilacs to complement the crab trees' spring show.

The Wedding Garden is found on the west side. Here, the landscapers from David J. Frank Landscaping plant unusual species like Golden Delicious salvia, annual creeping phlox, and pineapple plant, a bromeliad-looking tropical that resembles its name. Imagine looking at those luscious wedding pictures decades from now.

Perennials are primarily confined to the twelve side planters. Many of them are natives such as gaillardia, coneflowers, daisies, and black-eyed Susans. With Wright the father of the Prairie school of design, the plants are consistent with his philosophy of organic architecture. Planters can be found in the center of the garden as well as along Olin Terrace, the portion of the building that connects to Martin Luther King Boulevard.

COUNTY	Dane
ADDRESS	One John Nolen Drive, Madison
PHONE	608/261-4000 or 608/261-4049
WEBSITE	www.mononaterrace.com
DIRECTIONS	From I-90 east, exit U.S. Highways 12/18 (the Beltline) and go west. Exit John Nolen Drive and follow it toward downtown Madison. Monona Terrace will be on your right. There's underground parking available for a fee.
ADMISSION	Free
HOURS	Because the garden is used for events, call between 8 a.m. and 5 p.m. Monday through Friday to see if it is open or closed. Otherwise the garden is open from 8 a.m. to 10 p.m. Sunday through Thursday and from 8 a.m. to midnight Friday and Saturday. It's closed during inclement weather.
AMENITIES	Parking lot. Toilets and water available inside the building.

The Flower Factory

STOUGHTON

WHEN DAVID NEDVECK TURNED FIFTY, he decided he wanted a train set. Fortunately for David, his wife, Nancy, was willing to let her husband indulge his dream as long as it was done tastefully and outside at their perennial nursery.

So David installed not one, but two, G-scale garden railroads complete with natural landscaping at The Flower Factory. The garden railroads join a

A "green" roof at the Flower Factory

shade garden, rock garden, rooftop garden, and pond and stream gardens at the nursery located just outside of Stoughton.

Sedums and succulents are the mainstay in the two garden railroad displays. One resembles an Old West scene; the other has more of a woodsy feel. A group of hostas, astilbe, and a few daylilies morphed into a shade garden when a septic system had to be removed and Nancy didn't want to re-install grass. Sand beds surround the pond garden, growing anything that adapts to the space.

A groundcover and sedum garden features varieties such as *Knautia macedonica* ('Pink Bubbles') and *Agastache Foeniculum* ('Golden Jubilee'). Sedums are also found growing on the roof of a small red building near the entrance. And yet more sedums planted in hypertofa pots appear in the rock garden. Large plastic troughs filled with plants do a great job hiding propane tanks. A row of natives borders one of the hoop houses.

In a border garden set against the large red barn, conifers and evergreens are interspersed with peonies, penstemon, dianthus, and yucca. An established Harry Lauder Walking Stick anchors one end. Located between several of the hoop houses, eight raised beds contain water plants and eight more have sand as the base for the desert lovers.

"Frivolity" is how Nancy describes the purpose behind the display gardens and the art in them. The Nedvecks are collectors of garden art and willingly share their finds with the public. There are rusty flowers courtesy of Jurustic Park in Marshfield tucked under mature trees near the house; glass heads and hands sitting in the groundcover garden; antique ceramic planters of cars, trains, and cows scattered throughout the Western garden railroad layout filled with succulents; and bright colored ceramic chickens and rabbits in the border garden. Look for Whizzer and his friends just doing their thing next to the Port-a-Potties. None of the art is for sale, but it adds lots of interest to the landscape here. The little ones have a sandbox to keep themselves occupied while the adults shop.

While sedums and succulents form the foundation of many of the display gardens, the Flower Factory actually sells over 4,000 varieties of perennials, hostas, and ornamental grasses. From desert to bog, sun to shade, they're likely to carry it.

While you're in the area, head south on U.S. Highway 14 to Stonewall Nursery for a fabulous selection of dwarf conifers. Owners Ed Lyon and Peter Moersch have put together a comprehensive selection from the tiniest specimen to the largest one available. They also carry ornamental deciduous trees and shrubs.

> More than fifty community gardens around the state are part of FEEDS, *Food and Ecosystem Educational Demonstration Sites*. Funded by a grant from the University of Wisconsin-Extension, this project connects people involved in the gardens together to share information and resources. Visit the Web site at: http://feeds.uwex.edu.

Stonewall Nursery is a case where redecorating the yard got a bit out of hand and led to the development of a nursery. The duo is turning both the front- and backyards of the property into display gardens.

COUNTY	Dane
ADDRESS	4062 County Road A, Stoughton
PHONE	608/873-8329
WEBSITE	www.theflowerfactorynursery.com
DIRECTIONS	From U.S. Highways 12/18 (the Beltline), exit U.S. Highway 14 South (Oregon) for several miles. Turn east on County Road A. Stonewall is slightly south of A on the west side of Highway 14.
ADMISSION	Free
HOURS	April 21 to October 10, 9 a.m. to 7 p.m. weekdays and 9 a.m. to 6 p.m. weekends.
AMENITIES	Gravel parking lot. Toilets available.

House on the Rock

SPRING GREEN

PREVIOUS VISITORS to the two hundred-acre House on the Rock aren't surprised at the curiosities that Alex Jordan built into a one-of-a-kind attraction. But ignoring the collections and touring the house's gardens offers a new perspective on Jordan's unusual legacy.

The garden tour starts the minute you turn off of State Highway 23 onto the property's entrance. There, two enormous sugar-bowl-style strawberry pots, each twenty feet high, flank both sides of the road. The annuals in these pots compete for attention with the lizards (or perhaps they're dragons) that appear to creep along the pots' sides. Also in evidence are the thousands of daylilies that have multiplied from the eight thousand planted twenty years ago. There are thirty more of these fantastical pots either lining the driveway to the Gate House, where you can purchase tickets for a trip into Jordan's imagination, or on the property itself.

Outside the Gate House, landscape manager Ron Boley and his staff have planted a welcoming combination red salvia and dusty miller accented with spikes in two raised beds. Sandstone slabs form the beds' foundation. There's also an area filled with samples of some of the two hundred seventy five varieties of plants found on the grounds. Each sample is contained in a pot, like its peers, and labeled with the botanical and common names.

This site pushes the idea of container gardening into the stratosphere. The usual suspects are potted flowering annuals like geraniums and petunias, daylilies and coleus, all in portable six- to fifteen-inch taupe plastic pots. But there are surprises. Look for the potted Korean lilacs and the eight thousand

Pots and more pots at House on the Rock

Ron Boley

pots of amaryllis, which was Jordan's favorite flower. See if you can spot the Easter egg plant, which looks exactly like an egg hanging from a green leaf. Even ferns and hostas are contained in plastic. It might be difficult to find some of the more unusual types, given that the pots get moved around the location several times during the season.

And depending upon Boley's success in getting them to bloom, there may even be a few kangaroo paws, a rare Australian flower, scattered among the thousands of pots. Other plants in the audition stage are rose kale and the unusual one with the fabulous bloom called (at least according to the catalog photo) a bat plant.

Indoors, the world-famous Infinity Room, with its 3,264 windows, is lined with pots of amaryllis, orange Chinese lanterns, money plants, Boston ferns, ivy, calla lilies, and pink, green, and white caladium. The plants almost compete for attention with the view: the

More greenery at House on the Rock   Ron Boley

room hangs out two hundred eighteen feet over the Wyoming Valley.

Boley grows everything but the 20,000 annuals in greenhouses located across the road from the property. Of the approximately 250,000 plants displayed on the ten-acre grounds, there are representations from all of the continents except Antarctica.

Many of the locations for the pots will change during 2008 as the site undergoes a three-phase restoration. In Phase 1, scheduled for completion in 2008, an authentic Japanese garden, complete with four fourteen-foot waterfalls that will cascade into a pond, is scheduled. A Zen garden with dry falls and a dry river will be placed behind the waterfalls. This new garden will replace the Garden Café and the current waterfall.

Completion of Phase 2, scheduled to be finished during the 2008 summer season, will result in a new Asian garden to be located outside of a new Welcome Center. Designed to be a hillside and pond garden, the Asian garden will contain waterfalls that form a stream leading to a large central pond. Phase 2 also includes are plans for the construction of a four-season conservatory overlooking the Japanese Garden. The conservatory will contain delicate, rare, and unusual plants and be open year-round.

Phase 3, with an expected completion date of 2010, just in time for the site's 50th anniversary, will feature a new plaza space to showcase the containers now placed around the grounds.

COUNTY	Iowa
ADDRESS	5754 State Road 23, Spring Green
PHONE	608/935-3639
WEBSITE	www.thehouseontherock.com
DIRECTIONS	Located nine miles south of Spring Green and nine miles north of Dodgeville on State Highway 23 on the west side of the road. Watch for signs.
ADMISSION	Adults 18 and over: $11.50 per tour or $26.50 for all three tours. Ages 4-17: $7.50 per tour or $15.50 for all three. Children under 3 free.
HOURS	Daily, 9 a.m. to 5 p.m., 6 p.m. or 7 p.m. depending upon the time of the year. Closed mid-January through mid-March.
AMENITIES	Parking lot. Toilets, food, and water available in the complex.

Katie's Garden

PLATTEVILLE

LOCATED JUST WEST of Platteville's log-cabin-style Chamber of Commerce/ Visitor Center is a lovely memorial garden dedicated to the memory of Katie Rae Vaassen. Vaassen, a Chamber volunteer who contributed more than eight hundred hours of work, died in 2004 at age 23. To honor her efforts, the Chamber dedicated a garden in Vaassen's name on the property.

Considered the "gateway" to the new Platteville Community Arboretum and Rountree Gardens project, "Katie's Garden" is the first installment along the city's hiking and biking trail that runs from the University of Wisconsin through the city of Platteville. Various beds of flowers are planted along the Rountree Branch stream and trail between the Chamber office and Business Highway 151. Hardscape features include a four-sided redwood gazebo with a tumbled stone floor. The wooded rock bluffs act as a subtle backdrop for both the trout stream and the plants.

A row of red yarrow, yellow and white daisies, purple coneflowers, and other natives separates the garden from the highway. Spirea borders the garden and the Chamber parking lot. Miniature roses and tulips encircle a memorial stone engraved with Vaassen's picture. Two carved tree trunk "chairs" are ringed with foxglove, lilies, and other perennials. Hostas, naturally, are found in a shade bed. When mature, several evergreens will tower above the gardens and stand as a "tribute to rise above challenges."

Many of the oval- or kidney-shaped beds contain roses. Some feature a mixture of annuals and perennials including coral bells and hostas, deep red or yellow daylilies, even marigolds and petunias. A rose arbor with a bench invites you to stop, sit, and smell the blooms. Pink climbing roses surround the arbor using the lattice for support while two beds of pink and white rose bushes flank the structure. Community members donated many of the plants found in the garden.

COUNTY	Grant
ADDRESS	275 U.S. Highway 151, Platteville
PHONE	608/348-8888
EMAIL	chamber@platteville.com
DIRECTIONS	Located on the southwest side of Platteville at the corner of Business Highway 151 and Staley Avenue across from the Governor Dodge Hotel and Convention Center. The garden is located on the south side of U.S. Highway 151 and the west side of the Chamber building.
ADMISSION	Free
HOURS	Daily, dawn to dusk.
AMENITIES	Parking lot. Toilets and water available in the visitor's center.

Longenecker Horticultural Gardens

MADISON

HERE'S A TRIVIA QUESTION. What was the first plant installed in the University of Wisconsin Arboretum? The answer: lilacs. Professor G. William Longenecker, the first director of the University of Wisconsin's Arboretum, planted lilac bushes on Good Friday in 1935.

Since that first installation, the 1,260 acres have grown to include three conifer forests, four deciduous forests, two savannas, four prairies, and a marsh. Oh, and don't forget the fifty-acre Longenecker Horticultural Gardens, named after the professor who first planted the lilacs.

It's no surprise that the Longenecker Gardens contain one of the country's largest lilac displays. But it also includes many other top-notch collections of "woodies," specifically ornamental crab apples (the most up-to-date collection), viburnums, and conifers. Much of the credit goes to Professor

Longenecker Gardens

Edward Hasselkus, emeritus curator of the gardens, who expanded Longenecker's initial work into a premier collection of trees, shrubs, and vines. The 2,500 plants are arranged according to genus. All of the plants are labeled.

Located north of the Arboretum Visitor Center, you'll find various outdoor rooms filled with unique trees and shrubs. There are the gingko, honey locust, and beech trees. A new hybrid elm hopes to derail the damage done by the Dutch elm beetle.

On a hill is the Pinetum. Here, the conifers really show their stuff. There are collections of blue spruce, junipers, and pines. The other side of the hill showcases firs and hemlocks. Longenecker also includes a collection of mugo pines with their quirky shapes and a unique Japanese umbrella pine that prefers warmer weather, but seems to have adapted well to its Wisconsin home. Another Wisconsin immigrant that's actually thriving is the bald cypress tree, usually seen only in Southern climates.

In the shrub department, there are the lilacs and the viburnums, but magnolias, forsythias, and serviceberries are actually the harbingers of spring, blooming in late April. Later in May, the azaleas and rhododendrons erupt with enthusiasm. And rose lovers won't be disappointed when the rugosas, Canadian, and other hardy varieties say hello in June.

COUNTY	Dane
ADDRESS	1207 Seminole Highway, Madison
PHONE	608/263-7888
FAX	608/262-5209
EMAIL	info@uwaboretum.org
WEBSITE	www.uwarboretum.org
DIRECTIONS	From U.S. Highways 12/18 (the Beltline), exit 258A (Seminole Highway). Follow Seminole Highway north to the second right, which is Arboretum Drive. The Arboretum Visitor Center is one mile from this entrance. From the UW campus, take Mills Street south to Arboretum Drive. The Arboretum Visitor Center is 2.5 miles from this entrance.
ADMISSION	Free
HOURS	Arboretum trails and the Visitor Center parking lot are open daily, 7 a.m. to 10 p.m. Other Arboretum parking lots are open from dawn to dusk. The Visitor Center is open from 9:30 a.m. to 4 p.m. on weekdays and from 12:30 p.m. to 4 p.m. on weekends (excluding holidays).
AMENITIES	Parking lot. Toilets and water inside the Visitor Center.

❧ Gone, but not forgotten:

Several well-known gardens and greenhouses are no longer in business including:

Jones Arboretum and Botanical Garden, Readstown

Several floods during 2000 destroyed most of Royce Jones' arboretum and botanical garden. Bill Kappler and Lisa Ashley bought Jones' site and opened Read's Creek Nursery further down the road on Highway 14.

St. Coletta's Greenhouse, Jefferson

As the institution downsizes and prepares to sell its residential complex in Jefferson, the greenhouse, which provided work for the developmentally disabled, is closed.

Ashland Agricultural Research Station

At one time, this site had one hundred beds devoted to flowering plants. It closed in November 2006.

Outdoor Sunken Garden, Mitchell Park Horticultural Conservatory, Milwaukee

The reflecting pool has been filled in and grass has been installed in the area.

✿ *Little Norway*

BLUE MOUNDS

ONCE A NORWEGIAN PIONEER farmer's simple family homestead, Little Norway and its location captured the attention of Chicago insurance executive, Isak Dahle. He purchased it in 1927 for a summer home and called it *Nissedahle*, or Valley of the Elves. Dahle had a considerable amount of work done to the property, installing additional buildings and significant landscapes, eventually opening the private estate up for tours in 1936. The plantings around this outdoor heritage museum represent what was a group of elegant English-style gardens in the style of garden writer Gertrude Jekyll.

Time and neglect have rendered these gardens somewhat shabby, something that Shan Thomas, the heritage gardener hired to restore the landscape to its historic charm, is fixing. Because many of the gardens fell into disrepair over the years, some edges have naturalized. But Thomas has implemented some significant restoration plans.

Her intent is to take the gardens back to their heyday in the early 1930s, before Dahle died. Fortunately, she has lots of documentation available.

A cross honoring the summer solstice at Little Norway

Copies of old photos show a lushness that easily held its own against the back-drop of the intricate architecture of the historic buildings.

Thomas is focusing on thirty-eight beds scattered around ten acres. Within the Little Norway site you'll find a bog, sandy loam, lots of shade, and a stream with a waterfall. There are two ponds, one of which is a reflecting pond. A three hundred-foot stone wall is being restored as a rock garden, which was its original intent.

Currently, the property sports two arborvitae that are almost eighty feet tall and two fifty-year-old white hydrangeas, as well as natives, bulbs, perennials, and wildflowers. Some of Thomas' work has involved uncovering the hardscape that plant overgrowth had hidden.

> Resembling a French *potager*, or kitchen garden, the garden located next to the Creamery Café and the *Artisan Gallery* in Paoli contains a variety of herbs and edible flowers, which are incorporated into the restaurant's offerings.

For springtime interest, Thomas is planting additional bulbs so that the site could be open to garden lovers earlier than May 1. Spring is also when a lot of the natives and wildflowers bloom. Additional shrubs will provide interest in the mixed borders. Replacement perennials are being selected from a Midwestern palette to rejuvenate the borders. Most of the perennials will need to work well in shade and like moisture.

Thomas plans to focus more on the bog that surrounds the pond on the valley floor. Because of the bog, there are only a few varieties of trees on the property. One pond only exists in the summer. During the fall, the dam is removed and the water flows into a nearby creek.

Once Thomas finishes reclaiming and restoring the landscape in a year or two, Little Norway will be a stunning representation of the kind of English garden Jekyll would be proud to write about. In the meantime, it's great fun to watch how it progresses.

COUNTY	Iowa
ADDRESS	3576 County Highway JG North, Blue Mounds
PHONE	608/437-8211
FAX	608/437-7827
WEBSITE	www.littlenorway.com
DIRECTIONS	Located on County Highway JG off of U.S. Highway 18/151. Exit Cave of the Mounds Road between Mt. Horeb and Blue Mounds. Turn right on County Highway ID. Go one-quarter mile to Highway JG.
ADMISSION	$12 for adults; $11 for seniors 62 and older; $5 for children ages 5 to 12. A tour group of 20 or more is $10 per person.
HOURS	May 1 through the last Sunday in October. Open daily 9 a.m. to 5 p.m. in May and June and September and October; 9 a.m. to 7 p.m. in July and August.
AMENITIES	Parking lot. Toilets, water, and food inside the gift shop.

Miner Park

SHULLSBURG

SHULLSBURG'S MINER PARK was born from tragedy. Cheryl Fink's grandfather, Joseph Griffin, was one of eight miners caught in a cave-in at the Mulcahly Lead and Zinc Mine on February 9, 1943. Her father's dream was to do something to honor the memory of Griffin and the men who died in the worst mining disaster in Wisconsin's history. So Fink and her siblings approached the city to build a memorial park that would be filled with perennials, bulbs, trees, and shrubs. Miner Park was created on the 5,000-square-foot site of the former Burg Theater, which was destroyed by fire.

Located on the south side of West Water Street between Cindy's Quality Embroidery and the Pick and Gad building, Miner Park does an effective job balancing the softscapes and hardscapes in a square city lot outlined with a split-rail fence. You'll find flowering shrubs such as weigela and burning bush, 'Diablo' ninebark, and 'Gold Mound' spirea. Hostas, stella d'oro lilies, roses, and potentilla are just some of the other plantings woven among the conifers and arborvitae. Some additional color is added with rudbeckia, irises, and coreopsis. Tulips pop up in the spring. A serpentine path formed from red concrete leads to a gazebo with three wooden benches. A memorial stone is dedicated to the lost miners.

COUNTY	Lafayette
ADDRESS	West Water Street, Shullsburg
DIRECTIONS	From State Highway 11, turn east onto West Water Street.
ADMISSION	Free
HOURS	Daily, dawn to dusk.
AMENITIES	Street parking.

All-America Selections Display Gardens

In 1932 W. Ray Hastings, president of Georgia's Southern Seedsmen's Association, proposed the idea of All-American Selections, a program where trial gardens all over the country would test seeds for their hardiness and viability. Trial gardens plant new, unsold varieties of seeds, and gardeners report on their experiences at the end of the growing season. Wisconsin's AAS trial gardens can be found at:

Green Bay Botanical Garden, Green Bay
Boerner Botanical Gardens, Milwaukee
A. R. Albert and Villetta Hawley Albert Horticultural Gardens, Hancock
Rotary Gardens, Janesville
Harold S. Vincent High School, Milwaukee
University of Wisconsin Spooner Agricultural Research Station, Spooner
University of Wisconsin West Madison Agricultural Research Station, Madison

Montesian Gardens

MONTICELLO

LOCATED OFF OF STATE HIGHWAY 69 between the Bank of Monticello and the village's softball diamond, the Montesian Gardens offer a wonderful example of what community support behind an idea can accomplish.

The gardens began almost on a whim when two Monticello residents, Harold Baebler and Ann Saunders, created raised flowerbeds next to a sign honoring the high school girls' basketball team's state championship. Later,

Sign announces the Montesian Gardens

the duo, along with several community members, visited Monticello, Iowa, to see that city's concept of a community garden. Bringing back the idea to Wisconsin, they drew up the plan for adoptable garden plots with initial help from McKay Nursery in Waterloo. Then the Montesian Gardens committee sought and received approval from the Bank of Monticello to install the gardens on the bank's property.

The name Montesian comes from a combination of Monticello and artesian. There's an artesian well that supplies water for the local lake.

The original plan started with an open circle and pergola at the garden's north end and ended just past the "Welcome to Monticello" sign. Later work brought the path up to the softball diamond. A donation from a local resident added 10,000 red brick pavers that were installed in a serpentine path that entices visitors to move ahead to see what's around the corner.

Each garden plot or room brings many surprises. A wide range of annuals and perennials in various combinations can be found in the individual beds. You'll see the purple-topped stalks of the gayfeathers underplanted with dianthus, snapdragons, and moss roses. Some residents prefer the natives, daylilies, and hostas in their beds. Low-lying shrubs, evergreens, and a wide variety of trees represent the "woodies." Tree selections include birches, a Kentucky coffee tree, magnolia, several Washington hawthorns, and a linden. The soothing green of the grass keeps your focus on the blooms.

The majority of the beds have curved borders for easy upkeep. Some even contain sculptures created by area artist Sid Boyum.

There's a gazebo, several benches, and a larger pergola in the same design as the one at the garden entrance. Urn planters flank both sides of the second pergola and pink shrub roses peek through its slats. A concrete sidewalk picks up where the initial brick pavers left off. Along the gardens' east side is Brayton Creek, named for the family who owned the property during the nineteenth century.

COUNTY	Green
ADDRESS	400 West Coates Avenue, Monticello
DIRECTIONS	From State Highway 69, exit Coates Avenue to the east.
ADMISSION	Free
HOURS	Daily, dawn to dusk.
AMENITIES	Parking lot.

 ## Native Wisconsin Plant Garden

MADISON

AROUND THE VISITOR CENTER at the University of Wisconsin-Madison Arboretum is the four-acre Native Wisconsin Plant Garden with its hundreds of native species that will inspire any garden club or home gardener. Planting began in the garden more than five years ago after the Arboretum Visitor Center was completed. Designed by landscape architect Darrel Morrison, formerly a professor at the University of Wisconsin-Madison and dean at the University of Georgia's School of Environmental Design, this space is divided into eleven gardens representing southern Wisconsin plant communities. They include a dry limestone prairie, a fen, cedar birch hillside, wet prairie swale, a wetland, a mesic prairie, a dry mesic prairie, bur oak and black oak savannas, an oak hickory forest, and a maple basswood forest. But there are other garden spaces interspersed among them.

Natives are on display in the Front Entrance Garden along with Wisconsin's largest black gum tree. Look for bee balm, wild geranium, shooting star, and spiderwort. Ornamental grasses such as little bluestem and side-oats grama grass can be found along with flowering prairie plants like leadplant, asters, and prairie coreopsis in the Lime Prairie Garden. Flowers in the Rain Garden (sometimes referred to as the Fen Garden) include turtlehead, angelica, and cardinal flower, but there's also porcupine sedge and prairie cordgrass.

Located behind the Visitor Center is the Birch Cedar Glade Garden with the Shaded Cliff Garden nearby. Unusual species here are starry Solomon's plume, jeweled shooting star, dwarf bush honeysuckle, and sensitive fern. Not to be missed is the Friends of the Arboretum Terrace Garden, with its sweet black-eyed Susans, mountain mint, bluejoint grass, Culver's root, and gayfeather.

In the Bur Oak Savanna Garden located just east of the Terrace Garden, you will find bur oaks, hazelnut, and gray dogwood as well as drifts of giant purple hyssop, nodding wild onion, prairie dropseed, and asters. Prairie gardens are located east of the Visitor Center. Dry mesic species surround the overlook seating area at the top of the hill, and the mesic prairie garden is planted on the slope.

A large pergola identifies the Species Garden, where three hundred species of plants native to southern Wisconsin are planted in concentric beds. Most of the selections are perennials. For easy comparison and identification, plants are arranged by genus and family in this garden.

Nearby, the Black Oak Savanna garden includes dotted mint, goldenrods, and lupine. The Oak, Hickory, and Maple Basswood forest gardens are a good place to see shade loving plants and spring ephemerals.

Several gardens are under construction: a Sand Prairie Garden, a Water Continuum Garden, the Children's Garden, and the Homeowners' Demonstration Garden. Paved walkways link the eleven plant community gardens in this accessible area.

COUNTY	Dane
ADDRESS	1207 Seminole Highway, Madison
PHONE	608/263-7888
FAX	608/262-5209
EMAIL	info@uwaboretum.org
WEBSITE	www.uwarboretum.org
DIRECTIONS	From U.S. Highways 12/18 (the Beltline), exit 258A (Seminole Highway). Follow Seminole Highway north to the second right, which is Arboretum Drive. The Arboretum Visitor Center is one mile from this entrance. From the UW campus, take Mills Street south to Arboretum Drive. The Arboretum Visitor Center is 2.5 miles from this entrance.
ADMISSION	Free
HOURS	Arboretum trails and the Visitor Center parking lot are open daily, 7 a.m. to 10 p.m. Other Arboretum parking lots are open from dawn to dusk. The Visitor Center is open from 9:30 a.m. to 4 p.m. on weekdays and from 12:30 p.m. to 4 p.m. on weekends (excluding holidays).
AMENITIES	Parking lot. Toilets and water inside the Visitor Center.

 Olbrich Botanical Gardens

MADISON

EVERY YEAR the American Association of Botanic Gardens and Arboreta honors one of its five hundred member gardens with the Award for Garden Excellence. The award, sponsored by *Horticulture* magazine, is given to a public garden that best exemplifies the highest standards of horticultural practice while supporting and demonstrating the best gardening practices. It's the Oscar of the garden world, and in 2005 the award went to one of Wisconsin's own—Madison's Olbrich Botanical Gardens.

The Bolz Conservatory at Olbrich Gardens

A piece of tranquillity situated on the capital city's east side, Olbrich offers a year-round feast for the senses. In the summer, the ten outdoor display gardens shimmer with color, while during the cold months, the Bolz Conservatory entices visitors to come in for a little taste of the tropics.

Built in 1928 on the site of the former Garver Feed Supply, which had a previous life as a sugar beet factory, Olbrich has entertained and educated generations of Madisonians and visitors. Give credit to the vision of Madison attorney Michael B. Olbrich for keeping the area on the shores of Lake Monona pristine and undeveloped.

When you exit the Visitor's Center you'll pass the Flowering Grove filled with crab apple trees. Nearby is the entrance to the wisteria-covered, semi-circular Donor's Arbor with its stone columns and metal "roof." A walkway encircles the elliptical Great Lawn like the hub of a wheel. Additional paths, like wheel spokes, lead you to the various specialty gardens. The paths are placed so that you can't see the entire garden from one spot. There's always a surprise waiting around the corner.

A northern path filled with annuals, container gardens, and a shrub rose border leads away from the Great Lawn and the Donor's Arbor to the Event Garden. Olbrich plants five hundred containers each year, the largest being a recycled industrial cauldron.

Joe DeMaio

Rose Tower

Head east from the Great Lawn and you'll encounter the Rose Garden. Installed in 2005, this garden blends perennials, ornamental grasses, bulbs, and ornamental trees along with shrub, hybrid teas, grandifloras, and floribunda roses in mixed borders. Designed to be sustainable without the excess use of water, chemicals, or care, if a rose grows at Olbrich, southern Wisconsin gardeners can be assured it will thrive in their backyard garden.

Prairie-style hardscape features in this garden include a forecourt fountain with five water jets and a "weeping" wall with five mini-waterfalls. All were designed in a series of five to represent the five petals of a rose. The two-story, thirty-foot Rose Tower offers dramatic views of the Rose Garden and beyond. Trellises continue the shape of the tower and planters are upside down trellis shapes, which repeat the dimensions of the conservatory albeit much smaller, said Sharon Cybart, manager of marketing and public relations. This is the only garden with landscape lighting.

A one hundred and fifty-five-foot arched ornamental steel bridge leads you across Starkweather Creek and deposits you at the three-acre tropical Thai Garden installed in 2002. Much symbolism is contained in the plantings and hardscapes of this garden. The bridge represents and even resembles the body of a snake, which Thais believe gives rain and holds power over wind and thunderstorms. Loor for see the tail of the serpent in the design of the stone pavers.

Filled with ornamental grasses, several species of bamboo, and large-leaf shrubs and plants, the Thai Garden and its reflecting pools surround the exquisite gold-leaf-accented teak Thai Pavilion or "sala." The King of Thailand and the Thai Chapter of the Wisconsin Alumni Association donated the pavilion—the only one in the continental United States and one of four worldwide—to the University of Wisconsin. Nine Thai artisans traveled to Madison to reconstruct the building without nails or screws on the Olbrich site. All of the rooftop tiles have messages written on the underside.

Topiaries called "Mai Dat" mimic a Thai style of topiary. Plant selections are consistent with a tropical garden. Bronze and stone statues of elephants signify strength, wisdom, and victory. There's even a lion statue and a pile of stones that represents a miniature mountainscape.

Retrace your steps back across the bridge to the small Serenity Garden and Flowering Cherry Grove. Take the walkway leading west along the northern bank of the creek and stop at the Starkweather Creek and Atrium Shade Garden with its hostas, viburnums, ferns, and tree canopies.

Heading north from the shade garden, you'll encounter the Perennial Garden filled with mixed borders of blooming plants, trees, and shrubs generally planted in "hot" colors of reds and yellows. Hardscape features here include a waterfall leading into a stream and three pools filled with aquatic plants.

A wooden grape arbor signals the entrance to the Herb Garden with its seven specialty beds. Herbs are planted in representations of knot, kitchen, dye, touch, smell, medicinal, and courtyard gardens. A parterre outlines a formal garden anchored in the center with a sundial. Look for a mint garden growing varieties of grapefruit, apple, and orange mints; a wine and hops garden; and an Herbs de Provence garden. Nancy Ragland, the former director of the gardens, designed the grapevine-covered arbor. Italian immigrants who lived in the Greenbush area of Madison and originally brought grapevines from Italy donated some to Olbrich.

In the southwest corner, the Eunice Fisher Hosta, and Meadow, Wildflower, and Rock gardens surround Discovery Dock, which offers an opportunity to get closer to the water and see aquatic plants and frogs. The Hosta Garden boasts a rare collection of hostas hybridized by Wisconsin resident Eunice Fisher. Perennial grasses, bulbs, and wildflowers that pop up like little

Joe DeMaio

Thai topiaries in front of the teak Thai Pavilion

jewels in the spring offer a "lawn alternative" in the Meadow Garden. Only mowed three times a year, fescue grasses keep the "lawn" at manageable levels. Against the backdrop of the wildflowers in the Wildflower Garden you'll find species of ferns, native trees, and shrubs. A fiddlehead fern sculpture is set in the middle of a bed of ferns.

Alpine plants and dwarf conifers fill the nooks and crannies of the Rock Garden, one of the older gardens here. This space contains a waterfall and lots of spring blooms. Connecting the Wildflower and Rock gardens is the Lussier wooden bridge.

From the Hosta Garden, take the walkway north to the Sunken Gardens. Originally designed in 1935 as a rose garden, the Sunken Garden has been renovated into a formal, traditional English-style garden. It features a limestone terrace, perennial borders, and an eighty-foot long reflecting pool colored with, appropriately, beet dye. The dye keeps the water warmer, which reduces the algae. Even though the pool is only three-feet deep, "it gives you a feeling that the depth is endless," said Cybart. Looking out over the pool from the east, you can see Lake Monona in the distance. Even in winter, it's a popular destination with berries, barks, and grasses surrounding the pool.

The Sylvia Beckman sculpture *Spring* resembles tulip leaves and offers hope of warmer days. Beckman also has another sculpture, *Hosta Leaf,* located in

A sea of tulips at the Lussier Terrace

Jeff Epping

A butterfly at home in the "Glass Pyramid"

the Arlette Morse Terrace near the Visitor's Center. Also located near the Center is the "Ol' Bear Topiary" representing a family of bears having a picnic lunch.

The fifty-foot tall, 10,000-square-foot Bolz Conservatory, "the glass pyramid," features over seven hundred fifty species of plants from Florida and Central and South America. Children will delight in finding the lemon and orange trees and cacao (chocolate) and coffee bushes. Carnivorous plants are always entertaining. Various species of orchids are on display from Olbrich's collection of over eight hundred. They add bits of color to the various textures and intensities of green. See if you can identify the thirty different palms scattered around the space.

A waterfall, bamboo arbors, and a stream are a few of the features found in the Conservatory. Look for the "free flying" birds that entertain as well as work as part of the integrated pest management system. The space is a wonderful getaway during the cold winter months.

Currently at sixteen acres, Olbrich was able to purchase an additional twenty-two acres for future garden expansion.

COUNTY	Dane
ADDRESS	3330 Atwood Avenue, Madison
PHONE	608/246-4550; events: 608/246-4718
WEBSITE	www.olbrich.org
DIRECTIONS	Located on the corner of Fair Oaks and Atwood avenues on the eastern shores of Lake Monona. From U.S. Highways 12/18 (the Beltline), exit onto Monona Drive. Take Monona Drive around the lake to Olbrich (about four miles). Monona Drive becomes Atwood Avenue as it curves around Lake Monona.
ADMISSION	The outdoor gardens are free. Admission to the Bolz Conservatory is $1. Children 5 and under are free. Admission is free from 10 a.m. to noon Wednesdays and Saturdays.
HOURS	Outdoor gardens: April through September, 8 a.m. to 8 p.m. October to March, 9 a.m. to 4 p.m. Bolz Conservatory and Botanical Center, 10 a.m. to 4 p.m. daily and until 5 p.m. on Sundays year-round. The gardens are closed on Thanksgiving and Christmas.
AMENITIES	Parking lot. Handicapped accessible. Toilets and water inside the building.

Orchard Lawn

MINERAL POINT

FORMAL GARDENS AND A GAZEBO on the site of what was once known as the Gundry House make this a lovely spot to host a wedding. The 1868 Italianate sandstone mansion and grounds was home to three generations of the Gundry family for sixty-eight years. The Gundrys called it "Orchard Lawn" because of its large apple orchard, pasture, and gardens.

After nearly encountering a wrecking ball in 1936, the house was spared and eventually renovated in 1999. At that time a new set of formal gardens, designed by Buettner & Associates, were installed on the grounds.

Two long flowerbeds arc from each side of a white, wooden octagonal gazebo around the perimeter of the great lawn. You'll find a selection of annuals, perennials, and shrubs such as lantana, peonies, yarrow, dahlias, sedums, spirea, and giant phlox in lush abundance. Petunias and other annuals add continuous color. Two stone benches with carvings of acorns and tree trunks invite you to pause for a moment.

Besides the formal gardens, the nine-acre estate features thirty-eight varieties of mature trees, some of which are over one hundred years old. The Mineral Point Historical Society even has receipts for trees from 1868. The first catalpa tree planted in Wisconsin was planted on the grounds of Orchard Lawn.

COUNTY	Iowa
ADDRESS	234 Madison Street, Mineral Point
PHONE	608/987-2884
EMAIL	mphistory@mhtc.net
WEBSITE	www.mineralpoint.com/hist.html
DIRECTIONS	From U.S. Highway 151, take the ramp toward State Highway 39 (Mineral Point/Darlington) and turn left at U.S. Highway 151 Business Route. Continue on State Highway 23, which turns into Dodge Street in Mineral Point. Take a left on North Iowa Street and go about one block. Take another left onto Madison Street.
ADMISSION	Free
HOURS	The grounds are open daily, dawn to dusk. Tours of the home are held from 1 p.m. to 5 p.m. Fridays and Saturdays and from 11 a.m. to 2 p.m. Sundays from mid-May to mid-October.
AMENITIES	Street parking.

Orchids by the Ackers

WAUNAKEE

ENTERING THE FAMILY BUSINESS can be a blessing or a curse. Fortunately for Nancy Acker-Skolaski and her husband, Stan, there was never any thought not to do so.

In 1990, the Skolaskis bought Orchids by the Ackers from Nancy's father, Walter, who had purchased the business from a Madison doctor in 1964 for whom he had worked as a teen. The doctor had raised orchids as a hobby and when Walter purchased it, he initially focused on wholesale cut flower sales. The Skolaskis have returned the business to its roots so to speak, growing orchid plants, and have added annuals and perennials for spring/early summer sales.

While the spring sales make up a substantial part of the business, it's the orchids that steal the show. The largest family of plants with some 25,000 species, orchids occur in every climate except for Antarctica and the desert. Most prefer the warm, moist heat of the tropics although homeowners can grow most of these beauties with a little bright, indirect light. Add another 100,000 cultivars and hybrids to the initial 25,000 and you can see why they claim the award for the largest number of offspring. A little orchid trivia: perfume companies use orchids in scents and vanilla is produced from the seed pod of an orchid.

The Skolaskis generally have 30,000 or more seedlings and 20,000 mature plants available for sale, growing under 32,000 square feet of greenhouses just outside of Middleton. They stock the well-known and largest orchid, the cattleya, at one time the must-have flower for prom corsages and weddings. The Skolaskis have even grown plants from cuttings taken from the cattleya that Nancy's mother carried on her wedding day.

One of the newest varieties grown in the greenhouses is the phragmipedium. There are also the phalaenopsis and dendrobiums. Brush up on your pronunciation and spelling skills: the Skolaskis also carry examples of oncidiums, miltonias, zygopetalums, and paphiopedilums. Cymbidiums actually like it cool in the fall. Vandas tend to be the most challenging for home growers, probably because some require daily watering.

With so many species, potential orchid buyers can choose from a variety of colors, sizes, scents, and leaf shapes. Some flowers are so tiny you'll need a magnifying glass to see the details. Don't be put off by the plants' reputation for being finicky. Orchid clubs and growers like the Skolaskis are there to ensure success.

COUNTY	Dane
ADDRESS	4823 County Highway Q, Waunakee
PHONE	608/831-4700
EMAIL	orchids@chorus.net
WEBSITE	www.orchidsbytheackers.com
DIRECTIONS	From U.S. Highways 12/18, exit Airport Road/Century Avenue. Take Century Avenue east and go to the seventh stoplight, which is Highway Q. Turn left and go one-half mile. The greenhouses are on the left.
ADMISSION	Free
HOURS	The greenhouses are open all year. Spring hours from the last Sunday in April through the last Sunday in June are from 8 a.m. to 6 p.m. weekdays, 8 a.m. to 5 p.m. Saturdays, and 10 a.m. to 4 p.m. on Sundays. The rest of the year the greenhouses are open from 8 a.m. to 5 p.m. Monday through Friday and from 9 a.m. to 3 p.m. on Saturdays. They are closed on Sundays.
AMENITIES	Gravel parking lot. Toilets and water available.

Riverside International Friendship Gardens

LA CROSSE

THE LANGUAGE OF PLANTS transcends cultural boundaries. So when local La Crosse leaders wanted to celebrate the city's relationships with its foreign sister cities, it decided to install a series of gardens representing each of the cities. The result is the 1.2-acre Riverside International Friendship Gardens, located on the north end of Riverside Park. The current collection of four gardens mimics the style of those found in La Crosse's sister cities of Epinal, France; Luoyang, China; Friedberg, Germany; and Dubna, Russia.

Arborvitae and yew hedges surround the formal French garden, one of the first installed. A brick pathway leads past the parterres of the herb knot garden. Various herbs, including catmint and sage, fill the knot garden's interior spaces. Two geometric annual beds add a dash of color with astilbe, marigolds, and petunias upping the intensity. Trimmed topiaries suggest French royalty and Versailles. A stone bench overlooks the knot garden.

A three-tiered granite fountain set in an eight-foot pool is topped with a sculpture representing a famous statue located in Epinal. Two climbing roses, 'Image D'Epinal', were donations from the sister city.

Step inside the giant moon gate topped with two carved granite dragons and enter the world of Luoyang, the former capital of China. Free flowing describes the garden's layout with its emphasis on rocks, water, architecture, and plants. The Chinese garden is a tangible illustration of the principles of *feng shui,* the philosophy of attracting good fortune via the specific arrangement of the home's physical space and characteristics.

Rest a bit on the backless granite benches or take the meandering path leading past the 5,000-gallon pond with a waterfall and bridge. A small, stone

Dragons guard the archway to the Chinese garden at the Riverside International Friendship Gardens

Theresa Smerud

temple anchors one corner. A black, wrought-iron fence with Chinese symbols encloses the space.

The Asian influence is felt, not only through the hardscapes, but through the plant selections. There are Japanese iris, tree peonies, flowering plum, and Korean sun pear trees, as well as a gingko tree. Hostas, vines, spirea, clematis, and groundcovers supplement the Asian selections.

The German and Russian gardens opened in mid-2007. The German garden was created to showcase a sustainable landscape with four-season interest. A rock garden bordered on one side by a two-foot high, twenty-foot long seat wall was incorporated into the garden's design. Intended to simulate a dry alpine slope, the rock garden ably showcases hardy alpine plants and dwarf conifers.

A large pergola supports several types of climbing vines. Plants of interest here include hydrangeas, shrub roses, fern leaf peonies, hazelnut and elderberry trees as well as a selection of hardy perennials—asters, ladys' mantle, chrysanthemums, and wild geraniums. And in a toast to the country's beer industry, the garden features an ornamental hops vine.

Groves of trees, a traditional component of Russian gardens are part of the "casual" and "freestyle" look in the Dubna garden. Siberian iris, narcissus, and veronica represent some of the floral selections. Mass planting was used to create an impact as was the besedka, a Russian-style domed pavilion made from fiberglass. An open overlook terrace is set along the bank of the La Crosse River.

All of the paths within each of the gardens are made from the same material conveying the concept that we're all part of one world, said Chuck Hanson, a local attorney who's involved with the community project. "We want to express as a community that we're open to the wider world."

Since the project began, La Crosse has developed relationships with Bantry, Ireland, and Forde, Norway. Work is expected to begin on the second phase of the gardens in 2007 with a 2008 completion date.

While you're visiting the International Friendship Gardens, stop by the Centurytel Building just east of the park for a look at the company's landscaping. Strips of daylilies, ornamental grasses, and black-eyed Susans offer a nice contrast with the low-lying rockbeds containing pieces of granite. Hostas and grassy space complete the minimalist design.

COUNTY	La Crosse
ADDRESS	Riverside Park, La Crosse
PHONE	608/791-GROW (4769)
WEBSITE	www.riversidegardens.org
DIRECTIONS	From the south and east, exit State Highway 33. Go west to U.S. Highway 14/61, which is also Third Street. Go north on Third Street. Turn west on State Street and follow it into Riverside Park. From the north, exit U.S. Highway 53. Go south to La Crosse Street. Turn west on La Crosse Street and then south on Second Street. Turn west on State Street and follow it into Riverside Park.
ADMISSION	Free
HOURS	Seasonal. Daily, dawn to dusk.
AMENITIES	Street parking. Toilets and water located in the Convention and Visitors Bureau.

St. Feriole Island

PRAIRIE DU CHIEN

ST. FERIOLE ISLAND links the city of Prairie du Chien with the mighty Mississippi River. Once home to city's Fourth Ward prior to the Army Corps of Engineer's floodplain relocation project, it is quickly becoming a garden lover's playground. The two hundred forty-acre island, shaped like a slice of watermelon, features several gardens under construction as well as the historic plantings around Villa Louis, an historic Italianate home. There is also a significant perennial bed in Lawler Park, which borders the Mississippi.

On the island's north end sits Villa Louis, the opulent mansion of the Dousman family. Hercules Dousman arrived in the area in 1827 and amassed a fortune while working for the American Fur Company. His son, H. Louis Dousman, and his wife, Nina, built the now-historic Victorian home. The beautiful grounds include a number of flowerbeds, a vegetable garden, a pond, and an artesian well and fountain all done in the character of the 1890s.

Staff at the historic site plant cannas, roses, and other flowers based upon receipts left by Mrs. Dousman and her gardeners. The 'Jackmanii' clematis is

Linda Ginkel

The Mississippi flows past the flowers at Lawler Park on St. Feriole Island a copy of the exact one that was growing at the house while the Dousmans lived there.

The Victorians liked geometry, so some of the flowerbeds are in geometric shapes. There's a diamond one filled with heirloom bulbs that get replaced with old-fashioned bleeding hearts, phlox, and lilies after their spring bloom. The star-shaped bed generally contains red cannas and coleus. The round and oval beds are lined with coleus with a castor bean plant anchoring them. In a fan-shaped bed, something is always blooming.

Tuber roses like to wind their stems around a set of unique trellises in the rose circle located near the pond. The trellises are replicas of ones found in historic photographs. Weeping forms of larch and mulberry trees can be found on the grounds.

The garden spot near the rose circle is called the grotto. Staff try to keep a red and white theme with the flowers in that area. A ribbon bed that's planted with coleus lines the front walk. Because the Dousmans liked geraniums, there are pots of the annual scattered about. Elephant ears are also potted up for interest.

The property once contained a greenhouse where the Dousmans grew exotics such as gardenias, jasmine, and cacti. The staff has potted some Voodoo lilies, which would have been found in the greenhouse, for show. When in bloom, these plants, which are related to the corpse plant, have an unforgettable, and very unpleasant, smell.

South and west of Villa Louis is Lawler Park and a large, concrete-edged, octagonal planting bed filled with perennials, ornamental grasses, and shrubs. Centered in the bed are rosa rugosa bushes, hydrangea, and a bridal wreath shrub. Peonies, Shasta daisies, purple coneflowers, and monarda add height and color. Annuals such as moss roses, ageratum, dahlias, begonias, and snapdragons hug the perimeter. The planting bed anchors the Walk of History, which details the earliest periods of the city.

Across from Villa Louis on Villa Louis Road, lies the Mississippi River Sculpture Park, a work in progress. Three bronze sculptures—one of a Victorian woman, one of Chief Black Hawk, and one of Dr. William Beaumont and his son, Isaac—crafted by artist Florence Bird are the beginnings of what promises to be a nice collection of natural and handcrafted art. A fire pit with bronze plaques representing the various ethnic groups that settled or passed through the area acts as the focal point for the space. Sand colored contemporary stone seating areas are also part of the hardscape. Shrubs and plantings are just taking root.

South of the sculpture park between Blackhawk Avenue and Fisher Street are the bones of what will be the $1.7 million St. Feriole Island Memorial Gardens. The plan for these gardens includes shade and butterfly gardens, a prairie, a children's garden, a stream garden, a grand lawn, and perennial and annual gardens. Hardscapes will include a Victorian pergola that beckons visitors into the garden, a gazebo, and paths that meander around a spring pond and through the various sections. A backwater habitat garden will include a waterfall and reflection pool.

Some of the perennial beds have already been installed, and the walkways are scheduled for installation in 2007. Mature trees make the garden seem older than it actually is. A prairie is underway. Additional fruit trees have been added to the portion of the property that was an old orchard. Nonprofit status was achieved and fund-raising is in progress.

Throughout the island local groups are maintaining various planting beds including one along Blackhawk Avenue as it enters the island. The pink carpet rose, tree peonies, and a flowering crab are some of the selections found here.

COUNTY	Crawford
ADDRESS	Blackhawk Avenue, Prairie du Chien or **Villa Louis:** 521 Villa Louis Road
PHONE	608/326-2721
EMAIL	**Villa Louis:** villalouis@whs.wisc.edu; **Memorial Gardens:** pdcnellie@centurytel.net
WEBSITE	**Villa Louis:** www.wisconsinhistory.org/villalouis **Sculpture Park:** www.prairieduchiensculpturepark.com
DIRECTIONS	From State Highway 35, go west on State Highway 27, which is also Blackhawk Avenue.
ADMISSION	**For Villa Louis:** $8.50 for adults; $7.50 for seniors 65 and over; $4.50 for children ages 5 to 17. Two adults with two or more dependent children is $23. The rest of the sites are free.
HOURS	Seasonal. Villa Louis is open daily from 10 a.m. to 5 p.m. May 7 through October 31. The remaining gardens and beds on St. Feriole Island are open to the public daily, dawn to dusk.

  ## Shake Rag Alley/Pendarvis
MINERAL POINT

WHEN MINERAL POINT WAS FIRST SETTLED in the 1820s, Shake Rag Alley was its business district. Today the two-and-one-half acre settlement is home to an arts education center that includes historic buildings and gardens.

Legend has it that the name Shake Rag stood for Shake-Rag-Under-the-Hill. Wives of the Cornish miners would shake rags from their doorways to let their husbands know it was mealtime. Nine historic buildings, many used for classes and workshops, surround Federal Spring, the water feature that runs through the property.

During the 1970s, Al and Eadie Felly of the Madison-based Felly's Flowers, purchased several of the buildings, restoring them and adding an All-America Selections display garden. Since then, the property has changed hands and is now owned by a community group. There are remnants of the original gardens and the area is undergoing some restoration so things are in flux.

The trees give the property a woodland feel. Natives and perennials border Federal Spring, which bisects the site. There are hydrangeas and coneflowers, hostas and sedum, alpine plants and goldenrod. Rough-hewn benches are placed in front of some of the buildings, which have their own plantings. A rustic wooden arbor and trellis add to the hardscape. Small limestone slabs are used as bridges.

A tree, bent from the weather, has formed an "S" shape over the streambed. A red brick paver path leads from the Shake Rag Café past all of the buildings. The courtyard in front of the café features a selection of herbs, ornamental grasses, and perennials.

About a half-mile north of Shake Rag Alley at 114 Shake Rag Street is Pendarvis, one of a series of limestone and log miners' houses dating back one hundred fifty years. Nestled into the hillside, the property around Pendarvis and the other historic buildings has multiple limestone terraces. Perennials fill these handcrafted terraces, both for beauty and for erosion control. There are dwarf conifers, some alpine plants, hostas, natives, and stella d'oro lilies. A shaded footpath leads from Shake Rag Street up the hill through gardens of perennials originally installed in the 1930s.

Local residents Robert Neal and Edgar Hellum saved and restored the buildings occupying the Pendarvis site in the 1930s eventually opening up the Pendarvis House Restaurant. Part of the 1930s restoration included planting gardens reminiscent of what the miners would have planted nearly a century earlier. Look for hollyhocks, nasturtiums, poppies, violets, and lady's slippers, plants traditionally found in an English cottage garden.

COUNTY	Iowa
ADDRESS	**Shake Rag Alley:** 18 Shake Rag Street or **Pendarvis:** 114 Shake Rag Street Mineral Point
PHONE	**Shake Rag Alley:** 608/987-3292 or **Pendarvis:** 608/987-2122
WEBSITE	www.**ShakeRagAlley**.com or www.wisconsinhistory.org/**pendarvis**
DIRECTIONS	From U.S. Highway 18, take the U.S. Highway 151 exit into Mineral Point. Follow the signs to Shake Rag Street.
ADMISSION	Free for **Shake Rag Alley**. For **Pendarvis**: $8 for adults; $7 for seniors ages 65 and older; $4 children 5 to 17, $22 for a family with two adults and two or more dependent children.
HOURS	**Pendarvis:** 10 a.m. to 5 p.m. daily mid-May to the end of October. Check the Web site for specific dates. **Shake Rag:** Daily, dawn to dusk.
AMENITIES	Street parking. Toilets, food, and water inside local restaurants.

Shakespeare Garden

LANCASTER

IN THE WRITINGS OF WILLIAM SHAKESPEARE you'll find many references to gardens. So when members of the Grant County Master Gardeners decided to develop one to beautify the city of Lancaster, they took a page from Shakespeare and fittingly, located the garden along the east side of the Schreiner Memorial Library.

While the garden's objective was to add a touch of beauty, the master gardeners chose Shakespeare to provide an educational element to the project. The plants, most of which were donated, were selected to be as close to those that would have appeared in Shakespeare's time, with adjustments, of course, for climate and availability.

Some selections were made for their symbolic meanings based upon the Victorian "language" of flowers and plants. For example, the daffodil or narcissus that's referenced in the Bard's *The Winter's Tale* is a good spring choice since it provides images of joy and rebirth. It's also considered one of Shakespeare's meadow flowers along with violets, daisies, oxlips (primrose), and cuckoo-buds (ranunculus).

The garden includes other Shakespeare-related plants such as columbine, eglantine rose, pansies (also called Johnny-jump-ups), harebell (bellflower), and several varieties of herbs. Silver king artemisia was employed for wormwood.

Some less hardy plants like marjoram and rosemary were planted in pots and are brought indoors during winter. Although Shakespeare included references to weeds in his writings, the master gardeners did not intentionally install them. Hardscape features include a white arbor with a bench and several mosaic tiles.

While you're visiting the Shakespeare Garden, look for the Two Sisters garden that's located on the south and west sides of the library. It's named for two Lancaster residents, Josephine Morris and Mary Marm Wilson. Composed mostly of hostas and a memorial rock, the garden was established by the former mayor of Lancaster, Jo Pebworth, in honor of two of her relatives. Pebworth was also instrumental in creating the Shakespeare garden.

Also located in Lancaster is the memorial garden at the Grant Regional Health Care Center at 507 South Monroe Street. The hospital decided to utilize a donation of an angel statue as a centerpiece for a kidney-shaped memorial/healing garden located outside of patient rooms. There's also a line of more than twenty rose bushes planted just to the south of the memorial garden.

COUNTY	Grant
ADDRESS	Schreiner Memorial Library, 113 West Elm Street Lancaster
PHONE	608/723-7304
EMAIL	atollefson@swls.org
DIRECTIONS	Located at the corner of Madison and Elm streets. Madison Street is also U.S. Highway 61 and Elm Street is also County Highway A.
ADMISSION	Free
HOURS	Seasonal. Daily, dawn to dusk. The library is open from 9 a.m. to 8 p.m. Monday through Thursday, 9 a.m. to 5 p.m. Friday, and 9 a.m. to 1 p.m. Saturday.
AMENITIES	Parking lot. Toilets and water available in the library.

Sinsinawa Mound

SINSINAWA

OVERLOOKING THE DRIFTLESS AREA of southwestern Wisconsin, the Sinsinawa Mound complex is the headquarters of an order of Dominican sisters. The area's fertile soil sustains the four hundred fifty-acre site. It's apparent to visitors that the religious community takes its commitment of stewardship of the earth seriously.

On the grounds are a variety of gardens maintained by some of the retired sisters with help from Sinsinawa staff. Sister Sarah maintains the two small beds near what was St. Clara Academy. Most of the plantings were gifts or donations that she salvaged and replanted. Depending upon the year, there are hydrangeas, pussywillows, and hybrid columbine in the shade garden and miniature roses, larkspur, and four o'clocks in the sunny garden. Easter lilies are always part of the mix.

Sister Alessandra is the motivation behind the cutting garden and Our Lady's garden. These two gardens are also located on the Academy side of the grounds. The more formal cutting garden encircles a 19th century fountain with a calla lily design. Once a working artesian fountain that anchored a rose garden, it's now the focal point for various groups of perennials, including Siberian iris, pachysandra, snow-on-the-mountain, phlox, calla lilies, pampas grass, poppy-red daylilies, and hostas. The various textures, colors, and heights add interest no

The cutting garden and 19th century fountain at Sinsinawa Mound

matter what time of the season. The fountain is filled with annuals—generally geraniums, petunias, and marigolds—to give it seasonal color. A Victorian stone bench sits on a patio of bricks allowing a respite from one's labors.

Spring is when Our Lady's garden is at its finest. Hundreds of tulips announce the onset of the growing season. When the tulips lose their blooms, spirea and annuals pick up the slack.

In a courtyard just off the hallway between the chapel and the dining room is a Japanese garden that's under construction. Around the grounds you'll find various beds and planters, some anchored by religious statues. One of the trails on the grounds is named the Woodland Flowers Trail.

An interesting hardscape feature of the complex is the eleven-circuit outdoor labyrinth. Built in 1999, the sixty-foot diameter labyrinth was placed in a grove of mature trees. Volunteers set 6,000 limestone bricks, end to end, to form a perfectly round circle. The circle holds the symmetrical path leading to the center.

COUNTY	Grant
ADDRESS	585 County Road Z, Sinsinawa
PHONE	608/748-4411
FAX	608/748-4491
EMAIL	center@sinsinawa.org
WEBSITE	www.sinsinawa.org
DIRECTIONS	From State Highway 11, turn onto County Road Z.
ADMISSION	Free
HOURS	Monday through Friday, 10 a.m. to noon, 12:30 p.m. to 3:30 p.m., and by appointment.
AMENITIES	Parking lot. Toilets and water available in the main building.

 ## State Capitol Grounds

MADISON

A PARKLIKE SETTING envelops the State Capitol, softening the white granite building with shades of green and splashes of color. Landscape architect John Nolen designed the thirteen acres of grounds in 1919. He intended for visitors to sit and see the building from a distance. That's why the landscape contains few shrubs or large evergreens to obscure the view.

In the spring, 25,000 tulip bulbs make their presence known in thirty-five flowerbeds scattered around the building. Eight of those beds were original to Nolen's design. Once the spring show winds down, 30,000 annuals are planted, giving color throughout the summer and into the fall.

Over the years, the design of the beds has been both simple and complex. Begonias, geraniums, salvias, and impatiens are the most common plant selections, but Capitol gardeners have set trends, introducing the public to such varieties as

John Nolan's landscape design surrounds the Wisconsin capitol.

rose fountain grass, sun coleus, and dark opal basil for a deep purple accent.

Some thirty different varieties of trees, more than one hundred fifty in all, can be found on the grounds. Most, like the red oak and sugar maple, are native to Wisconsin; a ginkgo is one of the few exceptions. Nolen's design called for tree allees around the perimeter. Over time they disappeared, but with renovations on the building drawing to a close, the focus will be on the landscape. The intent is to re-establish the allees and balustrade planters that originally contained perennials.

The best time to see the tulips at their spring finest is at the end of April or the beginning of May. The annuals are at peak from mid-August to early September.

COUNTY	Dane
ADDRESS	2 East Main Street, Madison
PHONE	608/266-0382
DIRECTIONS	From U.S. Highways 12/18 (the Beltline), take the John Nolen Drive exit. Follow John Nolen to South Broom Street. Turn left. Go one block to West Wilson Street and turn right. Go one block and turn left onto South Hamilton Street. Go two blocks and turn right onto East Main Street.
ADMISSION	Free
HOURS	Daily, dawn to dusk.
AMENITIES	Street parking. Water and toilets in the Capitol building.

Storybook Gardens, Timbavati Wildlife

WISCONSIN DELLS

LIONS AND TIGERS AND BEARS, OH MY. Yes, there are now wild animals at the Timbavati Wildlife at Storybook Gardens, but don't overlook the plantings. One of Wisconsin Dells' most child-friendly sites is under new ownership and has changed its focus slightly, adding a live animal show to the mix of plastic and fiberglass storybook characters and planting beds.

An iconic statue at Storybook Gardens

One of the first tourist attractions that would change the future of Wisconsin Dells, Storybook Gardens opened in 1956 and remained pretty much unchanged until 2004 when Mark Schoebel and his wife, Alice, took it over. They are proceeding with an active reclamation of the fifteen-acre park, especially the gardens, most of which had fallen into disrepair.

From the original plantings, only the tiger lilies, hydrangeas, and some cardinal red weigelas still exist. So Alice, who was raised in a landscaping family, rose to the challenge. She's planted snow-on-the-mountain, coral bells, irises, and hostas, worrying about texture and color rather than blooms. Marigolds, hybrid daylilies, monarda, peonies, and cannas are added for highlights. There are flowering shrubs such as tree hydrangeas and dwarf pink lilacs, as well as ornamental grasses and trees. A forty-foot flowering crab really makes a statement in the spring when it blooms.

The trees and shrubs date back to the 1950s when they were first planted. A burning bush has actually morphed into a burning tree. Shrub hybrids, which were available half a century ago, can no longer be purchased but can be seen on the grounds. "Most have been miniaturized to fit suburban lawns," said Alice.

The hardscapes are endless. Four ponds, two with islands and a few with fountains, as well as a stream with cattails comprise the water features. A train, a carousel, bridges, and, of course, the iconic statues are also part of the landscape. Snow White and the Seven Dwarfs are perched on the bank of the stream. Cinderella, Jack and the Beanstalk, and Simple Simon are all there as generations of Dells visitors remember them. The Schoebels have built a stage to host wild animal shows and animal cages are scattered around the grounds.

COUNTY	Sauk
ADDRESS	1500 Wisconsin Dells Parkway, Wisconsin Dells
PHONE	608/253-2391
EMAIL	www.storybookgardens.net
DIRECTIONS	The site is located next to Noah's Ark on Wisconsin Dells Parkway, which is also State Highway 23/U.S. Highway 12.
ADMISSION	$10.95 for adults, $8.95 for ages 2 through 12. Under 2, free.
HOURS	Daily, 9 a.m. to 7 p.m. May 6 through Sept. 15. After September 15 call for hours.
AMENITIES	Parking lot. Toilets and water inside the park.

Taliesin

SPRING GREEN

WALKING A PORTION OF TALIESIN'S SIX HUNDRED ACRES is akin to walking on hallowed ground. You can't help but realize that wherever you are, Frank Lloyd Wright once was. Wright's vision is instilled in both the physical structures as well as the landscaping and gardens of his beloved Taliesin.

Taliesin, Welsh for "Shining Brow," is actually the name for the entire complex, including his aunts' Hillside Home School, Tan-y-deri House, Midway Farm, the Romeo and Juliet windmill, and the Unity Chapel, which are located on or near the property. But it's often used to refer to the building that housed Wright's studio, school, and principal home.

The green rolling hills provide the only conceivably appropriate backdrop to Wright's signature architecture and the landscape. "Mr. Wright was always tying it [the architecture] in with nature," said Margaret Ingraham, a Taliesin tour guide. Wright built Hillside in 1902 and began work on his principal residence in 1911, but seeing them now is like looking at today's designs in *Metropolitan Home.* And, of course, the landscaping and flowers look fresh and contemporary too.

"Juicy" is the term head gardener Frances Nemtin uses for the colors she prefers in plant selections. Nemtin, who came to Taliesin in 1946, worked closely with Wright on many projects. She volunteered to help with the gardens in 1978, after a stint in Iran where she was in charge of putting in the gardens for a Taliesin-designed villa that was being constructed for an Iranian princess.

The front garden bed located near Wright's home studio had phlox, asters, tiger lilies, and Solomon's seal. Keeping the original selections, Nemtin had

The gardens near the tea circle and courtyard at Taliesin

new soil installed to make the bed more productive and augmented the plants to increase their bloom time. Added to the mix were monarda, delphiniums, penstemon, ageratums, and verbena. Nemtin likes verbena 'Homestead Purple' for its ability to trail over walls and its bright purple color. She uses *verbena bonariensis* for its airy qualities.

Walking up the hill to Wright's home, you're suddenly graced by the sight of an unusual pergola. The red metal structure, formerly the pipes and stanchions from the barn at Midway Farm, covers the old horse and buggy path that once led to the carriage house. Overlaid with wisteria and grapevine, the pergola provides a cooling oasis from the exertion needed to get up the hill. The vines shade the mixed beds, which include hostas, ferns, coral bells, lilies, astilbe, and grasses with some begonias added for color. A plunge pool with a fountain located off of the terrace is one of several water features on the property. Another pond is located outside of the entry court and its gardens. Wright made the large lake on the property by damming a stream; the resulting waterfall was once used to generate electricity for Taliesin.

Thanks to Mother Nature, the gardens around the entry court have changed dramatically from the photos in even the more recent Taliesin tour books. In 1998, a storm blew down the historic oak tree that shaded the home's tea circle and courtyard. A new one was replanted on the site, but it will be many years before it reaches the majestic heights of its predecessor. The metal tea bell, now sitting a bit forlornly on the stone wall, used to hang from a limb of the old tree. But one of the twelve gardens on the property perseveres.

Red and pink cascading roses follow the wall surrounding the tea circle. Nemtin carries the orange and red along the wall and then adds color harmonies of red and purple dahlias to make it look rich. A bed of ferns sits outside of the entry court edged in a stone bed. A trellis outside of Wright's personal studio supports a clematis.

Outside of Hillside is an informal, one-hundred-foot-long mixed flowerbed filled with Russian sage, lilies, phlox, cleome, and irises, and underplanted with ageratum, zinnias, and begonias. The colors are softer here—pinks, purples, blues, yellows, and whites with just a few splashes of orange to shake things up. Mature trees anchor the bed with an evergreen trimmed in a bonsai shape next to the house. Wright was a proponent of Asian design and collected many pieces of Japanese art still seen on the property.

The bed at the Unity Chapel is undergoing renovation due to the local deer's penchant for lunching on the plantings. Wright's grave features an upright stone that resembles the state of Wisconsin and stands about 5' 6", the architect's actual height. The massive evergreen near his grave was Wright's way of honoring the great love of his life, Martha Borthwick Cheney, who was murdered at Taliesin in 1914.

COUNTY	Sauk
ADDRESS	5607 County Road C, Spring Green
PHONE	877/588-7900
EMAIL	tours@TaliesinPreservation.org
WEBSITE	www.TaliesinPreservation.org
DIRECTIONS	All tours begin at the Frank Lloyd Wright Visitor's Center located at the intersection of State Highway 23 and County Road C. Take U.S. Highway 14 and turn south on Highway 23.
ADMISSION	Ranges from $16 per person ($14 for seniors and students; children under 18 free when accompanied by an adult) for the one-hour Hillside Tour to $80 per person for the four-hour Estate Tour (no children under 12 permitted on this tour). A two-hour House Tour is $47 per person ($42 for seniors and students 12 and up) and a two-hour Highlights Tour is $52 per person (no children under 12 allowed). There's a $4 handling fee for phone, fax, or mail reservations.
HOURS	Tours begin at 9:30 a.m. with the last one leaving at 3:30 p.m. daily, May 1 to October 1. Call ahead to schedule tours because some are only offered at specific times. Walk-ins accepted as space allowed.
AMENITIES	Amenities: Parking lot. Toilets, water, and food available inside the visitor's center.

The Executive Residence

MADISON

WHILE MANY HISTORIC HOMES attempt to retain their original plant selections and design over the years, there have been a lot of changes to the gardens at Wisconsin's Executive Residence, including a complete renovation in 1993.

The six current gardens are located outside the garden room on the south side of the 1921 Classic Revival house. While they're all worthy of standing on their own, it doesn't hurt to have Lake Mendota as a backdrop.

There is the Walled or Formal Garden with its great lawn of grass. Perennial borders filled with black-eyed Susans, purple coneflower, garden phlox, and pearly everlastings hug the stone wall's perimeter. Red brick pavers define the edge between the garden and the lawn. The only annuals here are tucked under a magnolia tree on the garden's southwest corner or in terra cotta pots filled with bright pink mandevilla located at each of the four corners.

Matching white pergolas and two stone winged griffins are some of the Walled Garden's accessories. The pergola nearest the lake is bare; it seems a grapevine didn't like the microclimate. But a mature wisteria vine happily takes over the other one framing a view of the lake. The wisteria conceals two large terra cotta pots filled with annuals that are tucked under the pergola. A gazebo, located on the south perimeter of the Walled Garden, defines one portion of the Rock Garden, which contains miniature sedums, aquatic plants, and fish.

More than ninety-one varieties of hostas can be found in the Hosta Garden located on the property's far southwest corner. A nearby kidney-shaped bed filled with daylilies is one of the components of the Daylily Garden. This bed and two others like it contain varieties solely from Wisconsin hybridizers such as 'Mountain Violet', 'Pink Super Spider', and 'Blue Lustre.'

Along the far south fence, a curving border of Wisconsin Native Woodland plants features native prairie plants and spring ephemerals. May apples and trilliums celebrate the arrival of spring while wild strawberry, native prairie grass, and wild ginger join in the fun later. Mature trees anchor the expansions in each curve.

Like the Walled Garden, the Oval or Perennial Garden also features a great lawn. You definitely get a sense of place here amid the two black metal arbors, one with the word "Forward" in gold lettering and the other with "E Pluribus Unum" in the same gold typeface. These arbors break the circle of arborvitae surrounding this garden. A circle of red brick pavers again defines the edge between flower and grass. Several clematis plants are utilizing the Forward arbor as support while a climbing rose has overtaken E Pluribus Unum. Five stone benches provide a place for contemplation.

The former rose garden that was located in the front of the mansion is now filled with daylilies, spirea, and annuals. The roses were ousted because they didn't do well in that location although a few pink shrub roses do remain. Strips of common yew divide that garden into sections as well as encircle the large fountain.

There are mixed beds flanking the iron gate at the property's entrance; they continue to hug the circle drive. UW-red begonias fill a circular bed. It's hard to miss the largest tree on the grounds, a magnificent cottonwood. A nice example of hackberry and a gingko are just some of the other woody species found on the four-acre property.

COUNTY	Dane
ADDRESS	99 Cambridge Road, Madison
PHONE	608/246-5501
EMAIL	WERFFDN@yahoo.com
WEBSITE	http://jessicadoyle.wi.gov
DIRECTIONS	From I-94 West, exit State Highway 30 West. Follow Highway 30 and veer to the right on Aberg Avenue. Continue on Aberg Avenue and make a left on Sherman Avenue. Turn right on Lakewood Boulevard Follow Lakewood to Cambridge Road. Turn left. **From the north,** take I-94/I-90 toward Madison. Take the U.S. Highway 151/East Washington Avenue exit. Follow East Washington to First Street. Turn right. Follow First Street to East Johnson Street and turn left. Follow East Johnson to Fordem Avenue and turn right. Turn left onto Lakewood Boulevard and left again onto Cambridge Road. **From the south,** take I-90 East/I-94 West toward Madison. Exit U.S. Highways 12/18 West (the Beltline). Take the Beltline to the John Nolen Drive exit. Continue on John Nolen to East Washington Avenue. Turn right. Continue to First Street. Turn left. Continue on First Street to East Johnson Street. Turn left. From East Johnson Street continue to Fordem Avenue. Turn right onto Fordem Avenue. Turn left onto Lakewood Boulevard and left again onto Cambridge Road.
ADMISSION	Free
HOURS	1 p.m. to 3 p.m. Thursdays, April through October. Reservations are required for groups of 20 or more. Visit the Web site for the schedule.
AMENITIES	Parking in the circular drive. Some street parking available.

University of Wisconsin–Madison Botanical Garden

MADISON

WHAT COULD HAVE BECOME A VERY CLINICAL RESEARCH GARDEN with its emphasis on plant taxonomy has developed instead into a work of art. The 1.2-acre University of Wisconsin Botanical Garden serves as both an educational tool and an island of calm on the busy UW-Madison campus.

Developed by the university's botany department on the site of a former tennis court, this botanical garden has gone through several evolutions since its first incarnation in 1959. Construction on the current space began in 2004.

Everything that represents a world-class research garden can be found here, starting with multiple beds filled with plant species from around the globe. What's most unusual is that this garden is the first of its kind to use the new Angiosperm Phylogeny Group system of molecular classification of plants. Plants are arranged in evolutionary sequence according to their taxonomic classification from the lowest (ferns) to the highest (daisies). The garden's east side focuses on the monocots, while the west side is reserved for the dicots. This makes it easy for visitors interested in the genetic underpinnings to identify relationships between plants.

All of the plants are labeled with well-placed, informative signs containing the Latin name, common name, location of origin, and taxonomic classification. There's the native garden with its requisite coneflowers, cosmos, and black-eyed Susans interspersed with purple gayfeathers, yellow and orange marigolds, sunflowers, Shasta daisies, and fuzzy-topped ageratum.

The UW–Madison Botanical Garden is a world-class research garden

Fescue and sedge are underplanted around cannas and bananas in one bed. Lilies, grasses, an Adam's needle yucca, autumn crocus, and dwarf iris are combined in another. Caladium can be found mixed in with various species of daylilies. One bed features the sharp, pointed leaves of the gas plant ringed with begonias and petunias. There are more than five hundred species of plants here, including annuals, perennials, shrubs, and trees.

While ordering plants according to their taxonomy was the driving force behind this garden, there obviously was also a strong emphasis placed on design. Hardscapes include a gazebo, serpentine concrete paths, wooden pergolas, arbors, a water feature, even a dry riverbed. A brick and iron-rod fence outlines the garden.

Mequon artist Susan Falkman's hand-carved trio of Indiana limestone stone sculptures, titled *Essence*, features *The Seed*, *The Flower*, and *The Fruit*. *The Seed* represents the point where life emerges from the earth into the light. *The Flower*, strategically placed near the magnolia family, is actually a stone rendering of a *Magnolia solangiana* that's cut in half. The apple-shaped *Fruit* is located near the Newton apple tree.

The backdrop for the garden is the cream-colored brick of Birge Hall along with the site's mature trees and firs. It's truly an oasis on a bustling campus.

COUNTY	Dane
ADDRESS	University Avenue, Madison
PHONE	608/262-2235
EMAIL	mmfayyaz@wisc.edu
WEBSITE	www.botany.wisc.edu/Garden/
DIRECTIONS	Located on the north side of University Avenue between Chamberlain, Lathrop, and Birge halls. There is no parking along University and limited parking is available in the area. It's best to park in a metered ramp and walk over.
ADMISSION	Free
HOURS	Seasonal. Daily, dawn to dusk.
AMENITIES	None

The eighty-acres of grounds of *Yerkes Observatory* in Williams Bay contains two hundred forty rare and state-record trees, the Great Ellipse, and the South Lawn. Olmsted Brothers, a firm run by the son and stepson of Frederick Law Olmsted, the landscape architect of New York's Central Park, designed the observatory's landscape although much of it was not implemented due to budget constraints.

University of Wisconsin–Madison Botany Greenhouse

MADISON

IN THE PLANT WORLD, getting a *Titan arum* to blossom has got to be the equivalent of the Badgers winning the Rose Bowl. The large, slow-growing plant, which rarely blooms in captivity, attracts an enormous amount of attention when it does.

While the bloom is unusual, it's really the smell that makes this native Indonesian rain forest plant unique. The Titan is also known as the corpse plant for its overpowering aroma of rotting meat when it flowers. And no amount of pleasing fragrance can cover up its stench.

Three of these tall beauties can be found in one of the greenhouses of the University of Wisconsin-Madison's botany department. And occasionally one or more will decide it's time to poke its head out of the soil and send a shoot heading skyward eight or nine feet.

With a recent renovation and new addition, the eight greenhouses that encompass 10,000 square feet behind Birge Hall are home not only to the three Titans but also to over 1,000 species of aquatic, tropical, and desert plants. Papyrus grows in a pond in the tropical house. The orchid house is home to a selection of rare bromeliads. During the winter, the cold house showcases a nature bog.

Besides the Titan, there are other unique species to be found here including the Wollemi pine, a rare plant recently discovered in Australia; a Welwitschia, which grows in the African desert; and several species of carnivorous plants.

Some of the greenhouses grow plants specifically for classroom use. Others find their way into the university's botanical garden. A new addition to the complex has added high-tech options for plant experimentation.

COUNTY	Dane
ADDRESS	Birge Hall, 430 Lincoln Drive. Madison
PHONE	608/262-1057
FAX	608/262-7509
WEBSITE	www.botany.wisc.edu/greenhouse
DIRECTIONS	Located on the north side of University Avenue between Chamberlain, Lathrop, and Birge halls. There is no parking along University and limited parking is available in the area. It's best to park in a metered ramp and walk over.
ADMISSION	Free
HOURS	8 a.m. to 4 p.m. Monday through Friday when the University is open. Tours are available from 1:30 to 3:30 p.m. Mondays and Wednesdays and from 9 a.m. to 10:30 a.m. Tuesdays and Thursdays.
AMENITIES	Toilets, water, and vending machines.

West Madison Agricultural Research Station

VERONA

CARPETS OF COLOR announce the trial gardens at the West Madison Agricultural Research Station. Located on the north side of Mineral Point Road between Madison and Verona, the site overwhelms you with its riot of blooms in every tint, hue, and pigment of the rainbow—and then some.

The University of Wisconsin sponsors this five hundred seventy-acre site and eleven other agricultural research stations across the state. This particular station includes more than three acres of flower, fruit, and vegetable trial gardens. As the site's name implies, these gardens grow the latest and greatest offerings from the big breeders to see how well they hold up in southern Wisconsin climates. This research station installed its trial gardens in 1994.

Highlights include four hundred new selections of floral and vegetable annuals, a selection of ornamental grasses, a garden of all native Wisconsin plants donated by Prairie Nursery of Westfield, and a selection of perennials that are shade tolerant. Half of the shade garden plants are hybrids; the rest are Wisconsin natives.

Some of the test gardens growing the latest and greatest at the West Madison Research Station

A few of the four hundred varieties on display at the West Madison Agriculture Research Station

For those interested in food crops, there's a small selection of fruit trees, specifically apricot, apple, and plum as well as a new selection of winter hardy table grapes and twelve new raspberry cultivars. Since the West Madison station is a site for Renewing America's Food Traditions (RAFT), which helps preserve rapidly disappearing varieties of seeds, there's an heirloom bed filled with flower and vegetable contributions from Seed Savers Exchange.

The Wisconsin Daylily Society donated a huge collection of both new and old varieties. The research station also is home to some unusual trees and shrubs, for example, beech, birch, and Japanese maples. One of the perennial gardens is specifically designed with the busy gardener in mind with its display of easy-to-care-for perennials. Prairie Nursery also designed a rain garden on the grounds that features one hundred thirty-one plants.

A gazebo is used as an outreach center. There is also a wooden arbor and a bench on the property. Paths of gravel and grass lead through the gardens. In keeping with the center's educational emphasis, all of the plants are labeled.

COUNTY	Dane
ADDRESS	8502 Mineral Point Road, Verona
PHONE	608/262-2257
FAX	608/829-3074
WEBSITE	www.ars.wisc.edu
DIRECTIONS	From U.S. Highways 12/14, exit Mineral Point Road to the west.
ADMISSION	Donation; guided tours for 12 to 15 are available for a small fee. Call ahead to schedule.
HOURS	Seasonal. Daily, dawn to dusk.
AMENITIES	Parking lot. Toilets and water located in the office buildings, which are open from 8 a.m. to 4:30 p.m. Monday through Friday and on the two Field Days. Field Days are held from 10 a.m. to 3 p.m. the last Saturday in April and the third Saturday in August.

southeast Wisconsin

Al's Auto Body and Arboretum

WALWORTH

THERE'S NO DOUBT that hosta mania reigns at Al's Auto Body and Arboretum in the town of Walworth. Thousands of hosta plants are nestled among the mature oak, hickory, and walnut trees in owner Al Ritchey's backyard.

Ritchey calls his handiwork the "epitome of biodiversity." Like many business owners, Ritchey, who has run his body shop on five acres for the past twenty-eight years, wanted his place to look nice. So he reserved about three acres of his backyard to growing the cultlike hostas. Yes, there are the companion plants such as 'Northern Lights' azaleas, ferns, Japanese maples, woodland plants, and even some rhododendrons interspersed among the trees. But the hostas are the real stars of this location.

The arboretum is located in the Upland Conservation district, a fingerling marking the farthest reach of an ancient glacier. Past the shop, the land drops twenty to thirty feet. The "beds" take advantage of the dips and rises and the trails follow the land's natural contours. The juxtaposition of the towering trees against the multiple greens, creams, and yellows of the hostas is not to be missed and will remove any doubt that an arboretum is the ideal accompaniment to an auto body shop.

Over the years, Ritchey has planted some four hundred varieties of the popular perennial and is anxious to try more. His rarest variety is the 'Ice Age Trail' hosta,

A view of the arboretum at Al's Auto Body

which he planted from tissue culture and is on display at his annual Hosta Fest, generally held every Memorial Day weekend when the plants are at their peak.

While you're in the area, visit Millie's Restaurant and Shopping Village, just a few blocks around the corner from Al's. Located on South Shore Drive at Highway O, Millie's seven acres include English gardens in the courtyard and along the walkways as well as a Victorian gazebo. Whiskey barrels are planted with annuals, a row of peonies lines a white picket fence, and mature trees and shrubs dot the grounds. A starburst pattern of brick pavers and clipped hedges complements the gazebo.

COUNTY	Walworth
ADDRESS	W6886 North Walworth Road, Walworth
PHONE	262/275-2800
EMAIL	questions@alsautobodyandarboretum.com
WEBSITE	www.alsautobodyandarboretum.com
DIRECTIONS	From the south, take State Highway 67 to U.S. Highway 14 northwest and exit County Highway O. Turn right onto North Walworth Road. From the North, Take State Highway 11 and exit Highway O. Take Highway O south and turn left on North Walworth Road. While the mailing address is Walworth, Al's Auto Body is actually closer to Delavan.
ADMISSION	Donations
HOURS	Seasonal, daily, dawn to dusk. Call ahead for tours.
AMENITIES	Small parking lot.

 ## *Angel Museum*
BELOIT

THE PRESENCE OF ANGELS is not confined to the interior of the former brick church located on Pleasant Street in Beloit. There are angel statues and even a metal trellis in the shape of a celestial being scattered throughout the gardens at what is now the Angel Museum. Italian immigrants built the former St. Paul's Roman Catholic Church in 1914, which reopened as the museum in 1998.

The substantial collection of angels once belonged to Beloit residents Joyce and Lowell Berg. The Bergs donated some 13,000 angels and TV host Oprah Winfrey provided another six hundred black ones that fans had sent her.

Hostas comprise the majority of the landscaping on the east side of the building. Two stone memorial angels flank the sidewalk that leads to the building's former front entrance. Stone planters and flower boxes filled with annuals add flashes of color.

On the building's west side, volunteers constructed a garden in a ravine. Because the location gets lots of sun, hardy perennials were chosen for easy maintenance. There are stella d'oro lilies, several butterfly bushes, irises, daffodils, and a flowering pear. Potentillas hug the handicap-accessible ramp that leads down to the garden. Blue, white, and pink varieties of creeping phlox cover the boulders. Roses add extra color and beauty. Besides the concrete ramp, other hardscape features include stone benches and tables, and, not surprisingly, the requisite angel art.

COUNTY	Rock
ADDRESS	St. Paul on the Riverfront, 656 Pleasant Street, Beloit
PHONE	608/362-9099
FAX	608/362-2330
WEBSITE	www.angelmuseum.com
DIRECTIONS	From U.S. Highway 51, which is also Riverside Drive, turn west on Pleasant Street.
ADMISSION	Free admission for the garden. Admission fee for the museum.
HOURS	Seasonal. 10 a.m. to 4 p.m. Tuesday through Saturday and 1 p.m. to 4 p.m. Sunday June through August. 10 a.m. to 4 p.m. Tuesday through Saturday September through May. Closed Mondays and the month of January.
AMENITIES	Parking lot. Toilets and water inside the museum.

Beloit's Rooftops

BELOIT

INSPIRED BY THE BEAUTY of European rooftop gardens, inveterate tinkerer Don Mischo created a process for installing gardens on the roofs of buildings that's being applied all over Beloit. Mischo, director of special projects at ABC Supply Company, which manufacturers the products he uses in his process, began testing the concept in 2001 on the roof of his employer's corporate headquarters.

The modular GreenGrid Green Roof System, a cooperative venture between ABC Supply Company, Inc., and Weston Solutions, Inc., is easy to install and maintain. It also saves both heating and cooling costs and reduces stormwater runoff as well. Oh yes, it's as tasteful as it is practical.

The north rooftop garden at ABC supply

The company's 3,500-square-foot north garden is designed as a show garden. The water feature is a faux rock fountain. Also at 3,500 square feet, the south garden includes both a show garden with a pond and less structured plantings as well as a research space. Both gardens contain four-inch-deep modules preplanted with grasses, sedums, and wildflowers as well as eight-inch modules that support larger ornamental plants. These modules, similar to the flats found in greenhouses, are installed in raised or framed beds. The flats can be removed to access the roof or for winter storage. The company also makes two-and-one-half-inch modules for roofs with limited weight capacity. Recycled asphalt shingles compressed into spongy, square tiles are utilized for paths.

Beloit Memorial Hospital opened its new rooftop garden in spring 2007 using ABC's GreenGrid system. Located on the third floor directly off the cafeteria and adjacent to some patient rooms, the Neese Memorial Garden was the hospital's latest effort to create a holistic healing environment.

The hospital's rooftop garden holds a fountain with three spouts, raised beds filled with a variety of perennials, shrubs, and trees, and three sculptures. A limited palette of stella d'oro lilies, shrub roses, junipers, sedums, and catmint are on display in the raised beds. Staff, patients, and visitors use the teakwood benches and tables for meals or as a spot to rest. The rooftop is enhanced with a flat turtle mosaic, a copper sculpture of a DNA molecule created by a hospital employee, and *Sky Song,* a commissioned piece created specifically for the site by former Beloit College professor, O.V. Schaffer.

Schaffer also created a sculpture called *Silversong*, which can be found in the Welty Tribute Garden located on the hospital's front lawn. The Tribute Garden features perennials, trees, flowering shrubs, and evergreens.

Beloit College plans to install the GreenGrid system on the roof of its new science building. And Beloit Memorial High School also has plans for it. The system has been installed on buildings at the University of Wisconsin-Milwaukee, University of Wisconsin-Stevens Point, the Milwaukee Zoo, several corporate and retail establishments, and the Dane County Courthouse.

COUNTY	Rock
ADDRESS	One ABC Parkway, Beloit
PHONE	608/362-7777 or 608/362-6529
EMAIL	don.mischo@abcsupply.com
WEBSITE	www.abcsupply.com
DIRECTIONS	From I-94, exit the Beloit exit 185A toward State Highway 81 West. Follow Highway 81 to U.S. Highway 51. Turn east on Highway 51 to the ABC Headquarters. The hospital is located at 1969 West Hart Road.
ADMISSION	Free
HOURS	By appointment only at ABC Supply.
AMENITIES	Parking lot. Toilets and water inside the building.

 ## Bradley Sculpture Garden
MILWAUKEE

ONE OF MILWAUKEE'S BEST-KEPT GARDEN SECRETS is tucked behind a gray stockade fence along West Brown Deer Road in the village of River Hills. Once the home of Harry L. Bradley (one of the founders of the former Allen-Bradley Company) and his wife, Peg (an inveterate art collector), the Bradley Sculpture Garden is known worldwide to the art community, but most Milwaukee residents don't even know it exists.

Situated on forty acres, six of which are devoted to sculpture and gardens, the site is truly a jewel. Technically known as the Lynden Sculpture Garden, the site is open for tours by appointment only. Peg, whose art collection (excluding the garden's sculptures) can be seen at the Milwaukee Art Museum, convinced her husband to allow her to use the grounds as a canvas for sculptures from such artists as Henry Moore and Mark Di Suvero. They hired a landscape architect to create a botanical garden that would complement the contemporary sculptures.

The location features three acres of lakes, wooded paths, a meadow, expansive grassy areas, a native and perennial garden, and a formal garden. There are mature trees of all types, from the standard oak and elm to catalpa and an unusual weeping birch placed on the land with great care. Near one sculpture,

Scotch pines are sculpted like giant bonsai. There are groves of hawthorns and Kentucky coffee trees and even a few apple trees on the property.

The lakes glisten like glass, forming a mirror image of the trees and the sculptures placed nearby. One contains the elements for a waterfall that's occasionally turned on. A groundskeeper manages the vegetation on the perimeters of the lakes to keep the reflection crystal clear.

The formal garden overlooks what was the home's dining room. Originally filled with roses, borders of perennials now define the large oval lawn space and annuals fill terraced beds constructed of stone. The Bradleys were partial to lilacs and the bushes are interspersed with irises, Russian sage, weigela, anemone flower, and hydrangeas. Some shrub roses remain in the borders. The triangular-shaped terraced beds are filled with different themes each year. One year it was a mixture of zinnias and moss roses for color and cleome for height.

> *Alverno College* located on Milwaukee's south side won the 2006 Mayor's Urban Design Award for its updated landscaping, which features a sitting garden, a campus circle with a fountain, a prairie, and a water feature.

The terraced beds frame the one sculpture that Harry and Peg purchased together, Gerhard Marcks' *Bremen Town Musicians,* a bronze of the four animals in the famous children's story. Harry died soon after the purchase but Peg acquired another fifty pieces, most of which are on display on the grounds. A decorative weathered wooden gate, what's left of an original fence, bisects the southern border of the formal garden. Clematis is happily growing up the support posts and layers of concrete "pillows" form an almost pyramidal shape alongside the posts.

Clipped yew hedges frame most of the house. Although there is no evidence that the Bradleys wanted to mimic an English garden, the hedges could easily be the foundation for one.

Between two large sculptures crafted of Cor-Ten (a type of steel that rusts to a subtle, multi-colored patina), a small perennial bed contains spirea, cranesbill, hostas, and other perennials. A sculpture of a buck, a gift, is the only realistic art piece on the property. The buck once caused some consternation among the area's wild deer that fought with it, breaking off some of the antlers.

The estate was conceived of, first and foremost, as a home. Famous visitors who've graced the grounds and admired the gardens include the film star Buster Keaton and the artist Georgia O'Keeffe. There's a small cottage on the grounds that was used as a seasonal changing/warming house. Today, natives and perennials frame the structure. A great clump of black-eyed Susans pops against the weathered gray exterior. The beds surrounding the structure also contain a variety of textures in irises, milkweed, hydrangeas, lilies, lamium, aruncus, ferns, and gooseneck loosestrife.

Decorative trellises crafted from weathered vines and buckthorn are placed along the stockade fence near the parking lot and restrooms. The Paddock Garden, located in the same area, was once the Bradleys' cutting garden. It now contains natives and perennials.

COUNTY	Milwaukee
ADDRESS	2145 West Brown Deer Road, Milwaukee
PHONE	414/276-6840 or 414/962-3947
EMAIL	jcyoungman@wi.rr.com
DIRECTIONS	From central Milwaukee: Take I-43 north to exit West Brown Deer Road (exit 82B). Go west about three-quarters of a mile. At the crest of a small hill there is a left exit lane that takes you directly to the garden. A white lamppost and a silver sign (Lynden-Harry L. Bradley) mark the entrance. Watch for the stockade fencing. From the west, take I-45 and exit Brown Deer Road.
ADMISSION	$10 per person plus a docent fee.
HOURS	By appointment only, no walk-ins allowed. Appointments are available Monday through Friday. Reservations must be made seven business days in advance. A docent always accompanies visitors.
AMENITIES	Parking lot. Toilets and water available in the restroom building.

 ## Boerner Botanical Gardens

HALES CORNERS

KNOWN NATIONALLY as the "Father of the Parkway System," Charles Whitnall really left his mark on Milwaukee when he purchased a plot of farmland on the city's south side. Residential development now surrounds Whitnall Park, but tucked into the middle of the site is a treasure trove of plants, the Boerner Botanical Gardens.

Named for Milwaukee landscape architect Alfred L. Boerner, the English country-style gardens consist of a 1,000-acre arboretum that stretches along the Root River Parkway, five original gardens, and several additions to Boerner's master plan. Whether your taste runs toward more formal gardens or to groves of trees and shrubs arranged by plant family, there's something on the forty acres for everyone.

From the Garden Center, the Annual Garden quickly ushers you into the formal gardens. Also known as the walled garden, this ever-changing space features the best of new bedding plants especially those that have withstood Wisconsin winters in the Trial and Test Gardens. Designs and plants change from year to year with 10,000 annuals being installed every new growing season. The Water Garden located in the center of the Annual Garden is accented with four Pfitzer junipers, replacements for elms that succumbed to disease.

Many of the hardscapes were crafted with help from employees of the Works Progress Administration, the Civilian Conservation Corps, the

National Youth Administration, and Milwaukee County relief labor. WPA workers built the native stone wall that frames the gardens as well as the stone gazebo in the southeast corner. There is a series of statues of a boy and a girl, a sea crab and turtle, a sundial, and sculpted bench bases, all created by the students of the Layton School of Art (now Milwaukee Institute of Art and Design) under the auspices of the WPA.

Contemporary artist Susan Falkmann added *The Passages*, a series of limestone sculptures, to the garden. Her work can also be seen at the Botany Garden located on the University of Wisconsin-Madison campus.

A fountain at the end of the Annual Gardens simply means there are more formal spaces to explore. Adding color to each side of the grassy mall, the Perennial Borders were part of Boerner's original design. For staff horticulturists, the challenge here is to choose plants with varying bloom times so you'll see color all season long.

Tulips start the color in the spring, followed by miniature, intermediate, and tall bearded irises and peonies. Summer color is found in phlox and sunflowers with chrysanthemums blooming during the fall. Interspersed with these colorful offerings are geraniums, hosta, salvia, sedum, coreopsis, and lilies. George Adam Dietrich's statue, depicting a mother and two sons, can be found here.

The borders lead visitors to the famous Rose Garden where the color usually peaks during the third week of June. Shakespeare's Romeo famously observed that a rose by any other name would smell as sweet. With the popular floribundas, hybrid teas, grandifloras, miniatures, tree roses, and less well-known varieties such as shrubs, climbers, hybrid perpetuals, Chinas, and polyanthus, you can put the Bard's words to the test.

The formal European garden's design is the same as it was when the first roses bloomed there in 1939 although plant selections and bed sizes have been altered

Sundial at Boerner Botanical Gardens

John Ernst

since then. Some of the 3,000 plants representing three hundred fifty varieties came from Boerner's brother, Eugene, a nationally recognized rose expert, known by the nickname "Papa Floribunda." Eugene earned his moniker for his success in saving the rose's cutting stock from the Nazis during World War II.

Stroll the gravel walks around the Rose Garden or wander grassy paths through the beds. There's a large stone and wood arbor that supports varieties of climbing roses as well as two ornamental circular pools and one rectangular pool that hosts various types of aquatic plants and koi.

The Rose Garden is an official display garden for the All-America Rose Selections. Each year, the new selections tested in Boerner's Trial Gardens and awarded the title "All-America" are added to the display. A shrub rose collection, named for a founder and the first president of the Milwaukee Rose Society, can be seen in the meadow to the west of the Rose Garden.

Resembling a monastery garden, the twelve Herb Garden beds are tucked into a corner of the formal gardens behind yew hedges. The plants are divided according to their uses: medicinal, religious ceremonies, dyes, insect repellents, and flavorings. A "salad bowl" that was started as a Victory garden during World War II remains today with various vegetables grown for local food pantries. A statue of St. Fiacre, an Irish monk considered the patron saint of gardeners, watches over things. Many of the annual herbs are planted in geometric or knot designs. A theme bed gathers a variety of herbs under one subject such as the Peter Rabbit Garden or the Asian Herb Garden. Plants are well labeled and the labels include common uses.

Take the Daylily Walk from the Herb Garden, a serpentine path that runs south to the Bog and Rock Gardens. Various hues of daylilies can be found along the path, including some considered antique. The peak bloom time for these flowers is in July.

The junglelike Bog Garden is one of the closest things to an outdoor tropical environment Wisconsin can offer. A bridge over the garden entices you to stop and look at the skunk cabbage, marsh marigolds, and jewelweed that have taken up residence here. Because alkaline soil is sitting on top of a limestone foundation, the Bog Garden is actually misnamed; it should be called a Fen Garden. But no matter what it's called, the dampness provides a rich environment for these unusual plants.

Between 1934 and 1941, workers from the Civilian Conservation Corps built the Rock Garden. What was once a shallow gravel pit was landscaped with more than one thousand tons of limestone slabs from Currie Park to turn it into a "woodland grotto." The Rock Garden is filled with natives supplemented with trickling water. Although most of the garden is recessed, the overlook terrace crafted from limestone rock meets the formal Shrub Mall at the terrace level.

In the Shrub Mall, think English estate with an outdoor room. Here you'll find annuals, perennials, shrubs, trees, and vines surrounding an expanse of lawn.

Part of the Mall includes a collection of tree peonies. This variety has thicker stems than their herbaceous cousins. A pair of Amur chokecherry trees and the site's intermediate bearded iris collection can also be found here. The design for this area contains an optical illusion. The Mall is actually sixteen feet narrower at its south end, although you wouldn't see it unless you'd actually measure it.

Stop by the Peony Garden, also part of Boerner's original design, for additional fragrant blooms, including seven varieties that were hybridized in the 1800s. Three varieties of intersectional peonies, a cross between herbaceous and tree peonies, can also be found here. But those aren't the only types. Other varieties on display are Japanese, anemone, single, semi-, and full double. The unusual tree anchoring the garden is a Katsura tree whose fall leaves are said to smell like caramel corn.

Don't forget to stop at the Voight Trial Garden before heading to the Garden House. Here you will find the official test site for the All-America Rose Selections, the All-America Selections flower display and test garden, and the display garden for the All-America Vegetable Selections. The gardens are one of twenty-three rose test sites in the country.

COUNTY	Milwaukee
ADDRESS	9400 Boerner Drive, Hales Corners
PHONE	414/525-5600
WEBSITE	www.boernerbotanicalgardens.org
DIRECTIONS	**Coming from the north or downtown Milwaukee:** Take I-43 to I-894 West and exit 5A, (Forest Home Avenue). Once on Forest Home, turn left onto South 92nd Street. Continue on South 92nd Street to the entrance of the Root River Parkway (at College Avenue). Turn right onto College Avenue (into the Parkway). Turn right at the stop sign and then turn right at the entrance to the gardens.
	From the southwest: Take I-43 to I-894 West. Exit 59 (Layton Avenue) on the left toward State Highway 100. Stay straight to West Layton Avenue. Turn right on South 108th Street (also known as Highway 100). Go through the intersection of Highway 100 and Forest Home Avenue. Proceed to College Avenue. Turn left onto College. At the first stop sign, turn left. Then turn right at the entrance of the gardens and go up the hill.
	From the south: Take I-94 to exit 320 (Rawson Avenue/Highway BB). Turn west onto West Rawson Avenue and proceed to South 92nd Street (about five miles). Turn right onto South 92nd Street and follow the signs to the gardens (about one mile). Turn left onto College Avenue (into the Parkway). Turn right at the first stop sign and then turn right at the entrance to the gardens and go up the hill.
	From the west: Take I-94 to I-894/U.S. Highway 45 South. Take exit 60 (Highway 100) on the left. Stay right and merge onto South 108th Street (also known as Highway 100). Head south. Go through the intersection of Highway 100 and Forest Home Avenue. Proceed to College Avenue. Turn left on to College. At the first stop sign, turn left. Then turn right at the entrance of the gardens and go up the hill.
	From the northwest: Take U.S. Highway 41 South (which becomes U.S. Highway 45 in Milwaukee County) to I-894/U.S. Highway 45 South. Take exit 60 (Highway 100) on the left. Stay right and merge onto South 108th Street (also known as Highway 100). Head south. Go through the intersection of Highway 100 and Forest Home Avenue. Proceed to College Avenue. Turn left onto College. At the first stop sign, turn left. Then turn right at the entrance of the gardens and go up the hill.
ADMISSION	$4.50 for adults; $3.50 for Milwaukee County seniors ages 60 and up; $2.50 for children ages 6 to 17; $3.00 for the disabled of any age.
HOURS	8 a.m. to sunset, daily from April 21 through Oct. 14. The gardens are open in early November and early April, weather permitting. Call ahead. The gardens are closed from late November to early April.
AMENITIES	Parking lot. Toilets, water, and food inside the building.

Community Memorial Hospital
MENOMONEE FALLS

SOME THERAPEUTIC OR HEALING GARDENS ARE PRIVATE, meant solely for the use of patients, their families, and the institution's staff. Others, like Community Memorial Hospital, not only allow the public in; they encourage frequent return visits through a class offered by the Menomonee Falls Recreation Department. Master gardeners offer seasonal, monthly garden walks through the space. Walkers receive a book with color pictures and descriptions of what's planted in the garden.

Opened in June 2006, the hospital's healing garden has four objectives. It seeks to provide a unique healing environment; a place of beauty, silence, and serenity; a spot to experience the outdoors through the seasons; and a place to relax. The healing gardens are located between the ambulatory surgery parking lot and the hospital. There are also plantings in front of the hospital that surround a waterfall and pond.

The healing gardens are divided into two levels. As the public face of the garden, Tier 1 emphasizes masses of color and includes hostas and irises, stella d'oro and foxtail lilies, lily of the valley, and cranesbill. There are also hollyhocks, hibiscus, and bee balm for vertical interest.

The Tier 2 gardens are more "personal" and private. You're invited to wander and relax, have a conversation at the tables and chairs, or learn something new about plants as you follow the paths through them. Eight separate garden rooms can be found in the Tier 2 gardens. There are the butterfly and the herbs for butterflies gardens, the latter providing plants to support the insect in its larval stage. Daylilies, coreopsis, black-eyed Susans, as well as asters, zinnias, and cleome provide a varied menu for the butterflies. The larval stage must like to hang out in a spicy environment since the hospital provided them with their choice of a well-stocked Italian kitchen in dill, chives, thyme, parsley, and oregano.

A Fragrance Garden emphasizes the aroma of shrub roses, wallflowers, dwarf mock orange, and peonies. Dianthus, lady's mantle and other plants common to the nineteenth century are found in the Heirloom Garden. A few lilies, some salvia, roses, and peonies are thrown in for pizzazz.

The Hummingbird Garden woos the feisty flyers with columbine, butterfly bush, bellflowers, and bee balm. Veronica and lobelia are also part of the menu. A Medicinal Herb Garden features herbs that have been utilized to treat common diseases. Look for comfrey, mullein, valerian, feverfew, and betony. A few like foxglove, aconite, autumn crocus, and arnica are actually poisonous.

The classic rainbow colors of red, orange, yellow, green, blue, indigo, and violet can be found in their floral counterparts in the Rainbow Garden. Red peonies, orange phlox, yellow coneflowers, green coral bells, blue dwarf irises, and purple hydrangeas draw the eye along the color spectrum.

Trellises of clematis ('Niobe,' 'Warsaw Nike', 'Jackmanii', and 'Sweet Autumn') and hibiscus ('Southern Belle') provide the backdrop in the Native Plants Garden with its ornamental grasses, sedums, verbena, and gaillardia. Delphiniums add height while artemisia hovers closer to the ground.

Tulips, alliums, fritillaria, hyacinth, narcissus, colchicum, and crocus are the harbingers of spring. In the walkways, groups of plants such as weigela, lupine, campanula, and geranium are chosen for their complementary colors and textures.

All of the Tier 2 gardens are centered around a large pool with a fountain shooting jets of water. Mike Casper's sculpture, *Doves Taking to Flight* anchors the pool.

COUNTY	Waukesha
ADDRESS	W180 N8085 Town Hall Road, Menomonee Falls
PHONE	262/252-5302
WEBSITE	www.communitymemorial.com
DIRECTIONS	From the north, take U.S. Highway 41/45 south to Main Street exit. Turn west to Menomonee Falls. Follow Main Street approximately two miles to Town Hall Road. Turn left on Town Hall and follow it approximately three-quarters of a mile to the hospital, which is located on the west side of the road. From the south, take I-894 to U.S. Highway 45 north for approximately ten miles. Exit Appleton Avenue North (Menomonee Falls). The exit curves underneath Highway 45. Stay on Appleton Avenue until you reach the first set of stoplights, which is the intersection of Good Hope Road and Appleton Avenue. Turn left and go west three miles to Town Hall Road. Turn right and continue on Town Hall for one mile to the hospital, which will be on your left. LindenGrove Health Care Center is located in front of the hospital.
ADMISSION	Free
HOURS	Seasonal. Daily, dawn to dusk.
AMENITIES	Parking lot. Toilets, food, and water available in the hospital.

 Congdon Park Rotary Gardens

DELAVAN

WHEN THE DELAVAN ROTARY CLUB was looking for a service project in 2004, they wanted to do something that would visibly affect the community. By improving the landscaping at Congdon Park with the installation of its first of a set of formal gardens, they have succeeded admirably.

Tucked into a business park located between State Highway 50 and I-43, the 29.6-acre greenspace was intended to provide local residents with a place to relax. Although it already had a gazebo with picnic benches, a pond stocked with fish, and a series of walking trails, it really lacked an attractive centerpiece.

Delavan's Rotary Gardens have become a significant focal point in the middle of an expanse of grass. A large contemporary fountain set in a raised stone pool defines the gardens' center. Seven granite boulders symbolizing the

Courtesy of City of Delavan Parks and Recreation

Stone fountain at Rotary Gardens in Congdon Park

seven continents of the world form the structure of the fountain. The water depicts the world's oceans, the "connecting tissue" that holds those continents together. Sedum-covered rocks ring the pool's interior perimeter.

A brick pathway separates four small perennial beds that are placed around the fountain in a cardinal grid. The path leads to two garden rooms, one at the north end and the other at the south end of the gardens. The rooms, containing roses and hostas, are outlined with a semi-circle of ornamental trees followed by a V-shaped line of evergreens and another of trees that delineates the border between garden and park. Grass paths separate the four smaller beds from the larger ones. Herbs, perennials, small shrubs and trees, ornamental grasses, even a few granite boulders fill in the space. Annuals are added every year for spots of color.

The undulating perimeters of some of the beds soften the rigid lines of the formal gardens. Four contemporary concrete benches consisting of a slab perched on top of two round balls also help to ease the angularity of the design.

Looking east from the fountain, the concrete path leads to the gazebo. Future plans include the development of gardens around the gazebo and the addition of a "flag garden" around the existing flagpole, which borders the garden's south side. The ten- to fifteen-foot-wide flag garden will extend one hundred eighty feet along Highway 50 and when completed is expected to be about six hundred square feet in size. It will be isolated from the Highway 50 traffic and the I-43 off ramp. A prairie restoration and a Japanese garden are also being considered for future projects.

COUNTY	Walworth
ADDRESS	1528 Hobbs Drive, Delavan
DIRECTIONS	From the north or the south, exit I-43 to State Highway 50. Highway 50 is also called Geneva Street. Turn west on Highway 50 and right on both South Wright Street and Hobbs Drive. From the west, turn left on South Wright Street and right on Hobbs Drive.
ADMISSION	Free
HOURS	Seasonal. Daily, dawn to dusk
AMENITIES	Parking lot.

Cudahy Gardens

MILWAUKEE

WHEN YOU HAVE SUCH A GLORIOUS ARCHITECTURAL WONDER as the soaring, white Calatrava addition at the Milwaukee Art Museum, the landscape that surrounds it should be somewhat understated. That's just what landscape architect Dan Kiley did when he designed the museum's Cudahy Gardens.

Rather than replicate the swooping lines of the winglike Burke Brise Soleil, Kiley went in the opposite direction. The minimalist landscape features

Less is more: minimalist layout at Cudahy Gardens

geometric shapes of squares, rectangles, and diagonals of grass separated by both clipped yew hedges and a three-foot-wide water channel that runs lengthwise through the six-hundred-foot by one-hundred-foot space. Jets located within the water channel create a solid four-foot-high water curtain that's backed by fiber optic lights.

The water channel further separates the large, rectangular space into two perfect mirror images. The hedgerows continue the separation, dividing the long room into a sequence of five smaller ones with a granite-paved plaza at each end. Fountains anchor the water curtain at the north and south ends of the rectangular space climbing to thirty-five feet within a forty-foot pool. Granite benches abut the hedgerows. Named for Milwaukee philanthropist Michael J. Cudahy, the $8.3 million landscape parallels the entrance to the Quadracci Pavilion.

> All of those black-eyed Susans planted around the campus of the *University of Wisconsin-Milwaukee* represent the university's colors of black and gold. Look for some formal beds of annuals outside of Chapman Hall and the Edith Helfaer Conference Center.

While you're in the area, stop by and see the rooftop garden at the Hotel Metro (hotelmetro.com) at 411 Mason Street. Downtown Milwaukee's newest boutique hotel installed a Zen garden on the seventh floor for its patrons' use. But the garden is accessible to the public on specific days when there is no event scheduled. And it's worth the trip for those interested in small-space or Japanese gardening.

Called "Zen on Seven," the site emphasizes natural materials including bamboo, slate, and limestone in its design. A limestone fountain moves the water in the reflecting pool. The pool's water is dyed black to make it more reflective. Terraced planters are filled with perennials and ornamental grasses.

COUNTY	Milwaukee
ADDRESS	700 North Art Museum Drive, Milwaukee
PHONE	414/224-3200
WEBSITE	www.mam.org
DIRECTIONS	Because of the road construction through the Marquette Interchange, the normal routes to the museum and gardens are due to be closed until late 2008. For up-to-date travel information, visit www.mchange.org or call (888) 468-0037. From the north, exit I-43 at West North Avenue and take North 6th Street turning left on East Michigan Street. Go east to Lincoln Memorial Drive (which is also Art Museum Drive). From the south, take I-43/I-94 north to the Plankinton Avenue exit. Continue north on Plankinton to Michigan Street. Turn east on Michigan and proceed to Lincoln Memorial Drive. From the west, follow I-94 or I-43 downtown to I-794 east. Exit at Lakefront (exit 1F). The museum is located at the intersection of Michigan Street and Lincoln Memorial Drive.
ADMISSION	Free
HOURS	Daily, dawn to dusk.
AMENITIES	Street or ramp parking. Toilets, food, and water located in the museum.

DeKoven Center

RACINE

THE GOTHIC-STYLE SET OF BUILDINGS built in 1852 at Racine's DeKoven Center provides an almost theatrical backdrop for the five gardens located on its grounds. If you weren't paying close attention, you might assume you were walking part of an historic British estate.

Located on the shores of Lake Michigan, this former Episcopal boy's school is now used for conferences, ecumenical and artist retreats, and recreational events. Volunteers and some long-term tenants developed and work on the gardens, most of which were installed in 2000.

One of the biggest gardens on the property is a Zen Meditation Garden, lovingly tended to by members of the Original Root Zen Center. Located outside of the Great Hall, the space features a complex mix of Buddhas, perennials, and annuals. Most of the plants were donated, hence the abundance of colors, textures, and heights. North of the Meditation Garden is the Williamsburg-style Herb Garden that includes a few annuals for color and interest.

Kings Way—a concrete pathway named for Kingston Erlich, a local real estate developer—leads visitors directly to St. John's Chapel. This English-style cottage garden hugs both sides of the path that many brides take on their wedding day. Hydrangeas, roses, daylilies, irises, cosmos, purple coneflowers, and Shasta daisies are just some of the flowers that wish the newlyweds good luck.

The Secret Garden is tucked behind the chapel. Hardscape features include a limestone path, a wooden garden bench, and a metal garden bench crafted to resemble bent willow. Sit on one of the benches and contemplate the dwarf conifers, perennials, and annuals. Statues of St. Francis and Mary keep watch over things.

The recently restored Bishop's Garden, located to the south of Taylor Hall, is older than the other gardens. The former pond, which may have been installed when the school was built, was converted into a "rockery," a dry, rock-filled sunken garden with pots of petunias and impatiens for color. Hostas encircle the exterior rim of the sunken garden. A stone bench seems to issue an invitation to sit and meditate.

The eastern part of the Bishop's Garden includes perennials such as hostas, tiger lilies, ferns, and hens and chicks as well as verbena and petunias for color. These plants form a backdrop for several sacred statues. Hardscapes include three wooden benches, a stone bench, and a birdbath.

Mature trees dot the Center's grounds and provide many secluded spots. The western portion of the Bishop's Garden is framed with a variety of them. The property also contains a wildflower garden located near the south exit.

The Center has applied for membership in the Quiet Garden Movement, a worldwide movement based in England that encourages its 277 members to open their gardens up to the public for meditation.

A quiet place at the DeKoven Center

COUNTY	Racine
ADDRESS	600 21st Street, Racine
PHONE	262/633-6401
EMAIL	dekoven.center@juno.com
WEBSITE	www.dekovencenter.pair.com
DIRECTIONS	From I-94, exit at State Highway 11. Follow Highway 11 until it ends at Sheridan Road. Turn left on Sheridan Road and continue until you reach 21st Street. Turn East on 21st Street. The Center's entrance will be on your left.
ADMISSION	Free
HOURS	Seasonal. Daily, dawn to dusk.
AMENITIES	Parking lot.

Eble Farm and Gardens

BROOKFIELD

ON THE NORTH SIDE OF BLUE MOUND ROAD lies one of the last remaining rural parcels of land along the overdeveloped stretch of highway. The large white dairy barn, farmhouse, and outbuildings mark the site of the Eble Farm. The farm is no longer in operation, but the gardens offer a quiet reminder of what once was.

Until her death in 1995 at 91, Florence Eble, a granddaughter of a State Assembly representative, lived in the family home and tended to her gardens. Today, several members of the Southeastern Wisconsin Master Gardeners group and volunteers carry on Eble's gardening tradition, even planting red geraniums in pots and hanging them along the white picket fence like she would have done. Walk into the flower garden that's located east of the farmhouse and you'll feel like you've taken a step back into the past.

Springtime is show time for the two-tone pink, white, yellow, rust, and purple irises. They compete with the later pink, white, and fuschia peonies to see who can put out the best blooms. Hollyhocks and daylilies trim the side of the barn as they would have in Eble's day. Her cottage garden is getting a boost with the addition of various natives including purple coneflowers, black-eyed Susans, and daylilies.

Irises announce springtime at Eble Farm

Milkweed and other host and nectar plants were installed in the separate butterfly/herb garden, which features twenty-five varieties of herbs including borders of lavender and chives. An arbor trimmed with clematis and climbing roses signals the entrance to it. A flashy red and turquoise bird feeder stands in the center. There are plans to add literature boxes with information on how to harvest and cook herbs.

The Waukesha County Department of Parks and Land Use, which owns the property, donates various types of annuals that the volunteers plant around the property each year. Marigolds, impatiens, and zinnias add splashes of color after the early perennials have lost their blooms.

COUNTY	Waukesha
ADDRESS	19400 West Blue Mound Road, Brookfield
DIRECTIONS	From I 94, take Barker Road/Blue Mound Road (exit 297). Follow the signs for Blue Mound Road east. The gardens are located at the corner of West Blue Mound Road and Janacek Road.
ADMISSION	Free
HOURS	Daily, dawn to dusk.
AMENITIES	Picnic tables; parking in the Eble Ice Arena lot to the east of the farm.

Forest Home Cemetery

MILWAUKEE

THE GHOSTS OF VALENTINE BLATZ, Joseph Schlitz, and T. A. Chapman must be applauding from the great beyond at the new addition to Forest Home Cemetery. The two hundred-acre cemetery, the final resting place for many long-gone captains of Milwaukee industry, opened its formal Victorian Columbarium Garden in 2006.

Not that the cemetery wasn't beautiful before the addition, mind you. Many visitors have walked through the valleys and promontories, nooks and open lawn, mature trees, and even Indian mounds, all on the site of a glacial moraine. Forest Home was designed as a "garden cemetery," a place where Victorian families tired of the urban chaos could take the streetcar out on a Sunday afternoon to the verdant green lawns, fountains, and memorial markers and picnic near the family graves.

From a historical standpoint, the new garden makes sense. In keeping with the cemetery's one hundred fifty-plus year history, the concept and design

The Victorian Columbarium Garden at Forest Home Cemetery

are a must see, much like the cemetery was when it was first constructed. And the Victorian Columbarium Garden offers a nice balance to the established Chapel Gardens.

Potentilla, gayfeathers, phlox, and mums trim the asphalt walkway entering section 16 where the new garden was installed. White hydrangea bushes flanking the walkway appear to guard the garden's entrance.

Two marble columbariums are set among the flowers, trees, and shrubs. A white pergola frames one end of the garden, while parterres filled with roses and salvia anchor the other end. Two semi-circle borders filled with various annuals and perennials chosen for their predilection for sun or shade, connect the pergola with the parterres. Coleus, hostas, and begonias as well as lilies, ferns, mums, and petunias, fill in the borders. All of the flowers are occasionally interrupted by peonies and other flowering shrubs. Paths define the space between the grass and the borders.

> The *Milwaukee Urban Gardens* (MUG) organization assists local residents and volunteers in creating new urban gardens and preserving garden plots that have become casualties of development.

An allee of arborvitae interjected with annuals lines the walkway leading to a five-tier Victorian fountain set in a stone pond, a replica of one that originally graced the grounds. Four urns are filled with color.

There is also a formal space located in the Chapel Garden. This sunken garden located beneath the chapel contains an octagonal great lawn inside of walls of vaults topped with clipped hedges. A round bed of softly hued annuals has replaced the fountain that was originally constructed in the center of this garden. Ivy covers the chapel columns and hanging baskets accent the stained glass. The great lawn is edged with eight beds of roses, eight stone benches, and two beds of cannas surrounded by dusty miller and blue salvia. Permanent planters filled with dusty miller and petunias bisect the set of steps leading down into the garden.

COUNTY	Milwaukee
ADDRESS	2405 West Forest Home Avenue, Milwaukee
WEBSITE	http://foresthomecemetery.com
DIRECTIONS	From I-94, exit 308B (U.S. Highway 41 South). Go one mile. Highway 41 South turns into Miller Park Way. Go an additional mile and a half to West Lincoln Avenue. Turn left. Continue on West Lincoln for a little over a mile to Forest Home Avenue. Turn right onto Forest Home. Enter the cemetery off of Forest Home Avenue. The Victorian garden is located in Section 16. The Chapel Garden is located across the drive from the offices.
ADMISSION	Free
HOURS	Daily, dawn to dusk.
AMENITIES	Parking lot. Toilets and water available in the office.

Frame Park

WAUKESHA

ON THE EASTERN SHORES OF THE FOX RIVER, Frame Park sits as a bit of green respite in an otherwise urban environment. Andrew Frame understood the benefits of preserving land for the next generation, and in 1928 donated $75,000 to the city of Waukesha so it could acquire space for a park. This particular parcel once ran from Barstow Street to the White Rock Spring Bottling Company. Frame's donation turned essentially what was a dump for local industries into a park complete with a beautiful garden spot.

The one-acre Frame Park garden began as a formal rose garden, but over the years has evolved into a garden with roses as an integral component. Outlined with arcs of rounded privet hedges that help separate the site from the park's recreational components, the garden showcases annuals, perennials, and unique hardscape features in addition to the rose bushes. Tall, stone urns divide the clipped hedges into sections.

Several steps bring visitors down into the heart of the garden. Anchored at the eastern end with a pergola and trellises, wooden benches that overlook the plantings encourage you to sit and contemplate the view. A black metal fence marks the western end of the garden space.

Each year gardener John Sorenson selects the nine thousand or so annuals that will best showcase the preselected floral design. One year blue and white was the color scheme. Another year, the Wizard of Oz theme included a yellow brick road. Cement sidewalks and gravel paths were temporarily painted with yellow paint to lure visitors to, and through, the grass-bordered flowerbeds.

The pergola's stone walkway is original. Lannon stone columns that support wooden lathes and form the pergola are also part of the park's initial design. A water feature was removed some twenty years earlier. Other than changes in plant selections, the garden looks pretty much as it did during the 1930s and 1940s. Sorenson chooses plants based on their hardiness and tries to incorporate many All-America winners in the design. Black pearl ornamental peppers were a hit with the public the year they were planted.

White climbing hydrangeas have replaced the grapevines that once covered the pergola. The vines died when the elm trees shading the space had to be removed. Perennial beds filled with selections such as coleus, hostas, nicotiana, astilbe, and sedums add color, texture, and interest. Ornamental grasses add height and form a backdrop for many of the perennial choices. The Southeastern Wisconsin Daylily Society donated a selection of daylilies to the garden.

The garden and park are a popular spot for weddings. Permits are required for professional photography as well as for weddings.

COUNTY	Waukesha
ADDRESS	At the junction of Highways 164 and 18, Waukesha
PHONE	262/544-4111
DIRECTIONS	From I-94, take Highway F (exit 195) south to East Moreland Boulevard (also known as U.S. Highway 18). Turn left onto Moreland and go across the Fox River. Turn right into Frame Park.
ADMISSION	Free
HOURS	Daily, dawn to 10 p.m.
AMENITIES	Parking lot. Toilets and water available in the park shelter.

 Free S.P.I.R.I.T Equine Center

FOND DU LAC

THE SENSORY/HEALING GARDEN located at the Free S.P.I.R.I.T. (Special People In Riding Therapy) Equine Center serves many purposes. It acts as a respite for the parents or friends of riders who come to the center for equine therapy. It served as a rehabilitation opportunity for members of the Department of Corrections' Drug and Alcohol Correction Center who constructed the hardscape and the memorial gazebo. And the garden provides a constructive space for "sensory integration" for those with disabilities.

The facility, found on the north side of State Highway 23 just east of the city of Fond du Lac, is designed and maintained by the Master Gardeners of Fond du Lac County. Two local quarries donated the stone for the walls that support some of the raised beds. The raised beds allow those in wheelchairs to enjoy the garden as easily as their ambulatory peers. An apple tree anchors the base of a horseshoe-shaped raised bed filled with colorful annuals.

Plants and horses help heal at Free S.P.I.R.I.T.

As a sensory/healing garden, plants are chosen for their smell, their colors, their fragrance, and even their taste. The "scent" area contains lavender, heliotrope, and alyssum among other selections. A pond with a tiny waterfall and a set of wind chimes are hidden among the rose bushes in the "listening" area. In the "free to eat" garden, herbs and vegetables share space with sunflowers and nasturtium. The fuzzy tops of purple ageratum, the furry leaves of elephant ears, and even the soft petals of red geraniums can be found in the "touch" garden. For those whose sight is intact, the color therapy portion includes selections of red yarrow, hot pink petunias, yellow marigolds, and purple coneflowers.

A space for sensory integration

Calendula, hens and chicks, sedums, and coneflower attract birds to the bird sanctuary. A large wooden butterfly identifies the butterfly garden with its various cosmos, Queen Anne's lace, rose asters, and rudbeckia. The garden even contains a butterfly made from annuals. Thyme is utilized as a border around many of the sections.

In keeping with the center's mission, horse-themed objects are interspersed among the plants, shrubs, and trees. The memorial gazebo is trimmed with saddles and horseshoes. Worn cowboy boots have been recycled into birdhouses.

Hardscapes are not neglected in this garden. There are two inviting latticework arbors, several wood and stone benches, and a teepeelike trellis made from several old bamboo fishing poles. A wooden horse sculpture sits in the middle of a "pasture" of lamb's quarters. On the southeast and southwest sides are two four-sided trellises with four horse heads perched atop. Sweet peas wind their way up the trellis legs. Those who take advantage of this peaceful space are certain to come away rejuvenated.

COUNTY	Fond du Lac
ADDRESS	W3950 Highway 23 East, Fond du Lac
PHONE	920/924-9920
EMAIL	info@freespiritriders.org
WEBSITE	www.freespiritriders.org
ECTIONS	State Highway 23 east in the town of Empire. Located on the north side of the road.
MISSION	Free
HOURS	Daily, dawn to dusk.
MENITIES	Gravel parking lot.

The Garden Room

SHOREWOOD

NURSERIES, GREENHOUSES, AND RETAIL GARDEN STORES frequently install display gardens on their property to inspire their customers. But most of them aren't located smack dab in the middle of an urban area.

The Garden Room is set on a city lot and bordered, not by trees and grass, but by buildings and a parking lot. Owner Deborah Kern couldn't fathom a garden store without a garden so she looked toward the heavens for her inspiration.

The building, a car repair shop and a Buick dealership in its previous lives, had a flat wooden roof that needed replacing. Enlisting the creativity of Buettner & Associates, Kern simply had the 4,000-square-foot roof replaced with steel beams and a concrete deck covered with a Siplast Teranap roof membrane to support a plant-intensive garden with eighteen inches of soil and a glass conservatory.

The roof has three usable spaces: the conservatory area, the garden, and the arbor terrace. A fourth space houses the mechanicals and maintenance tools.

An oval walkway made from reclaimed brick pavers encircles the glass roof. A wooden arbor anchors the south end of the garden providing shade and a display for outdoor furniture. The glass conservatory acts as both the garden's entrance and the northern focal point. Four tree-filled, large terra-cotta pots are placed at each of the roof's four corners. Bulbs, perennials, and ornamental shrubs flank both sides of the brick walkway and cover 1,900 square feet. As both a safety and a decorative feature, an ornamental black iron fence outlines the glass roof.

Serviceberry, crab apple, and viburnum are the ornamental trees on display. Deciduous and evergreen shrubs include 'Dwarf Amur' maple, 'Knockout' rose, 'Magic Carpet' spirea, and 'Montgomery' spruce. The garden features several varieties of clematis as well as the 'William Baffin' climbing rose and Boston ivy. Salvia, sedum, geraniums, anemone, asters, and phlox represent perennial choices. Also included are several types of ornamental grasses.

Garden art rules here. There are Celtic crosses, sundials, and stone figures of animals tucked in among the greenery in four display areas. The glass conservatory is the annex for the Anaba Tea Room. Hanging plants are evident but not intrusive.

Other area roof gardens include ones at the Urban Ecology Center and at the Great Lakes WATER Institute connected with the University of Wisconsin-Milwaukee.

COUNTY	Milwaukee
ADDRESS	2107 East Capitol Drive, Shorewood
PHONE	414/963-1657
FAX	414/963-1138
DIRECTIONS	From I-43, exit Capitol Drive and go east. The store/garden is located on the south side of Capitol Drive just about a block after you cross Oakland Avenue.
ADMISSION	Free
HOURS	10 a.m. to 6 p.m. Tuesdays through Fridays, 10 a.m. to 4 p.m. Saturdays, 11 a.m. to 3 p.m. Sundays. Closed Mondays.
AMENITIES	Parking lot. Toilets, food, and water inside the store.

Grand Geneva Resort

LAKE GENEVA

THE BUNNIES AT THE GRAND GENEVA RESORT aren't the same ones that were hanging around the property during the 1970s when it was the former Playboy Club. Sure, both sets have furry tails, but that's where the resemblance stops. Playboy's Bunnies were considered attractions. Today's bunnies are, at the very least, nuisances. But who can blame them for adopting the resort as home with a regular buffet of thousands of flowering plants and ornamental grasses scattered around the property's thirteen hundred acres?

When the Playboy Club closed in 1982, the resort changed owners several times until 1993 when the Marcus Corporation took it over. As part of the plan, the company wanted to turn the site into a destination for tourists to come and look at the grounds, said Jim Crothers, Grand Geneva's director of grounds. That meant the condition of the landscape was as important as the look of the buildings. They've obviously taken that directive to heart.

The floral show begins at the property's entrance with drifts of color surrounding a fieldstone-supported sign. The fieldstone is significant. Frank Lloyd Wright used it in many of his buildings and the resort has emphasized the architect's famous Prairie style in its renovations and new construction.

Courtesy of the Grand Geneva Resort

Carpets of color at the Grand Geneva Resort

Courtesy of the Grand Geneva Resort

Some of the 100,000 plants at the Grand Geneva Resort

The Prairie style is carried over in the plant selections: lots of natives and ornamental grasses. You'll see the ubiquitous coneflowers, black-eyed Susans, and daisies in both perennial and annual form. The annuals planted in drifts or scattered around represent a small fraction of the 100,000 that are planted each year for a bold splash of color.

The carpets of color continue to dot the landscape along the road to the main entrance. There are thirty-five gardens located on the grounds, including those off the back of the golf course, in all the islands in the parking lots, and those dividing the main road. You'll also find some around the pro shop and outside the north and south wings of the resort's entrance. Blossoms abound around the timeshare units. The front of the spa features a small perennial garden. Crothers estimates that he and his staff are responsible for the care of two to three acres of plants.

The tower next to the resort's entrance and the fountain located in the same area are some of the property's significant hardscapes. There's a concrete path that leads from the entrance door, through the plantings, to a parking lot. And if that's not enough for garden lovers, there are seventy-one planters filled with annuals scattered around. Cannas are used for the backdrop with potato vines, verbena, coleus, and petunias that drape for color.

COUNTY	Walworth
ADDRESS	7036 Grand Geneva Way at State Highway 50 East and U.S. Highway 12, Lake Geneva
PHONE	262/248-8811 or 262/249-4763
EMAIL	info@grandgeneva.com
WEBSITE	www.grandgeneva.com
DIRECTIONS	From Milwaukee, take I-43 south and exit Highway 12 (Lake Geneva/Elkhorn). Follow Highway 12 to Highway 50 East/Lake Geneva (the second exit). Take the off ramp and continue east under the overpass. The resort will be on your left. From Madison, take I-90 south to Beloit/Janesville. Exit State Highway 11 (Delavan). In Delavan, follow Highway 11 to Highway 50 and head east to Lake Geneva. The resort will be on your left.
ADMISSION	Free
HOURS	Seasonal. Daily, dawn to dusk
AMENITIES	Parking lot. Toilets, water, and food in the hotel.

Hancock Agricultural Research Station, Albert Garden

HANCOCK

KNOWN AS THE "SMILE ALONG THE HIGHWAY," the Hancock Agricultural Research Station's two-acre fruit, flower, and vegetable demonstration gardens are a bright spot in the flat, sandy potato country of Waushara County. The gardens are named for A.R. Albert, a University of Wisconsin-Madison research professor, and his wife. Albert was the superintendent of the Hancock station from 1922 to 1947.

Located on the grounds of the agricultural research station on the west side of U.S. Highway 39, the Albert garden was initiated in 1991 as a "hook" to get people to stop by and check out the station's research on various Wisconsin agricultural products. One of twelve agricultural research stations around the state, this one specializes in research on potatoes and other food crops as well as poplar and jack pine trees.

When the gardens were first begun, they had a few dozen flower and vegetable varieties on display, all of which were started from seed. Since then, the varieties number over eight hundred annually. In 1995, the garden was designated one of seven All-America Selection Display Gardens in the state.

Each year what is selected to be planted in the garden is based on a theme. In 2006 the theme was Lifelong Gardening. Since 2007 celebrates the 75th anniversary of the All-America Selections program, the long rectangle boasted one hundred fifty past and present examples of the cultivars that were selected as improvements over previously existing varieties. AAS annuals on display included varieties of petunias, ageratum, celosia, nasturtiums, and verbena. The oldest annual on display was the Thumbelina zinnia, which became an AAS selection in 1963. The earliest perennial was an 'Early Sunrise' coreopsis from 1988. Other perennial selections included hyssop, gayfeathers, false indi-

"The smile along the highway"

go, mallow, poppies, and larkspur. A wooden pergola sheltered several hosta varieties and other shade plants. A series of small raised beds were filled with herbs including the 1987 'Purple Ruffles' basil. The oldest plant in the display was a vegetable—the 1935 'Detroit Dark Red' beet.

The little log cabin located at the entrance to the garden is the Brian Wallendal Visitor's Center. Named after a seven-year-old boy who died, the cabin, perennial gardens, and old-fashioned windmill are arranged as they might have looked on a typical Hancock farm in 1916. The perennial gardens flank the concrete sidewalk that leads to the cabin's front door. Here you'll find pasque flowers, hollyhocks, foxglove, and peonies as well as a forsythia bush. Check out the selection of cacti and succulents tucked under the base of the windmill.

There are other perennial gardens scattered throughout the property including one at the brick headquarters building. A special white trellis with a red W in the middle, a reminder of the UW's connection to the property, supports a clematis.

COUNTY	Waushara
ADDRESS	N3909 County Highway V, Hancock
PHONE	715/249-5961
FAX	715/249-5850
EMAIL	hancock@calshp.cals.wisc.edu
WEBSITE	www.ars.wisc.edu
DIRECTIONS	From I-39 North, exit at Hancock, exit 131, and follow County Highway V west. Turn south at the first dirt road.
ADMISSION	Free
HOURS	Seasonal. Daily, dawn to dusk. A Twilight Tour of the Gardens is held each August on the second Monday from 4 p.m. to 8 p.m. Group tours are available from 8 a.m. to 4:30 p.m. Monday through Friday. Call ahead to schedule a tour.
AMENITIES	Parking lot.

 Hawthorn Hollow Nature Sanctuary and Arboretum

KENOSHA

NAMED FOR A VALLEY FILLED WITH HAWTHORN TREES, Hawthorn Hollow was the summer retreat for two sisters, Ruth and Margaret Teuscher, who both taught in the Racine school district. Ruth earned additional money writing textbooks, allowing her to purchase forty acres of land in the town of Somers in 1935, which the two sisters then turned into a wildlife preserve.

Joy Morton, the creator of Chicago's Morton Arboretum, was contracted to design the site's arboretum, which greets visitors as they drive onto the property.

Ruth's lilac collection is planted along the south side of the property near the entrance road.

The nature sanctuary features a butterfly garden outside of the visitor's center. A trail leads you to a set of perennial gardens located in a grove of evergreens and mature trees. A flagstone walk curves through the larger perennial bed filled with coneflower, irises, bellflower, peonies, and milk-weed. A smaller bed contains daylilies and astilbe as well as some ornamental grasses. A bed of ferns peeks out from beneath the branches of a mature evergreen. A stone wall borders a portion of the grove.

A dwarf conifer collection of some thirty species is divided between the perennial beds and the arboretum area. A few beds filled with cannas and other annuals dot the landscape around the arboretum.

Hawthorn Hollow is in the process of developing a prairie garden that will be located near the site's restored prairie. An educational element will assist people in identifying the types of plants that are indigenous to a Midwestern prairie.

COUNTY	Kenosha
ADDRESS	880 Green Bay Road, Kenosha
PHONE	262/552-8196
EMAIL	hawthornhollow@wi.rr.com
WEBSITE	www.hawthornhollow.org
DIRECTIONS	From I-94, exit State Highway 50 east to Kenosha. Turn north on State Highway 31, which becomes Green Bay Road. The sanctuary will be on your left several miles ahead.
ADMISSION	$1 donation is encouraged.
HOURS	Seasonal. Daily, dawn to dusk.
AMENITIES	Parking lot. Toilets. Water inside the visitor's center.

 ## *Heritage Flower Farm*

MUKWONAGO

THE PHRASE, "EVERYTHING OLD IS NEW AGAIN," doesn't fully account for the popularity of Heritage Flower Farm located just south of Mukwonago. Some of the interest is also due to owner Betty Adelman's extensive research of the history behind her selections.

Adelman fell in love with heritage plants after moving to the seven-acre former farmstead and uncovering a lot of old plants on the grounds. "It piqued my interest in learning more about them and led me to specializing in heritage varieties," she said.

Adelman, who grows all of her perennials from seeds, has an eclectic selection of annuals, perennials, trees, vines, and shrubs on her property. She defines "heirloom" and "heritage" as plants that have been collected for gardens for one hundred years or more. There's the *Corydalis lutea,* a shade plant with tiny yellow blooms that was around during Roman times. The purplish gray blossoms on the bear's breeches inspired the design of the Corinthian column.

A tobacco plant seeded itself on her property, but Adelman points to pearly everlastings as the colonists' favorite brand of smoking material. The current popularity of zebra grass (two-striped *miscanthus*) belies the fact that the Victorians thought it was a nice addition to their gardens a century ago. Several of her selections, including an Osage orange tree, were first discovered on the Lewis and Clark Expedition.

Poet Emily Dickinson wrote extensively about plants and gardens, so Adelman installed a display garden in the poet's honor. You won't find the Shasta variety of daisy there; they weren't developed until several decades after Dickinson's death. Paths lead through other plant groupings giving you a hands-on history lesson.

Adelman has a wealth of knowledge about what she grows and is willing to share it. Don't tell the kids that the Joe Pye weed growing in your native garden was actually used as an aphrodisiac by a tribe of Native Americans. The Potawatomi used to grab some rattlesnake master before going off to play their games of chance, believing that the plant would bring them good luck. And the European version of Solomon's seal was thought to cure cuts and bruises for women "caused by stumbling on their hasty husband's fists." Hmmm....

Adelman arranges her retail plants by color. If you want something pink for that southwest corner, head toward the table that's painted pink and filled with plants in that hue. Ditto for the purples, blues, reds and the rest of the rainbow. The 1850s barn includes dried flowers for those whose green thumbs are fading.

> Stroll or drive along *North Lake Drive* between Whitefish Bay and downtown Milwaukee. This stretch of road contains hundreds of gardens planted by the residents of some of Milwaukee's oldest and finest homes. Lots of garden ideas here.

COUNTY	Waukesha
ADDRESS	33725 County Road L, Mukwonago
PHONE	262/662-0804
EMAIL	badelman@wi.rr.com
WEBSITE	www.heritageflowerfarm.com
DIRECTIONS	From State Highway 83, turn east onto County Highway L.
ADMISSION	Free
HOURS	9 a.m. to 5 p.m. Wednesday through Sunday, from April 14 through September 30 or by appointment.
AMENITIES	Grass parking lot. Toilets and water available.

Hilton Milwaukee City Center

MILWAUKEE

WITH EMPTY LOTS in downtown Milwaukee rarer than a ghost orchid, the Hilton Milwaukee City Center decided to beautify the footprint of its former parking garage in a natural way. It hired LandWorks, a local landscape architecture firm, to turn what essentially was a gravel pit into a hidden jewel.

The two-tiered garden goes from informal to formal as you progress down the stairs. The top level facing Sixth Street is informal with pink shrub roses, ornamental grasses including 'Heavy Metal' switch grass, and evergreens filling the bed and blocking out some of the street noise.

> Wisconsin's first "green street" is located in the *Josey Heights* subdivision in Milwaukee. The street, bioswales, and other green features are expected to absorb 100 percent of stormwater runoff.

One level below on the Sixth Street side, a border has more formal attitude with hostas, stella d'oro lilies, and various species of groundcovers including winter creeper filling the space. A concrete walkway separates the border from the more formal sunken garden.

The formal garden is outlined with cotoneaster hedges bordering an expanse of lawn and bisected by a red stone path leading to a gazebo. This combination exudes a simple elegance. Yews form four half-circles off the gazebo. Impatiens are underplanted along the hedges.

Annuals fill the window boxes along the wall on the garden's east side. Pots of ferns and banana trees are ringed with impatiens and chocolate soldiers. A few palm trees give the garden scale, offsetting the lower hedges. The banana and palm are being tested to see how well they withstand Wisconsin winters. Large crotons fill amphora type pots.

Choosing plants for this garden is challenging. With buildings bordering three sides, there are different microclimates to cope with. But the results are well worth the effort.

COUNTY	Milwaukee
ADDRESS	509 West Wisconsin Avenue, Milwaukee
PHONE	414/271-7250
WEBSITE	www.hiltonmilwaukee.com
DIRECTIONS	The garden is located on 6th Street, on the west side of the hotel. Because of the work on the Marquette Interchange over the next few years, on- and off-ramps may change. Contact the hotel for specific directions.
ADMISSION	Free
HOURS	Seasonal. Daily, dawn to dusk.
AMENITIES	Parking lot. Toilets, food, and water available in the hotel.

Horticultural Hall

LAKE GENEVA

THE 1912 CRAFTSMAN BUNGALOW located along Lake Geneva's main street has a special importance for gardeners. Once the social and educational gathering spot for the gardeners and foremen who worked on the luxurious Lake Geneva estates, Horticultural Hall and its open-air courtyard garden have seen their share of floral history.

The courtyard at Horticultural Hall in Lake Geneva

The Lake Geneva Garden Club used to plant and maintain the "secret" garden as the space is called, but now that task has fallen to local resident, Rosemary Divock. Divock has chosen plants to give the courtyard three seasons of color. Her goal is to add color with a variety of plants that live well together.

The plants trimming the building's exterior are bright and cheery—think tulips, daffodils, asters, and mums. Colorful annuals fill the windowboxes while ivy encircles the top of the front porch. Mature evergreens, magnolia trees, and tall hedges add height and a soft backdrop to the border of color that includes monarda, campanula, meadow sage, and bleeding heart.

Because the building is rented for weddings and parties, the colors in the courtyard borders are rather subdued. Silvers, pinks, and purples add a touch of formality without clashing with a bride's dress. Pale pink hydrangeas surround a fountain while hostas ring a circular stone sculpture. Trumpet vines snake their way up the side of the loggia walls that enclose the courtyard, providing a little color to the ivy concealing the walls. Mums, spirea, monarda, phlox, sedums, and coral bells are just a few of the perennials that are tucked into the borders surrounding the courtyard's "great lawn."

The hardscape also includes a flagstone patio that supports several stone planters and weathered benches. Pink rose bushes flank the steps leading from the patio down to the grass.

COUNTY	Walworth
ADDRESS	330 Broad Street, Lake Geneva
PHONE	262/248-4382
WEBSITE	www.horticulturalhall.com
DIRECTIONS	Broad Street, also known as State Highway 50, runs east and west along the north shore of Geneva Lake.
ADMISSION	Free
HOURS	By appointment only.
AMENITIES	Street parking. Toilets and water inside the building.

Kemper Center/Anderson Art Center

KENOSHA

LIKE THE DEKOVEN CENTER IN RACINE, the Kemper Center was once a private Episcopal boarding school. When the girls' school, St. Clair's, closed in 1975, the estate was converted to a park.

Lake Michigan borders the 17.5-acre property, home to several buildings including the Durkee Mansion, home to Wisconsin's first senator, Charles Durkee, and the Anderson Art Center. Around these buildings are various examples of garden spaces.

Parterres at the Anderson Art Center

In front of the former school, a wheelchair ramp is flanked with a mixed border of hostas, sedums, ornamental grass, and annuals. In spring, daffodils and hyacinths pop up around the buildings and the great lawn is covered with Siberian squilla turning it into a carpet of blue.

The Four Seasons Garden Club has created a Scented Garden for the visually and physically impaired on the south end of the estate. Raised beds and wheelchair-friendly concrete sidewalks allow all visitors a personal view of the plants.

The 9,000-square-foot Anderson Art Center set on 4.7 acres is located at the southern end of the Kemper Center property. The gray stone French Renaissance Revival home was built for James Anderson, an executive with American Brass, and his wife, Janet Lance Anderson, a former St. Clair alumnus whose grandfather founded the Simmons Mattress Company.

The grounds were originally landscaped befitting a corporate executive and an heiress. Mature trees dot the property with its expansive lawn. Clipped hedges form parterres around a slate patio on the home's southwest corner. Astilbe and hostas add interest while annuals in pinks and whites provide some color in the small formal garden. A cherub statue is also part of the design.

Adjacent to the art center's front entrance is a walled garden that the Andersons once utilized as an herb garden. The herbs have been replaced with a mixture of perennials and annuals including Russian sage, yarrow, pink begonias and geraniums, and coleus in red and green. Another cherub seems to have taken up residence in this garden.

COUNTY	Kenosha
ADDRESS	6501 Third Avenue, Kenosha
PHONE	262/657-6005
WEBSITE	www.kempercenter.com or www.andersonartcenter.com
DIRECTIONS	From I-94, exit State Highway 50 east to Kenosha. At the intersection of 75th Street (Highway 50) and 39th Avenue, Highway 50 will veer to the left. Continue straight on 75th Street. At Third Avenue, turn left and head north to 65th Street. Turn right onto the property.
ADMISSION	Free
HOURS	Seasonal.
AMENITIES	Street parking. Toilets and water inside the art museum.

Kneeland-Walker House and Gardens

WAUWATOSA

NAMED FOR THE FIRST TWO OWNERS OF THE PROPERTY, the Kneeland-Walker House is home to the Wauwatosa Historical Society, which purchased the 1890's Queen Anne-style home, coach house, and grounds in 1987. The one-and-one-half acre site features a Victorian garden dotted with various flowerbeds, a great lawn, and mature trees. While not an authentic replica of a period garden, the plantings are in keeping with the Victorians' preference for innovation, color, and form, said Carolyn Dressler, garden chair for the Historical Society.

Located at the corner of 74th Street and Hillcrest Drive, the gardens are tucked around the west and north sides of the carriage house. There are two tiers of trimmed shrubs running next to the sidewalk in front of the home giving an illusion of privacy while trimming part of the lawn. Shade plants such as hostas find the mature trees along the driveway to their liking. A bed just south of the porte-cochere has two conical arborvitae as anchors, with hostas filling the center.

A large evergreen provides a focal point for a perennial bed filled with traditional Victorian plants such as peonies, roses, bleeding heart, and lilacs. In keeping with the Victorian garden spirit of "embracing striking new plants," Dressler and her staff have added lisianthus, "which always attract attention and compliments," she said. An herb garden in front of the carriage house would have allowed the cook access to fresh spices for a meal.

Square stones form a pathway from the driveway around the carriage house to the backyard. A wooden bench is tucked among a bed of rose bushes. A metal arbor links two beds. A decorative birdbath has metal leaves winding around the base and the bowl.

You may recognize these gardens from television. Melinda Myers tapes many of the introductory segments to her Great Lakes Gardener program in these gardens. HGTV has also featured them in a segment of its Great American Gardens program. Volunteers, including members of the Southeast Wisconsin Master Gardeners, keep the site in tip-top shape.

While you're in the area, visit the Lowell Damon House, just a few blocks away on 76th and Rogers streets. While this 1841 historic home and gardens are not as elaborate as those on the Kneeland-Walker estate, they're worth a stop. A limestone path leads to a wooden arbor on the Rogers Street side. Mature trees and perennial beds filled with snow-on-the-mountain, hostas, lilacs, honeysuckle, and bulbs can be seen from the sidewalk. Two tree peonies anchor the southern part of the front bed. Steps leading to the beds from the backyard were reclaimed pavement. And yes, actor Matt Damon is related to the Damons who built this house. The house/grounds are open from 3 p.m. to 5 p.m. on Wednesdays and from 1 p.m. to 5 p.m. on Sundays.

COUNTY	Milwaukee
ADDRESS	7406 Hillcrest Drive, Wauwatosa
PHONE	414/774-8672
FAX	414/774-3064
EMAIL	Staff@wauwatosahistoricalsociety.org
WEBSITE	www.wauwatosahistoricalsociety.org
DIRECTIONS	From I-94 East, exit #305B (Fond du Lac) onto U.S. Highway 45 North. Take exit 40 (Watertown Plank Road/Swan Boulevard) onto West Watertown Plank Road heading east. Watertown Plank turns into Harwood Avenue. Turn left onto Harmonee Avenue (State Highway 181). Go approximately three blocks and turn left to follow Highway 181. Turn right onto Hillcrest Drive.
ADMISSION	Free
HOURS	Daily, dawn to dusk unless the house is rented for a private event.
AMENITIES	Street parking.

 # John Michael Kohler Arts Center

SHEBOYGAN

AS A LEADING MUSEUM OF CONTEMPORARY AMERICAN ART, the John Michael Kohler Arts Center is nationally acclaimed for its visual and performing exhibitions. With such an illustrious reputation, the gardens around the Center have to be equally remarkable, and there's no doubt that they are.

The Arts Center is comprised of three architecturally significant pieces. The Italian Revival style home, built in 1882, was constructed for the museum's namesake, who founded the Kohler Company. The glass-filled addition was added in 1999. The third piece, a stone wall, steps, and arch, remnants of the façade of the former Carnegie Library, was intentionally saved when the library was razed. In tying the three disparate sites together, Michael Beeck of Otter Creek Landscaping has had to honor the past while heading fast-forward into the future.

Nine garden areas comprise the Center's floral exhibits. The Arrival Garden, a collection of plantings set alongside the steps leading to the entrance, is designed specifically for four-season interest. Junipers and euphorbia mingle with Joe Pye weed, a Hinoki cypress, and ornamental grasses. Hardscapes include a birdbath and wooden benches and chairs. Even during the winter, this garden will look good.

Ten large terra-cotta pots filled with banana trees, tropical sugar maples, trellised jasmine, and elegant feathers for height, and nicotiana, coleus, and supertunias for accent adorn the front entrance. Of all of the plant materials used around the buildings it's the elegant feathers that receives the most attention with visitors regularly asking about the tall, fuzzy, lime green plant.

When planning the gardens, Beeck was given direct instructions to keep them interesting. In the Library Sculpture Garden he complied by adding Japanese maples, various species of hydrangeas, hardy bamboo, and the Seven Sons Tree, a Chinese shrub named for the white flowers that bloom in clusters of seven. Its bark shreds into a rugged texture and the green leaves turn purplish bronze in autumn.

The great lawn in the center of the garden fills in the original footprint of the 1904 library. It's purposely left open for seating for weddings and concerts. The arch and stage act as a focal point as well as an invitation for passersby to pop in and check out the blooms.

In the Library Sculpture Garden the emphasis is on unique individual plants, rather than mass plantings. Part of this was to complement the ruins of the library as well as to showcase the sculptures of Carl Peterson, which were introduced in 2006. Peterson, a self-taught artist who transformed his yard with concrete sculptures decorated with stones, glass, metal pieces, and paint, has created a miniature village complete with animals a la Dr. Seuss. Peterson's light fixtures in the library garden are actually wired to work.

Adding to the "Whoville" theme are two "wacky" birds from Thomas Every a.k.a. Dr. Evermor. Every, of Baraboo, crafts whimsical metal sculptures from castoffs, in this case musical instruments and other industrial pieces. Beeck surrounded the birds with a variety of grasses and natives reminiscent of their "home."

The large Festival Green hosts concerts and the art center's M.I.K.E. (Musically Integrated Kiosk Environment), a "transformable architectural structure" that functions as a digital recording studio and performance stage. The emphasis here is sculptural. There are clipped topiaries, hydrangea vines that look like a work of art growing up the brick walls, hawthorn trees, and white pines. Espaliered crab trees add to the 3-D effect.

The Tile Garden, set on the edge of the Festival Green, is the setting for the Wall of Donors tiles. With its grasses, pines, and perennials, the garden offers a subtle backdrop to the colorful tiles. Outside the Children's Educational Center is the Hosta Garden with a variety of hostas that look like they're feeding on steroids. Big doesn't even begin to describe their size.

Some of Carl Peterson's sculptures at the Kohler Arts Center

Mature dogwoods, hemlocks, maples, and even a hundred-year-old oak dot the grounds of the 1882 mansion, which was the original art center. Beeck plans to redevelop the space between the mansion and the new addition with an heirloom garden slated to include hollyhocks, bridal wreath, rose of Sharon, hydrangeas, and daylilies.

The Picnic Garden located outside of the café contains some unusual trees, most notably a Katsura, Japanese and American tamaracks, and a Yellow Wood. Cornish moss thrives in the partially shady area. Pots here are filled with calla lilies, more elegant feather, and begonias. Six additional Peterson sculptures, including a lighthouse with a working light, are found here. A Story Circle is scheduled to be revamped into a children's garden.

Bergenia and little bluestem are found in the parking lot as is a pear-shaped sculpture that serves as a support for a fleece flower. Walkways are composed of recycled, crushed glass that sparkles in the sunshine. Count these gardens as ever-changing to keep up with the art inside.

COUNTY	Sheboygan
ADDRESS	608 New York Avenue, Sheboygan
PHONE	920/458-6144
WEBSITE	www.jmkac.org
DIRECTIONS	From I-43, exit 126 (State Highway 23 East), which becomes Kohler Memorial Drive and then Erie Avenue. Continue east to Sixth Street. Turn right and follow Sixth Street four blocks south to New York Avenue. Turn right.
ADMISSION	The gardens are free. Donations of $4 for adults and $1 for children are suggested for the museum.
HOURS	Seasonal. Daily, dawn to dusk.
AMENITIES	Street parking. Toilets, food, and water inside the museum.

Lake Park

MILWAUKEE

REMEMBERED MOST OFTEN as the designer of New York City's Central Park, landscape architect Frederick Law Olmsted also contributed his prodigious talents to three Milwaukee landscapes: River Park (now Riverside Park), West Park (now Washington Park), and Lake Park. Newberry Boulevard, which connects Lake Park with River (side) Park, was also an Olmsted contribution.

Known as "gardens for the poor," these parks were earmarked for those urban residents who could not afford their own private lawns. Olmsted designed Lake Park in 1885 and work began in 1889 with the acquisition of land. The last addition, an exercise/jogging trail, was opened in 1978.

Borrowing from the great European parks with their open spaces, large trees, serpentine paths, and natural landscaping, Olmsted orchestrated a bit of heaven in this one hundred forty-acre park. He had some help, of course—the land already featured ravines with streams and Lake Michigan as a backdrop. Olmsted's design added paths, brooks, and waterfalls. A variety of famous names contributed the hardscapes. The Steel Arch and Brick Arch bridges were designed by Oscar Sanne and installed in 1893. Sanne also designed the notable "Lion Bridges" found in the park several years later.

Alfred C. Clas (of Ferry & Clas architects) designed the park's Pavilion, which opened in 1903. The lower level remains open to the public while the first floor houses one of the Bartolotta restaurants, the formal French Lake Park Bistro. One of the most impressive hardscapes is the Grand Staircase built in 1908. Located in back of the Pavilion and descending down to the bottom of a bluff, this Clas contribution connects the structure to Lincoln Memorial Drive. Ferry & Clas also supplied the concrete footbridge that spans Ravine Road.

Olmsted's plan called for "active" and "passive" sites. A six-hole golf course was installed in 1903 and expanded to eighteen holes in 1930. A children's playground was built in 1906 and tennis courts followed in 1909. Lawn bowling was added in 1919.

Trees, shrubs, and wildflowers grace the grounds, but there are several flowerbeds on the property. The Grand Entrance to the park located on Newberry Boulevard sports flowers along the median. An abandoned park flowerbed near the warming house that's used in the winter by ice skaters was restored in 2001 and expanded a year later into a butterfly garden. In 1999, plantings were restored to the planter in the Grand Staircase.

The Grand Staircase features a symmetrical pair of stairs that curves down the hillside. The staircases frame a white stucco "bowl" containing three columnar evergreens "bookended" with a flowering crab tree. A selection of annuals and perennials fill the base of the planter. Four stone pots filled with annuals rest on the railing.

In keeping with Olmsted's passive intent, sixteen "Central Park" style benches with short poetry excerpts are scattered throughout the grounds.

While you're in the area, visit Olmsted's work at River Park (now Riverside Park) at 1500 East Park Place. Located near the Milwaukee River, it was once used for swimming, boating, skating, and curling but industrial pollution of the river affected the park. In 1991, a grassroots effort led by a Riverside University High School teacher reclaimed the park turning it into the Urban Ecology Center (www.urbanecologycenter.org). On the twelve acres of land you'll find the Library of Sustainability, a Citizen Science Program, urban adventures, and the Neighborhood Environmental Education Project. The grounds also include a raccoon maze, a butterfly garden, and playground equipment. The Center recently added a satellite facility at the one hundred thirty five-acre Washington Park, another of Olmsted's Milwaukee legacies.

COUNTY	Milwaukee
ADDRESS	3133 East Newberry Boulevard, Milwaukee
WEBSITE	www.lakeparkfriends.org/history.shtml
DIRECTIONS	From I-43, exit Locust Street to the east. Take Locust to Lake Drive. Turn right at the "T" intersection of Lake and Locust. Take a left at the next possible intersection (Lake Drive and Newberry Boulevard), the entrance to Lake Park. From the west, take I-94 to downtown. Take the center lane (east) onto I-794. Take I-794 to the Lakefront exit, which becomes Lincoln Memorial Drive. Take a left on Ravine Drive. At the first and only stop sign on Ravine Road, turn left to enter the park.
ADMISSION	Free
HOURS	Daily, dawn to dusk.
AMENITIES	Parking lot in Lake Park. Toilets, food, and water inside the lower level.

 ## Lakeside Park

FOND DU LAC

STANDING LIKE AN AGING SENTINEL, the lighthouse on the southern shore of Lake Winnebago in Fond du Lac's Lakeside Park is one but not the only main attraction here. Nearby is an oval piece of land filled with some fifteen beds of bright blossoms. Here you'll find groupings of tiger lilies and formal beds of annuals filled with yellow and orange marigolds, multicolored snapdragons, and red geraniums to name a few selections.

Set in a grassy expanse of lawn dotted with mature evergreens and other trees, the lighthouse beds feature petunias in all colors, alyssum, impatiens,

City of Fond du Lac Parks

Bright beds of annuals fills Lakeside Park

One of the flowerbeds welcoming you to Lakeside Park.

City of Fond du Lac Parks

zinnias, and cannas. The city of Fond du Lac Parks Department plants the beds every year with the input of a semi-retired landscape architect. Fond du Lac High School students grow the annuals in exchange for seeds and materials. Hostas are tucked into the shady bower of the big trees.

Along with the annual beds, the four hundred-acre park provides gardeners with many inspiring plantings. A butterfly garden, situated on an island identified by a pool with a fountain and a double gazebo and filled with perennials, including a mix of large phlox, monarda, irises, alliums, ferns, and yarrows, entices the winged creatures. Hostas trim the pool's edge.

The four corners of the covered bridge feature calla lilies and other perennials. Perennials and shrubs mix it up near the boat dock. There's even a four-season perennial garden. Look for the tree peonies and you'll have found it.

An unusual "rock" garden can be seen at the park's western edge, just a short walk from the lighthouse beds. Constructed on the site of the former Fond du Lac zoo, the fake rocks were part of the mountain goat exhibit. They were relocated to their present location and used as the foundation for the tunnel for the children's train. The intent was to create a four-season garden on top of the tunnel, but damage from rabbits and geese changed that idea. Now the rocks are planted with dahlias, cannas, daisies, various perennials, and any annuals remaining from the lighthouse beds.

COUNTY	Fond du Lac
ADDRESS	West Scott Street, Fond du Lac
PHONE	920/929-2950
DIRECTIONS	Located at the end of North Main Street and West Scott Street. At various locations in the city, North Main Street is also marked U.S. Highways 151, 45, and State Highway 175. The park can also be accessed at West Scott Street and North Park Avenue, which loops around the lighthouse.
ADMISSION	Free
HOURS	Daily, 5 a.m. to 11 p.m.
AMENITIES	Parking lot. Toilets, water, and snack bar available in the park.

Lensmire's Village Gardens

PLOVER

SWEATY EDDY fell off an ore barge in Lake Superior about one hundred years ago and started digging. He broke through the sandy soil in Plover in 2002, missing a few fingers and teeth. At least, that's the story told about the over-sized humanlike sculpture located in front of Lensmire's Village Gardens just south of Stevens Point. Sweaty Eddy and a few other sculptures are highlighted in the pondless water feature at the garden center.

Warren Lensmire has been involved with the greenhouse business since 1973, but when he built Lensmire's Village Gardens in 2000, he wanted not only to sell the product and materials, but to show people how to use them successfully. A portion of the site is devoted to display gardens; a large peacock sculpture sports a tail comprised of several types of annuals including fuschia petunias, blue salvia, and white dusty miller. A twenty-foot wind chime is likely one of the largest ever created, with a four-hundred-pound hand-turned weight.

Mary Lou Santovec

Cherubs line the gazebo path at Lensmire's Village Gardens

Various garden rooms showcase different styles of gardening. There are wildflower borders along the eastern portion of Porter Court. Grass paths separate mixed borders and beds. Hummingbirds love the portion with monarda, gayfeather, petunias, and evergreens. Annuals, cherub statues, and ornamental grasses border a red gravel path that leads to a gazebo and eventually to a pond and a waterfall. Look for a small version of Nessie, the Loch Ness Monster, in the pond.

One of the more unusual hardscapes is a series of small wooden buildings. Originally built as a Christmas display for the Woodward Governor Company, they were later acquired by the Stevens Point Brewery. Lensmire found a home for them on his property and named them after local landmarks: Isherwood School, McDill Mill, Mosier General Store, and St. Bronislava Church. During the summer they're part of the hosta shade garden. In the winter, they're lit to portray a small Christmas village.

Look for the Native American-inspired cross set in the middle of the meditation garden. A Japanese garden is divided into sections representing tranquillity, harmony, and peace. And don't forget to stop by and say hello to Dolly the llama and the goats.

While you're in the area visit Curiosities, a folk art and country keepsakes store, located at 2600 Church Street, Stevens Point. The cottage garden in the front yard of Curiosities is ample distraction from the charming home accessories inside. Curiosities owner, Kathy Blake, inherited the garden when she took over the lease and opened her store. Not a gardener, she's been educating herself on the various plants left in her care. There's bee balm, salvia, bachelor buttons, daylilies, and daisies for color. The bittersweet regularly threatens to overrun the lilacs. The miniature roses, irises, and peonies, along with the lilacs and Russian sage, encourage passersby to stop and sniff the air for their fragrance.

COUNTY	Portage
ADDRESS	2811 Porter Court, Plover
PHONE	715/341-4577
EMAIL	wlensmire@charter.net
WEBSITE	www.lensmiregardens.com
DIRECTIONS	From I-39, take the HH exit, exit 15, and go west to Business Highway 51 (Post Road). Turn south on Post Road. Turn east onto Porter Court.
ADMISSION	Free
HOURS	9 a.m. to 7 p.m. Monday through Friday in June. 9 a.m. to 5 p.m. on Saturday and 9 a.m. to 4 p.m. on Sunday. From July through September, Lensmire's is open from 9 a.m. to 5 p.m. Monday through Saturday and from 10 a.m. to 3 p.m. on Sunday.
AMENITIES	Parking lot. Toilets and water available.

Milwaukee County Zoo
MILWAUKEE

BESIDES BEING A FREDERICK LAW OLMSTED LEGACY, West Park, known today as Washington Park, has another claim to fame. In 1892 it became the West Park Zoo, the precursor for the Milwaukee County Zoo.

By 1937, the twenty-three acre Washington Park Zoo had become one of the most popular zoos in the country, with attendance reaching over one million visitors. But decline in the infrastructure and no room for expansion encouraged city fathers to plan for a new location. Construction began on the Milwaukee County Zoo in 1958, and it opened officially on May 13, 1961.

The zoo's location was once a virgin oak forest. Remnants of that forest include some pre-Civil War trees located on the grounds. You'll also find examples of tulip and sweet gum trees, and a tri-colored beech along the east side of the Peck Center.

There are three official "gardens" on the two hundred acres, but many more planting beds add splashes of color to the site. A Heritage Garden filled with selections of African, Native American, European-Hispanic, and Asian vegetables is located behind the large red dairy barn in the Stackner Family Farm area. A butterfly garden is part of the vegetable garden and the Southeast Wisconsin Master Gardeners maintain both of them.

Also in the Heritage Farm area is a zoo-maintained butterfly garden. A large butterfly topiary identifies the space, if the free-range peacocks don't get your attention before that. Shasta daisies, bee balm, and gaillardia provide a nice meal for the flying beauties.

For the children and the young at heart, zoo horticulturist Ann Hackbarth and her colleague, Noah Huber, have made sure that color is key in every bed. They plant 35,000 annuals every year, many of which are alternanthera, a member of the amaranth family and native to the Florida swamps.

King of the topiary jungle at the zoo

The somewhat unusual flower comes in many colors, including red, yellow, green, and pink.

In choosing alternanthera, Hackbarth is using an old technique that was popular in Europe. The plants are placed in patterns and trimmed or hedged so that the pattern can be seen. Disney uses the plant for its flowerbeds on the grounds of Walt Disney World.

Hackbarth and Huber have filled a forty-foot bed over near the polar bear exhibit with floral penguins and the words "Milwaukee County Zoo." There's also one that spells out "Zoo" in the front mall. The penguin flowerbed contains 10,000 plants and is placed at an angle so the design is visible.

Animal topiaries, crafted from rebar and covered with creeping ficus, are scattered around the grounds. Prisoners in the Milwaukee House of Corrections weld the frames that hold the vines. Look for the giraffe, rhinoceros, and lion topiaries in the same bed as the alternanthera covered "Zoo." Ornamental grasses are utilized for the manes on the lion and giraffe. A train topiary highlights the Safari Train station. Whimsical topiary sea horses decorate the front of the Otto Borchert Family Special Exhibits Building.

There's also interior landscaping done in the bird house and around the ape exhibit. "The birds are tough customers and relatively destructive," said Hackbarth. "They like to peck at things and rip things apart." Plant material is changed out whenever the exhibit switches bird species. During a renovation of the lion and giraffe animal exhibits grasses were added to give them an African safari look. The monkeys on Monkey Island have their own annual border located around the moat. A bed located between the elephant house and the rhinoceros display mimics the pattern found in some nearby wooden giraffe displays.

Potscaping is popular. There are baskets hanging from the pergola outside of the Ralph Evinrude Landing and large pots scattered around the grounds. The zoo is showcasing environmentally friendly practices having installed a green roof of sedums on top of the Karen Peck Katz Conservation Education Center.

COUNTY	Milwaukee
ADDRESS	10001 West Blue Mound Road, Milwaukee
PHONE	Phone: 414/771-5500 or 414/771-3040
WEBSITE	www.milwaukeezoo.org
DIRECTIONS	From I-94, exit 304B (State Highway 100 North). Turn onto Blue Mound Road. The Zoo entrance is about eight blocks from the Highway 100 exit.
ADMISSION	From January 1 to March 31 and from November 1 to December 31: $9 for adults, $6 for children ages 3 to 12 and free for children 2 and under. Senior citizens age 60 and over are $7.50. From April 1 to October 31: $10.50 for adults, $7.50 for children ages 3 to 12 and free to children 2 and under. Senior citizens age 60 and over are $9.50. Milwaukee County residents (with ID) receive $1.75 off of regular Zoo admission every day. On Wednesdays, Milwaukee County residents (with ID) are admitted at a reduced rate of $5.25 for adults and $2.75 for children ages 3 to 12.
HOURS	From October 1 to April 30, 9 a.m. to 4:30 p.m. daily. From May 1 through September 30, 9 a.m. to 5 p.m. Mondays through Saturdays and 9 a.m. to 6 p.m. on Sundays and holidays.
AMENITIES	Parking lot. Toilets, food, and water inside the zoo.

Zoos with Gardens

Lincoln Park Zoo, 1215 North 8th Street, Manitowoc, 920/683-4685

NEW Zoo, 4378 Reforestation Road, Green Bay, 920/434-7841,
info@thenewzoo.com, thenewzoo.com

Racine Zoological Gardens, 200 Goold Street, Racine, 262/636-9189,
info@racinezoo.com, racinezoo.com

Milwaukee County Zoo, 10001 W. Blue Mound Road, Milwaukee, 414/771-3040,
milwaukeezoo.org

Wildwood Zoo, 608 West 17th Street, Marshfield, 715/486-2056,
http://ci.marshfield.wi.us/pr/zoo

Wisconsin Rapids Municipal Zoo, 1911 Gaynor Avenue, Wisconsin Rapids,
715/421-8240, wisrapids.com/index/zoo.html

Menominee Park, Zoo and Little Oshkosh Playground, Hazel Street and Merritt
Avenue, Oshkosh, 920/236-5080

Mitchell Park Horticultural Conservatory

MILWAUKEE

POISED LIKE A TRIO OF SILVER BEEHIVES just south of I-94, the Mitchell Park Horticultural Conservatory offers Wisconsin residents the flavor of both the tropics and the desert without ever having to leave the state.

The current Conservatory, also known affectionately as the Domes, opened in phases during the 1960s. The show dome was the first to open in 1964 followed by the tropical one in 1966 and the arid one in 1967. Former First Lady Ladybird Johnson dedicated the facility.

Each beehive-shaped (not geodesic) dome is one hundred-forty feet across and eighty-five feet high and covered with 2,200 panes of one quarter-inch thick wireglass imported from Germany. In total, one acre of land is under glass.

The show dome rotates through five shows each year. Themed shows are held in spring, summer, and fall. There's a holiday show in December and local garden railroad clubs turn the site into a haven for train buffs during the winter. Each show displays thou-

View from inside the Domes   John Ernst

sands of individual seasonal plants that contribute to the overall theme, including lilies, poinsettias, azaleas, chrysanthemums, tulips, cyclamen, and geraniums.

The show dome also features a waterfall that culminates in a pond. A streambed connects the pond with another water feature that's lined with rocks. An elevated viewing shed provides a place for photographers to shoot that once-in-a-lifetime picture.

The arid dome highlights the variety of desert flora of the American Southwest. Here you'll also find plants that normally reside in the deserts of Africa, Madagascar, South America, and Mexico. Cacti, palms, succulents, and grasses are just some of the species found here. There's also the welwitschia from Africa, jade and dragon trees, and for color, bougainvillea, bird of paradise, and the tabasco plant. The rarest of plants are found in the Madagascar collection.

One of the most striking plants in the arid dome is the Zululand cycad. Although the plant first produced a single cone about seven years ago, it bloomed in late 2006 producing two bright red cones.

The arid dome includes an oasis for displays and plants that don't fit into the represented geography. Free-flying birds make their home in both the arid and tropical domes.

The tropical dome showcases seven hundred fifty species of tropical plants including a variety of orchids and food and economic plants. Look for the guava and avocado, the banana, orange, and macadamia nut trees. A cacao tree called Ol' Methuselah, was transplanted from the original Mitchell Park Conservatory that was torn down in 1955. For the next decade, its home was the Milwaukee County Greenhouse Center until the tropical dome opened.

A kapok tree, whose white, fluffy seed covering was used for packaging as well as stuffing for life vests, is the largest tree in all of the domes. In the wild it can grow to one hundred fifty feet or more. It once grew through the top of the tropical dome before regular pruning became part of its schedule. Other plants of interest here include curare, a poison applied to darts, and the chicle tree, which produces the latex found in Chiclets gum.

COUNTY	Milwaukee
ADDRESS	524 South Layton Boulevard, Milwaukee
PHONE	414/649-9830
DIRECTIONS	The Domes are located on South Layton Boulevard, which is also South 27th Street, a major thoroughfare. Due to construction on the Marquette Interchange, some of the traditional routes may be blocked. Go to www.mchange.org for up-to-date road information. From the west, take I-94 east to 26th Street/St. Paul Avenue (exit 309B). Turn left onto St. Paul at the first traffic light and drive one block west to 27th Street. Turn left and go south through the viaduct. The parking lot is on your left. From the east, take I-94 West to 22nd and Clybourn streets (exit 309B). Turn left at the traffic light and go west on Clybourn until you reach 27th Street. Turn left and go south through the viaduct. From the south, take I-94 west over the High Rise Bridge to 22nd and Clybourn streets (exit 309B). Turn left at the traffic light and go west on Clybourn until you reach 27th Street. Turn left and go south through the viaduct.
ADMISSION	$5 for those 18 and up; $3.50 for Milwaukee County seniors ages 60 and up with proof of residency; $3.50 for people with disabilities and for those ages 6 to 17. Admission is free for all Milwaukee County residents with proof of residency from 9 a.m. to 11:30 a.m. Mondays (excluding major holidays).
HOURS	Daily, 9 a.m. to 5 p.m.
AMENITIES	Parking lot. Toilets, water, and food inside the Domes.

Monches Farm

COLGATE

SEVERAL DECADES AGO, Scott Sieckman began his horticultural career by growing flowers to sell at Madison's Farmers Market. Customer feedback encouraged him to branch out into potted perennials and eventually to onsite sales. So, twenty-eight years ago he purchased fourteen acres with an original farmhouse in Washington County and created Monches Farm. Today, three businesses operate out of that property outside of Colgate, all symbiotically intertwined: a perennial nursery; a gift shop that includes dried flowers, many grown and dried onsite; and garden design and installation.

Until recently, Sieckman lived in the farmhouse, to which he had attached an old log cabin that he disassembled and moved to the property. With plants, art, and antiques as his passions, his former personal gardens have provided a canvas for this Renaissance man to indulge in his love of plants.

This is no case of the shoemaker's kids going barefoot. Sieckman definitely has a green thumb. The home's backyard is filled with hidden spaces and paths wind from one direction to another. There's always a surprise waiting around a curve from stone architectural replicas to a former formal knot garden that has evolved into a rather eclectic composite of formality and informality. Trimmed balls of boxwood and espaliered pear trees share space with a willy-nilly compilation of plants, as if the ghosts of a great English estate had taken over a ho-hum backyard but left unexpectedly. A handmade picket fence crafted from small logs, borders the former knot garden. You hear the water feature, a lily-filled pond with a small waterfall, before you can see it. A canopy of mature trees has provided a very welcoming home for some of the larger hosta varieties.

The front yard has a Victorian air about it. Multiple beds of perennials have almost hidden the front of the house, sheltering several classical statues of women. Curving borders of perennials around the lawn feature selections of daylilies, shrub roses, cranesbill, euphorbia, hollyhocks, and ferns.

There's a glass house on the property that Sieckman found in Milwaukee, dismantled, and moved to the farm. It houses a collection of succulents and several aviaries. Chickens, sheep, even a peacock could be considered part of the landscape.

The farm specializes in more than three hundred varieties of daylilies and two hundred of hostas. The plants are potted and then sunk into the ground to overwinter in the Wisconsin cold under harsher conditions than you'd find in a private garden. Native plants are also grown in the same way. Unusual annuals including scented geraniums and kiss me over the garden gate as well as tropicals such as elephant ears, coleus, and other foliage plants are also for sale.

COUNTY	Washington
ADDRESS	5890 Monches Road, Colgate
PHONE	262/966-2787
WEBSITE	www.monchesfarm.com
DIRECTIONS	**From the east:** Take U.S. Highways 41/45 north, exit County Highway Q. Go west on Q to Monches Road. Turn to the right. **From the west:** Take I-94 and exit State Highway 83 (Hartland/Delafield). Go north to Highway Q. Go east on Q to Monches Road. Turn to the left.
ADMISSION	Free
HOURS	**Winter hours:** (January 25 to March 31), 10 a.m. to 4 p.m. Thursday through Sunday. Closed Monday, Tuesday, and Wednesday. **Growing season hours:** (April 1 to November 30), 10 a.m. to 5 p.m. Tuesday through Friday, 10 a.m. to 4 p.m. Saturday and Sunday, closed Mondays. **Holiday hours:** (December), 10 a.m. to 4 p.m. Monday, Saturday, and Sunday. 10 a.m. to 5 p.m. Tuesday through Friday. Closed on Easter, July 4, Labor Day, Thanksgiving, Christmas Day, and New Year's Day.
AMENITIES	Gravel parking lot. Toilets and water available on the property.

Northwind Perennial Farm

BURLINGTON

DO YOU HAVE THUGS IN YOUR GARDEN? No, not the bunnies and deer that like to eat the tender shoots of your favorite perennials. I'm talking about those sneaky plants that looked so tiny in the pots, but when planted turned into Audrey II, the man-eating plant from the Little Shop of Horrors. Thug plants devour all of the space around them leaving no room for anything else to grow.

Roy Diblick, one of a trio of owners of Northwind Perennial Farm outside of Burlington, aims to get rid of garden thugs. And the farm's display gardens provide an attractive visual of how to do it.

Diblick subscribes to what Dutch landscape architect Piet Oudolf calls "New Wave Planting" style. Relaxed and natural, this style tries to create an

"New Wave Planting" at Northwind

"idealized view of nature" with an emphasis on "form, texture, and the natural harmony of plants." The objective is to create easy-to-care-for spaces and four-season interest.

Diblick calls his system "Know Maintenance." Too many gardeners will buy what catches their eye without a thought as to the care that the purchase will require, he said. Utilizing the "Know Maintenance" premise, plants that like to be together in the same space are grouped to create a plant community that supports life rather than one that continually fights for resources. Think of a prairie, said Diblick; it's a closed community so it doesn't have weeds.

At Northwind, Diblick and his colleagues, Steve Coster and Colleen Garrigan, have created four contemporary "Know Maintenance" garden communities: Out of Bohemia, Another Morning, A Celebration within the Leaves, and One Gorgeous Day. Each one comes with instructions on how to replicate it in an eight-foot by twelve-foot space at home. In the Out of Bohemia garden for example, there's echinacea, saliva, alliums, asters, daylilies, and amsonia mixed with ornamental grass and blue false indigo. There's a sign that lists the amount of hours staff have contributed to weed the communities. It's less than you'd expect for such a large space.

The garden communities are set in beds around a serpentine path that leads to a stone pyramid placed in a circular bed of gravel. That's another of Diblick's ideas for sustainable gardening. Taking a page from the Germans, the natives and grasses are planted around the pyramid in four inches of gray gravel. They live or die on their own without water or care. During the second year, the hardiest plants will fill in and cover the gravel, which acts as a natural weed barrier.

From the stone pyramid, the path changes from wood chips to flagstones and meanders around several water features, with and without waterfalls. The plantings around the water features are a bit more controlled. Whimsical garden art, including a half-submerged mermaid and a metal sculpture of a bloodhound with his catch of the day, graces one of the ponds. Several varieties of dwarf conifers are set along this portion of the path.

Northwind, located on the site of a century-old dairy farm, includes several small red outbuildings with gardens placed around them. One of the mature trees near the chicken coop is hung with glass balls. The large barn features a collection of garden gifts and books. Look for the large urn filled with cut flowers inside the stone silo.

Mature black walnut trees provide the canopy for the site's woodland garden. Diblick wants to disabuse the public of the notion that nothing will grow under a black walnut. Granted, many annuals and vegetables have difficulty because of juglone, a chemical that the trees produce, but most perennials tolerate it quite well. Lots of examples of Victorian-style garden art are tucked among the hostas and ferns.

The farm's perennials have gotten rave reviews from some important customers. Northwind supplied all of the plantings for Chicago's Lurie Garden at Millennium Park as well as the Grand Geneva Resort in Lake Geneva.

COUNTY	Walworth
ADDRESS	7047 Hospital Road, Burlington
PHONE	262/248-8229
WEBSITE	www.northwindperennialfarm.com
DIRECTIONS	From Milwaukee, take I-43 south to State Highway 120/Lake Geneva exit. Turn left/south onto Highway 120 and continue for eight-and-one-half miles to Hospital Road. Turn left and go one-quarter mile. From the south, take I-94 West to State Highway 50 West. Stay on Highway 50 West for thirty miles to Lake Geneva. In Lake Geneva, turn north on Highway 120 and continue for three miles to Springfield. At the bottom of the hill, turn right on Hospital Road.
ADMISSION	Free
HOURS	9 a.m. to 5 p.m. daily, mid-April through mid-October. Northwind is also open from 10 a.m. to 4 p.m. daily mid-November through mid-December for their Christmas events. It is closed on Thanksgiving.
AMENITIES	Gravel parking lot. Toilets.

❧ Old World Wisconsin

EAGLE

LOVERS OF HERITAGE GARDENS will find much to enjoy at Old World Wisconsin located just outside the village of Eagle. There are thirteen heirloom gardens scattered among the twelve historic sites on this 576-acre living museum.

John Ernst

To represent life in various towns in Wisconsin during the 1800s, the costumed interpreters at each ethnic site grow what the immigrants would have grown during a particular year. With food critical for survival, most of the gardens showcase heritage or heirloom varieties of vegetables and fruits; however, there are flower and herb gardens worth noting at several sites.

The Sanford House has the most extensive gardens. Representing the homestead of a well-to-do Yankee farmer in 1860, the home and grounds are located in the Yankee Village at the first stop for the tram. Here, vegetables are planted in straight lines in a large rectangle. A formal herb garden is carved out of the rectangle. Triangular raised beds filled with a variety of herbs are arranged

A scarecrow in period costume at Old World Wisconsin

to form a star pattern. A sundial, placed in the center of the star, acts as a focal point. A cutting garden is also part of the Sanford House gardens. Flowers were grown to dry and hang inside the house.

Second only to the Sanford House are the gardens at the Schulz Farm, an 1856 structure located in the German section. Here, a walkway bisects the frontyard. On the left, outlined with rocks and split with a path, are the flower gardens. A series of squares are planted with vegetables, herbs, and some flowers to the right of the walkway. Flax is one of the herbs found in this garden. An interesting fence crafted from tree branches encloses the property.

In the wealthier 1893 Ketola House, a Finnish homestead from Bayfield County, two strips of blue and white cornflowers capture attention. Cardamom, dill, and sweet marjoram are grown here. Across the road at the Rankinen House, another Finnish example from Bayfield County, a bed of pinks, irises, and wild roses grows in front of this 1892 home. Beds of tiger lilies can be found around many of the homes.

A "walking onion" and other herbs can be found in the garden at the 1872 Pedersen house in the Danish area. The 1848 Kvaale House in the Norwegian section features gooseberries, plants for dyeing wool, and teasel, a plant that when dry would be used for carding wool.

Seeds for the gardens are acquired from several places including the Seeds Savers Exchange, Seeds of Change, and Forbes Seeds. Stock plants are used to propagate plants for the garden. The park's staff also collects seeds from the plants in the gardens.

The museum is located on what was a pine plantation planted by the Department of Natural Resources. Along the gravel road linking the villages, trees representing both northern and southern Wisconsin are evident. One side has hardwoods and blue spruce found in southern Wisconsin. But look across the road and you'll swear you're up north with the stately pines towering over the land.

The Southeast Wisconsin Master Gardeners group plants the gardens located in front and back of the Clausing Barn Restaurant as well as those located at the entrance to the gift shop. There's a shade garden with ferns, coleus, impatiens, and bush violets. Other shade beds hold ligularias, bleeding heart, hostas, and native plants. A birdbath in the sunny cottage garden is encircled with heirloom annuals and perennials. Chocolate mint, lemon grass, and bronze fennel are some of the varieties found in the herb garden, which the cooks harvest for use in the restaurant. The fence screening the patio has rugosa roses, black-eyed Susans, purple coneflowers, and other butterfly attracting plants. Swiss chard, scented geraniums, and petunias fill five large wooden pots. The gardeners have recently installed a 9/11 Memorial Garden on the property.

COUNTY	Waukesha
ADDRESS	S103 W37890 State Highway 67, Eagle
PHONE	262/594-6300 or 262/594-6342
EMAIL	oww@whs.wisc.edu
WEBSITE	http://wisconsinhistory.org/oww/details.asp
DIRECTIONS	Located 1.5 miles south of Eagle on State Highway 67.
ADMISSION	$14 for adults, $12.80 seniors, and $8.50 for children 5 to 17. Family price: $39 for two adults and two children; additional children, $3 each. From September 4 through October 31, buy one, get one free on weekdays.
HOURS	The park opens May 1. Between May 1 and July 1 call or visit the Web site for specific hours and times. 10 a.m. to 5 p.m. Monday through Saturday and noon to 5 p.m. Sundays from July 1 through September 3. 10 a.m. to 3 p.m. weekdays and 10 a.m. to 5 p.m. Saturday and noon to 5 p.m. Sunday from September 4 through October 31.
AMENITIES	Parking lot. Toilets, food, and water available in the Clausing Barn Restaurant. Some toilets and water are available on the grounds.

 Pauquette Park

PORTAGE

NESTLED INTO THE CURVE of State Highway 33 as it enters the city of Portage from the west is the 8.8-acre Pauquette Park. A terraced flower garden with a water feature and waterfall are some of the features that can be found in this historic park.

Named for French fur trader Pierre Pauquette, the park was originally a brickyard that manufactured the bricks that built many Portage homes. Landscape architect John Nolen was instrumental in the park's layout. The brickyard was eventually dredged to form the pond mentioned in author Zona Gale's fictional short story, "Bridal Pond," which was based on a true story about a young couple on their honeymoon who missed the curve on Highway 33, drove into the pond, and drowned.

An inmate at the Waupun Correctional Institute made two new wrought iron bridges. View the entire park from the gazebo. There are walking paths and mature trees that ring the pond and a spray of water that juts up from the pond's surface. The memorial wooden bridal arch is attached to a stone wall on the park's east side.

The community garden was installed during the 1990s and a local Kiwanis Club took the lead in its restoration. Now various organizations, families, and Kiwanis each sponsor a small portion of the raised beds. Sponsors' efforts are rewarded with handpainted signs.

Gravel walkways are edged with fieldstone. Since it's an adopt-a-plot garden, the beds are eclectic. You'll find ornamental grasses, Siberian irises, lilacs, tulips, hostas, and daisies just to name a few of the community members' favorite plants. A small waterfall ends in a water garden ringed with cattails and aquatic plants.

COUNTY	Columbia
ADDRESS	West Conant Street and State Highway 33, Portage
DIRECTIONS	From I-39, take Highway 33 (exit 87) and head east. Turn left on Conant Street.
ADMISSION	Free
HOURS	8 a.m. to 10 p.m. daily, year-round.
AMENITIES	Parking lot. Toilets and water available.

 ## Watertown High School International Peace Garden

WATERTOWN

ALL GARDENS BY THEIR VERY NATURE ARE PEACEFUL. However, the two-acre International Peace Garden enjoyed by staff and students at Watertown High School takes the peace aspect a bit more literally.

The garden had two inspirations: the Canadian botanist Henry Moore who presented his idea for a peace garden to a national association of gardeners in 1929 and the International Peace Garden located between North

Meridian 1 is set among the plantings at the Watertown High School International Peace Garden

Dakota and Canada. Cognizant of both Moore's speech and the international site, Steve Jacobson, a social studies teacher at Watertown High School, thought the idea of a peace garden would make a positive contribution to learning. The garden, located in front of the high school's entrance, is open to the public.

Anchored on the north end by a three-tiered semi-circle stone amphitheater and on the south end by *Meridian 1*, Edward McCullough's innovative sculpture on the circle of life, the garden offers a welcome respite for all who enter it. Granite benches set on red brick pavers are carved with various quotes relating to peace. Other hardscapes include a bronze crane sculpture, an oversize kaleidoscope planter, and a sundial.

Various plants, shrubs, and trees frame an expanse of grass that invites students to lie down and ponder the mysteries of life. Plant selections include both annuals and perennials. The original intent was to select plants with some international connection such as Japanese lilacs and a Chinese rose bush. Eventually, through memorial and other donations, the garden took on a life of its own. Spirea, peonies, hostas, petunias, columbine, lilies, and sedum are just some of the varieties giving life to the garden's public and private spaces.

Jacobson hopes to expand the garden's intent by planting trees along the boulevard leading from the highway into the high school driveway. A prairie restoration is underway across the north side of Endeavor Drive.

Teleidoscope planter at the Peace Garden

COUNTY	Dodge
ADDRESS	825 Endeavor Drive, Watertown
PHONE	920/262-7500
DIRECTIONS	From State Highways 26/16, go west on Endeavor Drive. The high school is located on the north side of Watertown.
ADMISSION	Free
HOURS	Daily, dawn to dusk.
AMENITIES	Parking lot. Toilets, water, and vending machines located inside Watertown High School.

Village of Kohler, Botanical Gardens
KOHLER

AS THE FIRST FULLY DEVELOPED GARDEN COMMUNITY in the United States, the village of Kohler provides a testament to sensible urban planning. The story began in 1913 when Walter J. Kohler, Sr., head of the Kohler Company, traveled abroad to view the work of Sir Ebenezer Howard, the god-father of the garden community movement. The movement, a backlash against the Industrial Revolution, emphasized designing limited-population communities with the exterior edge reserved for industry and transportation and the internal portion devoted to residential homes and parks.

Enamored of the concept, Kohler hired the Olmsted Brothers' firm to design, based on Howard's vision, the layout of the green spaces that beautify the Village of Kohler and the Kohler Company. After the initial fifty-year mas-ter plan expired in 1977, the Frank Lloyd Wright Foundation was hired to update it for fifty more.

In 2004, the village applied for and received approval from the American Public Gardens Association to become a registered botanical garden. As part of the approval process, the village had to identify places where people could view garden areas. Various gardens are scattered throughout this bucolic community.

The gateway to the gardens is the Kohler Gardener, located at The Shops at Woodlake. With its butterfly garden filled with natives, ornamental grasses, and annuals, the space attracts caterpillars and hummingbirds as well as but-terflies. Look for the usual suspects: purple coneflowers, black-eyed Susans, gaillardia, and lamb's quarters. There are also some unusual offerings, howev-er, including 'White Swan' echinacea, globe thistle, and fireweed. Grass paths lead through the space.

The emphasis on gardens continues. More than twenty-five stores in The Shops are bordered with beds of pink shrub roses. Masses of color are splashed around the parking lots.

Just south of The Shops is the Arts/Industry Walk, a three-quarter mile path past thirty-two outdoor sculptures and flowerbeds. Artists who partici-pated in the Kohler Company's Arts/Industry program created all the sculp-tures. This collaboration invites artists to work side-by-side with employees of the Kohler Company and utilize the company's materials and technologies. Look for *Glove Fish*, a collection of discarded factory workers' gloves assembled in the shape of a fish and then cast in bronze.

If your taste runs to less-structured groups of plants, take the Prairie and Arboretum Walk. Beginning at the Inn on Woodlake, the walk takes you west through the prairie. The twenty-acre arboretum is located northeast of the intersection of Greenfield Drive and Woodland Road southwest of The Shops. The arboretum is home to more than one hundred fifty varieties of shade and ornamental trees. One of the most magnificent varieties is the white pine.

Once the largest and longest-lived tree in Wisconsin, the forests of white pine that once covered much of Wisconsin fell to the lumberman's axe from the 1880s to the 1930s. The ones in the arboretum are not quite one hundred years old, but they nonetheless tower above all the other trees.

The Arboretum is one of four community parks that include Ravine Park. Designed by the Olmsted Brothers, the Nature Theater in Ravine Park received the American Society of Landscape Architects' National Medallion Award in 2000 for design and long-term preservation of the space.

At the Kohler Design Center, potscaping is the rage. Every set of doors is flanked with large pots filled with caladium, begonias, cannas, and other annuals. There are also beds full of colorful shrubs and flowers placed around the building's front and sides. Some are formal, like a parterre of clipped hedges. Flowers are interspersed with sculptures. The emphasis here is on creativity in keeping with the trend-setting design going on inside the building.

The center, which showcases designer kitchens and the company's bath products, covers a complete city block. The building also contains the Appleby Theater, the Wellness Business, and the Kohler Waters Spa.

There are various gardens at Waelderhaus, a rendition of the ancestral Kohler family home in the Bregenzerwald region of Austria. Free guided tours are conducted daily at 2 p.m., 3 p.m., and 4 p.m. except on holidays, and you're able to explore the grounds and gardens at your leisure.

The woodland trails of River Wildlife that run through more than five hundred acres of land are open only to guests of The American Club, the Inn on Woodlake, or with a private membership. Those hitting the links at Blackwolf Run or the PGA championship Whistling Straits golf courses will find an abundance of natural landscaping that's heavy on ornamental grasses. The entry road to Blackwolf Run is meant to be a driving garden with massed plantings of native and prairie plants. The Kohler landscapers describe the 27,000 perennials planted there like a "Monet painting." Nine varieties of narcissus appear in the spring. Visitors are welcomed at the clubhouses.

Courtesy of The American Club

Several gardens at The American Club

The emphasis on floral artistry really peaks at The American Club with its eight striking gardens. The Midwest's only Five Diamond resort hotel certainly doesn't skimp when it comes to plants.

Ever-changing entrance and exit flowerbeds greet guests as they drive onto the grounds of The American Club. 'Krossas Regal' hostas are offset with ageratum, alternanthera, and geraniums. Unusual conifers can be found in the American Classic Garden. Peonies, daylilies, ornamental grasses, and roses are mixed with broadmoor juniper, nest spruce, weeping Norway spruce, and Swiss stone pine.

A large cedar arbor covered with porcelain vine, clematis, and Engleman ivy is located in the Wisconsin Room Garden, a foyer for the Wisconsin Room restaurant. The bluestone terrace is surrounded with perennials such as Christmas fern, thorn apple, foam flower, and veronica. Holly, privet, and smoke bush shrubs provide some vertical interest.

Arborvitae hedges and a canopy of four littleleaf linden trees enclose the outdoor dining area of the Linden Terrace. In surroundings planted to resemble an English country garden, diners will find colorful window boxes filled with impatiens, sweet potato vine, asparagus fern, and coleus. The lindens are supplemented with serviceberry, magnolia, and arborvitae turning the site into a shade lovers' paradise. The requisite hosta thrive here, as do the lungworts, great Solomon's seal, wintercreeper, and lilies.

A replica of an early twentieth century gazebo is the focal point of the Gazebo Courtyard. Tables and chairs provide intimate seating around annual beds planted with alternanthera, begonias, alyssum, creeping Jenny, verbena, and coleus. Elephant ears are added for height along with boxwood, yew, and dwarf bottlebrush shrubs. A few perennials, specifically chives and lamb's ear, are thrown in for good measure. Circling the gazebo is a display of caladium, dicondra, and impatiens. Ferns, lilies, hostas, and clematis add both height and texture. Look for the contorted filbert's unusual structure.

Across from the Gazebo Courtyard are the Cloister Walk and Fountain Courtyard with the *Scarf Dancer* fountain as the focal point. The courtyard gardens feature a colorful backdrop of annuals, perennials, shrubs, and trees with a few groundcovers supplementing the designs. You'll find lantana and cannas, junipers and yew. In the perennial garden, roses are prevalent as are natives and hostas. This space includes The Greenhouse, an English antique solarium that was dismantled and reassembled here. It's a treat to savor your coffee and dessert with some natural eye candy.

The Lantern Courtyard is named for the handcrafted copper lanterns filled with leaded glass hanging on hand-hewn cedar poles topped with pointed finials. The American Club's architecture is complemented in the poles' design. Here the focal point is a specimen Scotch pine. The fir, along with several pear trees, provides privacy for the guest rooms that overlook the garden.

Perennials are added for seasonal impact. Look for the large-leafed gas plant (*dictamus albus*), several species of peonies including a fern-leaf variety, and ornamental grasses. Climbing hydrangea, twelve varieties of shrubs, and a dwarf fothergilla fill in the space. California is a distance away, but the redwood tree seems to like it here.

A stream meanders through the Prairie Woodland Courtyard, home to Midwest natives—Wisconsin trees, shrubs, and wildflowers that blanket the space. Look for monkey flower, trilliums, and wild sasparilla. Viburnums and witchhazel represent the middle layer, while beech, filbert, and hornbeam trees add vertical interest.

The latest addition to the gardens is technical rather than natural. Self-guided tour wands have multiple tour stops with audio information highlighting the flowers and plant life featured in a particular section. Historical information is included when applicable. Each of three garden tours is color-coded on a map you receive when you rent the hand-held wand. Wands can be rented at multiple locations, including The Kohler Gardener and the Inn on Woodlake, located at The Shops at Woodlake Kohler, and at The American Club. The cost is $10 and the wand can be used for the entire day.

COUNTY	Sheboygan
ADDRESS	1115 West Riverside Drive, Kohler
PHONE	920/458-5570
EMAIL	BotanicalGardens@kohler.com
WEBSITE	www.DestinationKohler.com
DIRECTIONS	From I-43, exit 126 (Kohler).
ADMISSION	Free
HOURS	Open 24 hours a day, year-round.
AMENITIES	Street parking. Toilets, food, and water inside the retail shops.

Poetry Garden, Beloit College
BELOIT

WRITERS OFTEN USE POETRY to capture the beauty of a flower. What better place to try your hand at some verse than at the Poetry Garden located on the campus of Beloit College.

The garden anchors the south end of the campus next to the Logan Museum of Anthropology and functions as a destination for both the campus and the community. Designed by Minneapolis-based artist, Siah Armajani, for the courtyard of the Lannan Foundation in Los Angeles in 1992, the garden was reinstalled on the Beloit campus in 1999 after the foundation moved its headquarters. Armajani also designed some of the sculptures found around campus.

A Prairie-style set of gates in blue-green steel defines the garden entrance on Bushnell Street. This same design theme and materials are utilized throughout the garden and across campus. A Prairie-style steel fence topped with four book holders borders a rectangular space in the garden. Plants and ceramic urns reside inside the space.

Near the Bushnell entrance is a "hidden" garden room featuring a wooden picnic bench. An oak tree provides the shade for the hostas that surround the wooden walkway leading to the table.

The 14,000-square-foot garden contains a variety of plantings, including daylilies, lamb's quarters, irises, daisies, and hostas. Perennial borders line the walkway leading to the garden from College Street and outline the spaces within the garden. In the spring, more than 10,000 tulips bloom. A beautiful bougainvillea clings to the corner of the oldest portion of the anthropology museum on the west end of the garden.

The garden is frequently utilized for events including classes, weddings, college receptions, and, of course, poetry readings. Three "picnic benches" provide various-sized platforms for speakers, teachers, and performers. Wooden single and double chairs set on brushed steel frames are arranged in orderly fashion on the brick patio. Elsewhere, the chairs are placed in more intimate configurations. The garden is open and lit around the clock for quiet reading, meditation, or simply observing. The college hopes to install more than 6,000 new plantings over the next five years eventually making this garden truly an urban oasis.

Elsewhere on the campus, the Pierpont J.E. Wood Conservatory greenhouse is open by appointment. Annuals and perennials can also be found in two oversized concrete planters on campus, one next to the greenhouse and the other that fronts "The Wall" a popular student gathering spot. The flowers in the planter located next to the greenhouse provide a supportive backdrop to Arnold Popinsky's large cast aluminum sculpture.

COUNTY	Rock
ADDRESS	Beloit College, located at the corner of College and Bushnell streets, Beloit
WEBSITE	www.beloit.edu
PHONE	608/363-2215
DIRECTIONS	From I-90 South, take the South Beloit exit and drive west to the third stoplight, which is Park Avenue. Turn right onto Park Avenue and drive north through two stoplights. Continue up the hill until you reach Chapin Street. Turn left on Chapin and you'll see Middle College two blocks ahead. Continue on Chapin until it intersects with College Street. From State Highway 81 West, follow the highway until it crosses the Rock River. Turn south on Pleasant Street. Turn east on Bushnell Street followed by a left turn at College Street. From I-43/State Highway 81 exit off of I-/90; I-43 ends and becomes Milwaukee Road. Follow it into Beloit and after crossing the railroad tracks, veer left to remain on Milwaukee Road. Follow it to Chapin Street and turn right.
ADMISSION	Free
HOURS	24 hours a day; the garden is lit at night.
AMENITIES	Street parking. Tables and chairs. Toilets and water located inside campus buildings.

Regner Park Labyrinth

WEST BEND

ARCHAEOLOGICAL EVIDENCE points to the existence of labyrinths as far back as 3,500 years ago. The labyrinth in West Bend's Regner Park has taken the past, updated it a bit, and become a real presence in the city.

Installed in 2005 the walkable grass pathways in this seven-circuit, Cretan-style labyrinth are lined with bulbs, perennials, annuals, and herbs. It was the brainchild of Barbara Robertson, whose daughter-in-law was involved in creating a similar labyrinth in Montana.

Community members maintain this interactive garden. Cantaloupe-sized rocks mark each two-foot by fifteen-foot section so that the volunteers know how much maintenance they're responsible for. Irrigation was installed so that the garden's beauty wouldn't have to rely on Mother Nature. The hardscapes are minimal: engraved "celebration" stones that outline the labyrinth's exterior, brick pavers that frame each circuit, a small bench, and a trellis in the middle of this ninety-foot diameter structure.

Gateway Technical College has installed eight new Horticulture Learning Lab gardens for student use including Butterfly, Southeast, Spring, Formal, Cottage, Fall, Wisconsin, and Dwarf Conifer gardens. Each garden provides students with a design challenge and an opportunity to study plant identification and maintenance.

Those who use the garden for meditation are treated to a selection of seasonal blooms: irises and daffodils in spring; columbine, phlox, sedum, chives, dianthus, and carnations later on.

While you're in West Bend, stop by the Robert J. Steiner Enabling Garden, a sensory garden for the blind and disabled located at The Threshold, a few miles away from Regner Park at 600 Rolfs Avenue. There you will see various beds filled with ornamental grasses, flowering shrubs, junipers, and boulders. Planters surrounding a gazebo are filled with annuals. Three latticework arbors support clematis and vines. A wishing well disguises a fountain.

Another small flower labyrinth can be found at St. Joseph's Catholic Church, 1619 Washington Street, Grafton. A birch tree anchors this structure, which consists of circuits flanked with clumps of yellow stella d'oro lilies and grass pathways. The labyrinth is located on the east side of the church. A small stone bench completes the site.

COUNTY	Washington
ADDRESS	Regner Park, 800 North Main Street, West Bend
PHONE	262/338-6903
EMAIL	Info@westbendlabyrinth.com
WEBSITE	www.westbendlabyrinth.com
DIRECTIONS	From State Highway 33, turn north onto State Highway 114. Regner Park is on the west side of the street. Look for the big bronze sculpture called *Tableau in Steel* that identifies the park's entrance.
ADMISSION	Free
HOURS	Daily, dawn to dusk.
AMENITIES	Parking lot. Toilets and water at the park.

Greendale Village Center

GREENDALE

ONE OF THE THREE GREENBELT TOWNS developed under the administration of President Franklin D. Roosevelt during the 1940s, Greendale's urban center was framed with a "greenbelt" of gardens, parks, and farms. And thanks to Roy Reiman, founder of Reiman Publications, it has a new status as "The Best Blooming Town in the Country."

Since 1988 when Reiman decided to move some flowers from the company's corporate headquarters to the village, more than 40,000 flowers have been planted along Broad and the other Village Center streets each year. Color is key so you'll likely find geraniums, coleus, zinnias, and impatiens planted in boulevard beds. Pots might be full of begonias, impatiens, dichondra, phlox, and spikes. You could find baskets hanging from the globe streetlights full of petunias, verbena, vinca, and sweet potato vines. The selections change each year.

Head south down Broad Street to Dale Park where you'll see an archway on your left. A bridge will take you over Dale Creek to a large daffodil garden planted in the shape of a rising sun. To make the village the "Daffodale Capital of the United States," subscribers of Reiman's *Birds and Blooms* magazine were asked to send in one daffodil bulb. Overwhelmed with the 54,000 bulbs it

Reiman Publications

"Daffodil Capital of the United States"

received, the publishing company planted 7,000 of them, creating one ray for every state in the Union and one for Canada. The extra bulbs were given to local residents. During the summer, annuals, usually red salvia, replace the sun's daffodil rays. The roses in Dale Park are the 'Knockout' variety, named Rose of the Year in 2001.

COUNTY	Milwaukee
ADDRESS	Broad Street, Greendale
PHONE	414/423-3080 or 414/423-3111
WEBSITE	www.greendale.org
DIRECTIONS	**From the north, east, and west,** take I-894 and exit 60th Street. Head south about a mile to Grange Avenue. Continue south as 60th Street becomes Northway and curves right into the downtown where the flowers are located. **From the south,** take South 51st Street north until you reach Grange Avenue. Head west and then take 60th Street south to Northway.
ADMISSION	Free
HOURS	Seasonal. Daily, dawn to dusk
AMENITIES	Parking lot. Toilets, water, and food inside the Reiman Visitor's Center, which is open 9 a.m. to 5 p.m. Monday through Saturday. Other options can be found along Broad Street.

Riverside Park

BELOIT

BACK IN THE 1930S, Riverside Park was a popular playground for the city of Beloit. Photos from that time show highly stylized sunken gardens; unfortunately those gardens were filled in and the space used for industrial activities. Once industry moved out, the space was all but abandoned.

Six decades later, Jeff Adams and a group of citizens calling themselves the Friends of Riverside thought that the park, hugging the banks of the Rock River, should be restored to its former glory, albeit with a different set of priorities. With that in mind, the group has set out to reclaim the space with plantings and public art, two components that attract the most attention.

 Along Highway 33 just east of Beaver Dam is the *Crystal Creek Dairy.* The owners have developed a large tiered garden that includes a gazebo, benches, and gravel paths just to the west of the building. Perennials, annuals, trees, and shrubs decorate the hillside.

It's hard to miss O.V. Shaffer's thirty-one foot sculpture called *Celebration.* Created for the fiftieth anniversary of the Warner Electric Company in Roscoe, Illinois, the company donated it to Beloit as a centerpiece for the park. Wildflowers and prairie grasses, specifically little bluestem, were chosen for their symbolism. "Beloit is at the edge of the metal banding part of the country and the start of the prairie," said Adams. The sculpture honors the city's industrial history and its location near native lands.

Across from the Beloit Inn on a wall that's part of the old Beloit Iron Works are murals representing the people who worked in the factory. Further west, Siah Armanjani, who designed the Poetry Garden at Beloit College, added his creativity to the locomotive atop of the trestle bridge.

The city contains many turtle effigy mounds. Artist Marina Lee, with help from Beloit's fifth graders, crafted a turtle geoglyph that's placed on the park's northeast end. The mosaic tiles are interplanted with a variety of alpine plants including creeping thyme. Shaffer continued the amphibious theme with *Source*, a golden turtle sculpture sandwiching a copper rectangle. It sits at the entrance to the Rotary River Center, encircled with colorful annuals.

The twenty three-acre park features a three-and-one-half mile recreational paved path that's bordered with beds of annuals and perennials. The red and pink 'Knock Out' variety of roses planted at the park's entrance coupled with some 'Carefree Beauty' varieties for height bid a cheery welcome.

The gates and picnic shelter near the Whitman Street bridge feature 'Karl Forester' grass, 'Purple Wave' petunias, and 'King Humbert' dark-leaved cannas, a plant from the Victorian era that accents the green ironwork and red brick

Jeff Adams

Celebration sculpture is part of the reclamation efforts at Riverside Park from which all the park structures are made, said Loris Damerow, a master gardener who was in charge of the plantings. A multi-season perennial garden sits at the base of the Rotary flags.

A fountain with four jets of water rising from the lagoon makes a stunning statement. Wetland plants hug the lagoon. Many concrete pots filled with annuals are placed along the river in back of the Rotary River Center.

COUNTY	Rock
ADDRESS	Pleasant Street and Riverside Drive, Beloit
PHONE	608/362-0964
EMAIL	friendsofriverside@yahoo.com
DIRECTIONS	The park is located on Riverside Drive, which is also U.S. Highway 51. Highway 51 bisects the city on the east side of the Rock River.
ADMISSION	Free
HOURS	Seasonal. Daily, dawn to dusk.
AMENITIES	Parking lot. Toilets and water available on the grounds.

 ## Rotary Gardens
JANESVILLE

WHAT WAS ONCE A NEGLECTED PIECE OF LAND with substantial natural resources has become a premier Wisconsin public garden. It all began in 1988 when Rotarian Robert Yahr wanted to do something with a dilapidated city-owned site in Janesville. Yahr's vision of a place of beauty in an area filled with sand and gravel evolved into Rotary Gardens, an internationally themed botanic garden dedicated to peace and friendship.

The twenty-acre site, containing two spring-fed ponds connected by narrows, boasts eighteen unique, luscious theme gardens along with several smaller ones. There's the international group of English, French, Italian, Scottish, and Japanese gardens. The drifts of color around a great lawn in the English Cottage Garden start just outside the Rath Environmental Center. A stone pedestal connects the eye with an identical pedestal set between the two pergolas at the far end of the French Garden.

The informality of the Cottage Garden is juxtaposed against the adjacent Italian Garden, with its clipped-hedge parterres filled with annuals. A rectangular stone pond filled with water plants and koi is found here. Along the west side of the Italian Garden is an herb garden accented with statuary.

Leave Italy and head to France to see a formal rose garden. Wander through the semi-circles of teas, shrubs, polyanthus, floribundas, and grandifloras. Two wooden pergolas repeat the geometry of the rose garden and frame a fountain.

The Royal Botanic Garden in Edinburgh approved the design and plant selection in the Scottish Garden. All of its two hundred species of perennials are

Ed Lyon

Overview of the European formal gardens at Rotary Gardens

native to the country. Some 400,000 bulbs burst forth at the first sign of spring in a tribute to the flowering history of the Netherlands. Ornamental grasses and perennials take center stage in the North American Perennial Garden.

While there are a number of Japanese gardens scattered throughout the state, the one at Rotary Gardens is likely the largest. This garden is home to Rotary's outstanding collection of moss and ferns (two hundred fifty varieties) as well as a "dry sea," a common feature of crushed rock raked to create waves. The large rocks represent islands while the trees and shrubs symbolize the forests. China isn't forgotten—there's a pavilion and a small pond tucked in among the trees.

Brides like the beauty of the Sunken Garden with its expanse of lawn and perennial borders. The Gazebo Garden is also a popular spot for weddings. The lilac collection in the Entrance Garden is a teaser providing highlights of what is to come. When in bloom, the plants in the Rhododendron/Azalea Garden burst with electric color. Sedums and alpine plants seem to enjoy the microclimate of the Alpine Garden. With more than one hundred varieties of hostas, Rotary was named as a National Display Garden for the American Hosta Society.

Some 100,000 annuals are installed every year. A Demonstration Garden holds the All-America Selections. In 2006, the garden displayed seventy-five years worth of winners. Salvias were the featured display in 2007 in the Seasonal Display Area. Plantings in the Larch area follow an annual color theme. There's also a half-acre prairie and an arboretum with sixty varieties of trees and shrubs on the property.

If you're interested in a monochromatic garden, four "color rooms" contain forty varieties of almost two hundred perennials in a specific color. Yews divide the beds and provide color and texture during the winter.

The gardens' signature sculptures are unforgettable. There's O.V. Shaffer's three-part, twenty-foot bronze sculpture named *Dialogue: World Peace through Friendship* that begins your tour of the garden. Shaffer, of Beloit, also did *Biota* found in the garden's southeast corner. *The Druid* came from Janesville's Mercy Hospital. George Parker created the *L'Chaim* sculpture found in the Sunken Garden.

An ornate 1919 Tudor-style stone arch from the former world headquarters of the Parker Pen Company can be found at the entrance of the Sunken Garden. Volunteers recycled curved light poles from the city's former wastewater plant into an authentic Japanese bridge that's painted bright red. With its twists and turns, the crooked footbridge in the Japanese Garden keeps evil spirits away. The Japanese believe that evil spirits are only able to go in a straight line.

There are trellises, paths, benches engraved with garden quotations, a gazebo, even a small pavilion scattered throughout the grounds. Water features include a waterfall and a fountain along with the two ponds. Brick paths connect some of the gardens.

Like all botanical gardens, Rotary is home to several plant collections. One of the few Fern and Moss Gardens in the United States is housed here. There are substantial collections of narcissus, hostas, daylilies, and alliums. The gardens also feature eighty varieties of nicotiana (flowering tobacco), over one hundred fifteen varieties of celosia, and more than forty different varieties of morning glory plants.

COUNTY	Rock
ADDRESS	1455 Palmer Drive, Janesville
PHONE	608/752-3885
FAX	608/752-3853
WEBSITE	www.rotarygardens.org
DIRECTIONS	From I-90, exit 175A (State Highway 11). Turn left at the first stoplight (Palmer Drive) and go about one-half mile.
ADMISSION	Free; donations of $3 for children, $5 for adults are recommended.
HOURS	Daily, year-round during daylight hours.
AMENITIES	Parking lot. Toilets, water, and gift shop inside the visitor's center.

Schoolhouse Park

WHITEFISH BAY

A PLOT OF LAND at the junction of three streets in the village of Whitefish Bay, boasts a small, formal flower garden. Known as Schoolhouse Park to the locals, the garden is planted on what was the site of the first schoolhouse in the community, which was destroyed by fire in 1918.

The garden is designed on a cardinal grid with a low octagonal fountain in the center. Most of the beds are filled with annuals. There are the common marigolds and begonias, but cleome and cannas are added to give some vertical interest to a bed that's enhanced with a variety of coleus. Fuzzy purple-topped ageratum and red and blue salvias can be found in several of the beds.

Fountain at Schoolhouse Park

Trimmed hedges outline the garden, while peonies, irises, and ornamental grasses add some early interest. An occasional spike is thrown in for a bit of drama. Asphalt paths and several memorial benches complete the space.

Also in the village is a private garden at 6350 Santa Monica Boulevard that's open to the public. In 1988, Polly Rabion replaced her home's frontyard with a wheelchair accessible garden and opened it to the public. Called *Le Clos*

Fleuri (The Enclosed Garden), the space features a wide circular path of pavers around an oval bed, terraced beds, a water feature, and mature trees all installed on a seventy-five-foot by seventy-five-foot plot of land. Explaining her reasons behind the investment, she said, "I started it for some segment of society that has become somewhat invisible."

After her husband, Guy, died, Rabion moved to this site and hired a landscape architect to design the garden. Filled with mostly perennials in color drifts from pink to lavenders to blues as well as yellows, oranges, and reds all interspersed with white, the beds do contain some annuals. A woodland space borders the driveway with ferns, May apples, wild geraniums, and trilliums that herald the arrival of spring.

The plants are wheelchair friendly. Many, like lavender, lilies, and woolly thyme, are scented. And they generally remain less than three feet tall so that the wheelchair bound can both see and smell the blooms. A sign in front of the garden welcomes visitors to stop in and wander among the flowers.

COUNTY	Milwaukee
ADDRESS	Located at the intersection of East Birch Avenue, North Marlborough Drive, and North Idlewild Avenue, Whitefish Bay
DIRECTIONS	From I-43, exit Silver Spring Drive. Turn south on North Marlborough Drive. Schoolhouse Park is several blocks south of Silver Spring Drive. To get to Le Clos Fleuri, turn north off of Silver Spring Drive at Santa Monica Boulevard.
ADMISSION	Free
HOURS	Seasonal. Daily, dawn to dusk.
AMENITIES	Street parking. Toilets and water available across the street inside the Whitefish Bay Library.

Settlers Park

SHEBOYGAN FALLS

ORIGINALLY THE SITE OF A DILAPIDATED FACTORY no longer needed by the Bemis Company, Settlers Park has now reclaimed much of its natural ecology with native plant landscaping. When the Sheboygan Falls-based Landmark Landscape was hired to collaborate with John Herzog of the Bemis Company on the plan for the reclaimed space, a skeleton of 5,000 perennials formed the backbone. The skeleton of natives was accentuated with other ornamental plants and shrubs that would bloom at different times during the season ensuring that visitors would have something to look at no matter what time of the year they came through. Plant selections were also based on maintenance issues since local volunteers maintain this municipal garden space.

Herzog and David Majerus of Landmark Landscape chose bayberry and Korean spice to enhance the area around the pump house. Yews and gray and red dogwoods can be found scattered throughout the site. Purple coneflowers, Russian sage, ornamental grasses, black-eyed Susans, and ferns are just some of the native species planted in various beds around the property.

The natural water feature is a "dam" good one. Settlers Park hugs the Sheboygan River on its western side; bluffs run along the river's eastern edge. From the redwood gazebo and overlook, you can watch the geese and the migratory birds hanging out at the dam. Benches are placed along the concrete pathway. A fence was used as a barrier between the park and the river.

COUNTY	Sheboygan
ADDRESS	Broadway Street, Sheboygan Falls
PHONE	920/467-7900
DIRECTIONS	From I-43, exit 123 (Sheboygan/Sheboygan Falls). Turn left onto State Highway 28 West. Go two miles. Turn right on Broadway. The park is at the north end of Broadway.
ADMISSION	Free
HOURS	Daily, 5 a.m. to 10 p.m.
AMENITIES	Parking lot.

Sharon Lynne Wilson Center for the Arts

BROOKFIELD

THE LANDSCAPING at the Sharon Lynne Wilson Center for the Arts is a wonderful application of formal design to a very limited palette of native plants. Because the site is located in Mitchell Park, a conservancy park, natives were a natural choice. The design, inspired by children at play, was a way to showcase ordinary plants in an unusual way.

Mowed grass paths lead to big sweeping organic beds of one plant species. The selection includes ornamental grasses like big bluestem, butterfly weed, liatris, and New England asters. The beds are arranged to feature various heights, textures, bloom times, and colors. Two bronze sculptures, George Lundeen's *Joy of Music* and John Rawlins' *Dancing Cranes*, peek out from between the beds.

In the center of Soerens Circle Drive, which leads from Mitchell Park Drive to the building's entrance, is a formal garden planted in the shape of the sun. A maple tree anchors the space and low evergreen hedges surround it. Red petunias color the sun's rays.

From the parking lot, two rows of maples flank a concrete sidewalk. Limestone boulders are interspersed between the trees. A honey locust anchors a bed of pink roses.

COUNTY	Waukesha
ADDRESS	19805 West Capital Drive, Brookfield
PHONE	262/781-9470
FAX	262/781-9198
EMAIL	events@wilson-center.com
WEBSITE	www.wilson-center.com
DIRECTIONS	From I-94, take exit 297 and follow the County Highway Y/Barker Road signs. Follow Barker Road north past North Avenue until you reach the railroad tracks. Immediately after the railroad tracks, turn right onto River Road. Go one-quarter mile on River Road and turn left onto Mitchell Park Drive. Follow Mitchell Park Drive until you see the large, contemporary building. Soerens Circle Drive forms a semi-circle in front of the building.
ADMISSION	Free
HOURS	Daily, dawn to dusk.
AMENITIES	Parking lot. Toilets and water available when the center is open.

Sisson's Peony Garden

ROSENDALE

IN JAPAN, it symbolizes "wealth and prosperity." The Chinese call it "the king of flowers and the flower of kings." Artist Edouard Manet preferred it above all others. The flower receiving all the kudos is the peony.

Recently listed on the State and National Registers of Historic Places, Sisson's Peony Garden is a wonderful example of how a small niche-market flower grower can have a substantial impact on a species. A white picket fence outlines the remnants of Wilbur Sisson's retirement project in Rosendale, a small town in Fond du Lac County.

Courtesy of Emajean Westphal

Ranks of peonies at Sisson's

After retiring in 1918, Sisson, the former manager of the Ripon telegraph office, moved in with his sister in Rosendale and used her yard for his collection of gladiolus, irises, and, of course, peonies. What started out as a hobby, eventually grew into a full-scale nursery and mail order business.

Sisson, who died in 1950, left the gardens to Jesse Phillips, who had been helping him with the business for more than two decades. Under Phillips, who expanded the business, the gardens developed a regional reputation. When Phillips retired in 1979, the business declined and in 1988, most of Sisson's original gardens were sold for development.

What remains today is the Windmill Garden, so named for its large, field-stone windmill with distinctive blue wooden blades. Planted in the middle of a residential area, the garden currently features somewhere between one hundred fifty and two hundred varieties of Sisson's passion.

Rows of herbaceous peonies are separated by grass paths. Looking like soldiers at attention, when they begin blooming at the end of May, the scent and sight remind you of why they became a very popular addition to home gardens. Peonies also run along the fence line.

Six recently installed raised beds located between the windmill and the rows will feature the newer varieties of peonies anchored with a tree peony in the center of each bed. The new varieties will be organized by color; single beds of red, white, lilac and mauve, and pink. There will be two beds of salmon and orange.

A gazebo is placed in the back of the garden. An old Sisson's sign hangs on the fence. The former entrance gate with its fieldstone and mortar foundation and wooden arched roof is still part of the hardscape but is not used as an entrance.

COUNTY	Fond du Lac
ADDRESS	207 North Main Street, Rosendale
PHONE	920/872-2131 (This is the hardware store. If no one is available, leave a message.)
EMAIL	bluemkes@centurytel.net
DIRECTIONS	Main Street is also State Highway 26. Go one block north on State Highway 26 when it intersects State Highway 23.
ADMISSION	Free
HOURS	Seasonal. Daily, dawn to dusk
AMENITIES	There is no street parking or parking lot but Wisconsin Street, just three houses south of the gardens, has street parking on both sides.

Warren Taylor Memorial Gardens

KENOSHA

WHAT BRIDE wouldn't want her outdoor wedding set among the blossoms in Kenosha's Warren Taylor Memorial Flower Gardens? Since these formal gardens were dedicated in 1965, many couples have exchanged vows amongst the beauty of the sunken garden that's set in a park-like environment. Located in Lincoln Park and named for a former Kenosha park director/city planner, the steps leading down to the formal beds give the space a feeling of intimacy.

Annual beds are framed with manicured grass paths

Laid out in avenues that form axes with strips of bright annuals contrasted with manicured grass paths, the gardens resemble a carpet of flowers. Thirty-one formal beds including a circular one in the center are filled with some fifty varieties of annuals including cannas for height, geraniums, petunias, impatiens, marigolds, ageratum, and salivas for color. Four benches flank the center bed and look out toward the rest of the garden.

The focal point is a white pergola crafted of cement block pillars with wooden slats and trimmed with a gingerbread edge. The pergola, placed at the gardens' west end, is outlined with hedges. A row of hostas defines the hedges.

As you travel Highway 50 (75th Street) toward downtown Kenosha, don't miss the large, chocolate-kiss-shaped bed located at Pershing Boulevard. It's filled with a pattern of annuals that changes annually.

COUNTY	Kenosha
ADDRESS	7010 22nd Avenue, Kenosha
PHONE	262/653-4080
EMAIL	parks@kenosha.org
DIRECTIONS	From I-94 East, exit #344 (Kenosha/Lake Geneva). Continue east on 120th Street for about a block. Turn left on to 75th Street (also known as Highway 50 East). Go six miles. Turn left on to 22nd Avenue for three blocks.
ADMISSION	Free
HOURS	Seasonal. Daily, dawn to dusk.
AMENITIES	Parking lot. Toilets in the park.

  Ten Chimneys

GENESEE DEPOT

TAKE A WALK BACK IN TIME to a more refined era at Ten Chimneys, the Genesee Depot estate of the late actors Alfred Lunt and Lynn Fontanne. Considered the greatest acting team in history, the Lunts left behind a legacy of their style in the gardens of their Genesee Depot home.

Various garden spaces dot the sixty acres. Alfred Lunt, an avid flower and vegetable gardener, could be found out in the gardens no matter which famous friend happened to be visiting. "The Lunts' entire philosophy was taking time to tend the gardens, literally and metaphorically," said Sean Malone, president of the Ten Chimneys Foundation. "The reason the Lunts chose Genesee Depot and the rolling Kettle Moraine was because of the nature."

Upon entering the grounds, guests could expect to be greeted with the first of many flowerbeds in the arrival court located to the side of the main house. Here mixed borders, clematis, and Virginia creeper have been planted with a pink color scheme.

Curved borders around the main house feature pink begonias and white alyssum. Some even contain pink roses. A retaining wall is topped with pots of pink geraniums and vines.

From the house, a flagstone path leads to the red and white cottage. Geranium-filled pots hug the path. Similar pots can be found throughout the grounds just as they would have been when the Lunts were in residence.

The garden along the cottage's exterior features polka-dot plants, coleus, and hosta. More red and white geraniums fill the window boxes. Following the Scandinavian theme of the main house and outbuildings, many of the annuals that Alfred would plant in containers were red, a nice juxtaposition to the various shades and textures of green on the estate. Preferring geraniums, impatiens, and petunias, Lunt would often add white and blue as accent colors.

The tips on the pickets of the white fence adjacent to the cottage are also painted red. A variety of perennials such as hollyhocks and hostas fill a border between the steps and the picket fence. A rock wall was added to help control erosion.

From the cottage, a path winds past the Lunts' in-ground swimming pool and studio building to the newly restored greenhouse and Fontanne's English cutting garden. This garden, originally designed by Chicago landscape architects Root & Hollister, was installed in 1939.

Historic photographs show three rectangular beds, each approximately thirty feet long and six feet wide. Between each of the beds was a three-foot grass corridor. There are now seven individual beds with grass paths, four with approximately twenty-five types of annuals and three with some fifteen varieties of perennials. Two annual beds are planted in cool colors and the remaining two are devoted to warmer hues. Plants such as celosia, zinnias, amaranthus, and cosmos provide lots of summer color. There are sunflowers, lisianthus, globe thistles, and German statice in the three perennial beds. Some of these flowers are cut to decorate the home's interior, much like Fontanne would do when she was living here.

Alfred Lunt was meticulous in keeping lists. The Southeast Wisconsin Master Gardeners have tried to restore the gardens according to his intent as much as possible, making substitutions only for hardiness and the canopy of trees. The trees that the Lunts planted during the 1930s have now grown up. Flowers that would have worked well seventy-five years ago would not have enough sun to thrive now.

COUNTY	Waukesha
ADDRESS	Depot Street, Genesee
PHONE	262/968-4110
WEBSITE	www.tenchimneys.org
DIRECTIONS	I-94 to exit 287 south (State Highway 83). Continue south on Highway 83. Turn west on Depot Street.
ADMISSION	$35 for the full estate tour; the main house tour is $28.
HOURS	Usually around May 1 through November 10. Call ahead or check the Web site for the exact dates.
AMENITIES	Parking lot. Toilets and water in the Visitor's Center.

Troha Garden

KENOSHA

THIS HOURGLASS-SHAPED GARDEN is much less formal than many of the flowerbeds around the city of Kenosha. But it replaces the formality of both Wolfenbuttel Park and the Warren Taylor Memorial Gardens in Lincoln Park with exuberance. Pink geraniums and fuschia impatiens share space with yellow marigolds, purple chrysanthemums, and yellow and purple lantana. You'll find hydrangeas and Russian sage, red roses and purple coneflowers. Chaos is controlled. Colors in this mix of perennials and annuals tend toward the feverish. There are no shrinking violets here.

The curving paths wind their way to the center, which contains a round bed filled with varieties of rose mallow. One quarter of the garden is annuals; the rest are perennials.

Located in the Harbor Park Development between the Southport Marina and the Kenosha Public Museum, Troha is one of the more than forty gardens maintained by citizen volunteers as part of the Keep Kenosha Beautiful "Adopt-a-Spot" garden program. A black granite marker located on the garden's west side honors Dennis Troha and his family for their contributions to the city. To the northeast is the red Kenosha lighthouse. Lake Michigan is on the east side.

While you're in the area, go over to the Eighth Street Small World Garden. An empty corner lot in an urban Kenosha neighborhood was transformed into a charming garden to honor the late civic leader Dr. Thelma Orr. Members of the Lincoln Community Neighborhood Alliance plant and tend the garden that reflects the neighborhood's diversity. Curving mixed borders run the length of the garden's east side. Two formal circular beds are both encircled and connected with a gravel path edged with brick. Tall cannas rise up from the center while begonias, coleus, and ageratum play a supporting role. Garden art is simple—rocks allow the eye to rest a bit among all the color. Three mature trees add shade to the south side of the space. A fence borders the east while a sidewalk frames the north and the west. The garden is located at the corner of 15th Avenue and 65th Street.

COUNTY	Kenosha
ADDRESS	On the trolley line between the Southport Marina and the Kenosha Public Museum, Kenosha
PHONE	262/653-4080
EMAIL	parks@kenosha.org
DIRECTIONS	From I-94, exit State Highway 158, which turns into 52nd Street in the city of Kenosha. Go east on Highway 158 to Sixth Avenue (about eleven miles). Turn right onto Sixth Avenue for two blocks to 54th Street. Turn left onto 54th Street and go five blocks east to First Avenue. You will end up at the Kenosha Public Museum. There is parking here and Troha Park is in back of the museum. The museum also has one of the forty community flowerbeds in the front.
ADMISSION	Free
HOURS	Seasonal. Daily, dawn to dusk.
AMENITIES	Street parking. Toilets and water inside the public museum.

Two Fish Gallery and Sculpture Garden

ELKHART LAKE

NOT WANTING TO SEPARATE ART FROM NATURE, Patrick Robinson and Karen Koehler Robinson, owners of Two Fish Gallery and Sculpture Garden have turned their early twentieth century Arts and Crafts home into garden nirvana.

The Elkhart Lake gallery houses the work of some fifty artists. But gardeners will know there's a kindred spirit in the house the minute they see the front yard filled with woodland and native plants in pinks and purples. Karen, a biology teacher at Sheboygan South High School and the designer of the gardens at the John Michael Kohler Arts Center, is the driving force behind the natural exterior spaces. Besides the ones in the front yard, gardens have taken over the entire property, essentially eliminating every blade of grass from the lot.

Entrance to main gardens at Two Fish Gallery

The couple began transforming the space in 1998. Taking out their lawn piece by piece over a four-year period and adding seven yards of red oak mulch every year, the Robinsons were able to convert a moraine of rock into a Garden of Eden. "The purpose was to have a garden to discover bits of artwork as you make your way through," said Karen.

Enter the main gardens through a gate constructed from rebar and bamboo on the east side of the house and prepare to be immersed in color, fragrance, and art. Plant selections guarantee that the garden changes every day. In addition to the 8,000 bulbs the Robinsons have planted, there are several thousand fall crocus bulbs that get mulched with pine boughs so they survive the first frost and bloom till Christmas.

Leaf size, color, and texture drive some of Karen's planting decisions. There are holly and evergreens, hibiscus and hydrangeas, hollyhocks and shrub roses. Bluestem and zebra grass is interspersed with coral bells, alliums, and cannas. One of the most unusual plants is a purple variety of angelica that turns magenta when it opens.

In the kiln yard, a back building that's used for classrooms and Patrick's ceramics, are grapevines, cherry trees, and plants for cutting. The pergola and tea garden were designed to mirror the style of the cranberry-colored Arts and

Crafts home. From the "dark garden" filled with dark leaves and/or blooms near the pergola, you move toward the teahouse. The yellows and purples surrounding the teahouse help make the transition from the dark garden to the rose garden. A moon gate made from a sixteen-foot section of a hog fence, identifies the entrance to the pond garden. Later, a converted sheep trough holds water plants, which are moved to the pond during the winter. In the American garden you'll find American perennials including the purple angelica.

Because city rules require no street parking during the winter, many of the plantings are in containers so they can be moved to make room for the couple's cars. Raised beds on the west side of the house contain morning glory plants, coleus, and sunflowers. There is also an herb garden for kitchen use.

Paths made from Colorado blue stone, Mexican beach stone, and limestone signal the start of new gardens. A small bridge adds interest as does the plethora of garden art tucked into nooks and crannies around the yard.

COUNTY	Sheboygan
ADDRESS	244 East Rhine Street, Elkhart Lake
PHONE	920/876-3192
EMAIL	twofish@excel.net
DIRECTIONS	On State Highway 67, turn west onto East Rhine Street
ADMISSION	Free
HOURS	10 a.m. to 5 p.m. Saturday, noon to 4 p.m. Sunday and by appointment. Call for extended summer hours.
AMENITIES	Street parking. Toilets and water in the gallery.

 UW–Stevens Point, Raymond E. Specht Forum

STEVENS POINT

FLANKED BY THE COLLEGE OF NATURAL RESOURCES, the Albertson Library and the Noel Fine Arts Center at the University of Wisconsin-Stevens Point, the area around the Raymond E. Specht Forum, also known as the Sundial, was once a concrete jungle. A few grassy spots were the university's idea of softening the hardscape, without taking away from the beauty of the unusual, four-story, ceramic-tile mosaic on the wall of the College of Natural Resources building. But the mosaic, sundial, and buildings are all various shades of beige and brown and they needed some color to make them pop.

Over the past few years, the area bordering all of the buildings has been transformed with spring bulbs, natives, and perennials. In the spring some two hundred fifty varieties of bearded irises bloom along the side of the Fine Arts building. Once the irises, the campus flower, are finished blooming, they're replaced with selections such as purple and yellow coneflowers, purple liatris, Russian sage, salvia, and delphiniums.

In the shaded area underneath the side entrances to the Noel Fine Arts Center are ten varieties of astilbe, five varieties of coral bells, and more than twenty varieties of hostas. It doesn't matter that the canopy providing the shade is concrete. To the flowers, shade is shade.

Along the perimeter of the College of Natural Resources are seven varieties of echinacea, three species of liatris, New England asters, queen of the prairie, and Culver's root. There are also native grasses, yucca, and willow blue star. Many of the selections in the beds are in the school's colors of purple and gold.

Other gardens of note on campus include the hosta walk in front of Old Main. A dozen varieties border one side of the curving concrete walk while coleus adds a bit of sizzle to the other side. The hosta walk leads to a sunny bed filled with balloon flowers, rudbeckia, salvia, tree and bush peonies, as well as two rain gardens, which flank either side of the historic red brick building. There's the pin oak garden along Fremont Street, which contains the largest pin oak ever recorded in Wisconsin, and the Iris Fountain garden between the University Center, Communications Building, Student Services Building, and Old Main, which contains a bronze bearded iris fountain. Currently the site of some building construction, the Iris Fountain garden will contain peonies, hibiscus, roses, delphiniums, coneflowers, ornamental grasses, and of course, the requisite bearded and Siberian irises when construction is complete.

> *Gateway Technical College* has installed eight new Horticulture Learning Lab gardens for student use including Butterfly, Southeast, Spring, Formal, Cottage, Fall, Wisconsin, and Dwarf Conifer gardens. Each garden provides students with a design challenge and an opportunity to study plant identification and maintenance.

COUNTY	Portage
ADDRESS	University of Wisconsin Stevens Point, Stevens Point
PHONE	715/346-3407
EMAIL	pzellmer@uwsp.edu
WEBSITE	www.uwsp.edu
DIRECTIONS	**From the north or south** take I-39 to Stevens Point. Exit U.S. Highway 10, which is also Main Street, and head west. Turn north onto Business Highway 51 (also known as Division Street). Turn east onto Portage Street. Drive several blocks and you'll be in the back of the Noel Fine Arts Center. There is some metered parking in the lot across the street.
ADMISSION	Free
HOURS	Seasonal. Daily, dawn to dusk.
AMENITIES	Street parking and parking lots. Toilets, food, and water inside buildings.

~ Villa Terrace Decorative Arts Museum

MILWAUKEE

WITH VILLA TERRACE, Milwaukee has its own bit of formal Italy overlooking Lake Michigan. As a remembrance of their Italian honeymoon, Milwaukee industrialist Lloyd R. Smith built the Italian Renaissance-style villa and gardens for his wife, Agnes, in 1924. After his death, his family donated the site to Milwaukee County for a decorative arts museum.

Boston landscape architect Rose Standish Nichols designed the original gardens in conjunction with the Villa's architect, David Adler. The gardens

The hillside gardens at Milwaukee's own Italian villa

eventually fell into disrepair. During the 1970s, when federal money was available for institutions to upgrade their facilities, a Milwaukee County landscape architect designed another set of gardens. But lack of money and flooding from an extremely high Lake Michigan later ruined a lot of plantings from the 1976 garden.

In 1997, Dennis Buettner of Buettner & Associates was asked to do a master plan for the garden. A year later, a team of three hundred volunteers, along with assistance from Buettner and Mike Marek of Marek Landscaping, began the work of creating a garden suitable for an Italian villa. The gardens were completed in 2002.

Until Lincoln Memorial Drive was installed in 1932, the gardens went down to the lake. Now with the lake as its backdrop, the sixteenth century Italian garden is as authentic as one can have in Wisconsin's climate. Extensively researched before it was put in, the plantings and the hardscape features combine for a breathtaking view, whether you're looking down from the house or up from the ironwork gate facing Lincoln Memorial Drive.

The fun begins as you enter the home. A marble statue of Mercury anchors the Mercury Courtyard. Parterres of clipped boxwoods are filled with groundcovers. Three terraces, Terrace D'Luna, Parnassus, and Nymphaeum, located off the back of the house provide a space to take in the view before heading down to the *prato*, or great lawn. *Putti* (cherubs) statues on the Parnassus Terrace represent the four seasons and the arts. A lead dolphin located in a small grotto on the Nymphaeum Terrace, identifies the home's source of water.

In the Italian tradition, most hillsides were planted as orchards or with grapevines. Villa Terrace is no exception. Four varieties of dwarf flowering crabapples are planted in three terraces on the hillside along both sides of the water stairway. Called the "Bride's Orchard," brides who were married at Villa

Terrace donated them as a remembrance. Their spring blossoms are reminiscent of the flowering fruit trees in the Italian countryside. The trees are underplanted with a native species of narcissus that, according to Buettner, predate the large Dutch daffodils. Some 30,000 pop their heads up every spring.

The Mercury courtyard at Villa Terrace

The *scaletta d'aqua* (water stairway) and the *vasca* (fishpond) were two of the site's original features. Inspired by the water feature at Villa Cicogna in Lombardy, the water stairway acts as an arrow drawing your eye down to the lake or, if you're standing on Lincoln Memorial Drive, up to the mansion. At one time, all of the water, two hundred gallons a minute, would drain into Lake Michigan. Now a three hundred-gallon storage tank recycles the water. The stairway water is caught in a semi-circular pool on the Herm Terrace. Nearby are benches called *scalinata double*.

The fishpond is also standard in Italian gardens. A granite lion's head hanging on a wall now spouts water into the pond. A fountain consisting of three fish represents Milwaukee's three rivers.

As you walk through the gardens, you're taken from small, intimate spaces to long, narrow ones, and finally to big rooms. The South Roundel, located in the southeast corner of the site, contains a secret garden (*giardino segreto*), which encases a sculpture of Diana and her quiver of arrows. Directly across the yard is the North Roundel with the statue of Hercules. The arborvitaes that encase the sculptures are trimmed so that only the statues' heads can be seen.

Two allees of trees act as escorts from the base of the hill to the roundels. At the end of the south allee is a statue of Ceres, the goddess of agriculture.

A double row of large ornamental shrubs called *ragnaias* creates thickets for shade and privacy (during the Renaissance they were also used to catch birds for food). These run north and south and are bisected by the Neptune

Court, the open area in front of the massive Neptune Gate. The traditional ironwork gate, one of the largest pieces of ironwork done in the past century, contains Greek and Roman images. The *ragnaias* also lead to a pair of *excedras* (semi-circle benches).

The temple, a former chicken coop, was renovated for restrooms. The eight-passenger, motorized tram is available for those who do not want to walk the steps down the fifty-five-foot hill to the *prato*.

Plantings are sixteenth century in inspiration, but Wisconsin hardy. There are culinary and medicinal herbs, potted citrus trees, scabiosa, roses, and geraniums. Grapevines cover the arbors as a temporary measure until the ironwood trees grow larger and become a living arch.

COUNTY	Milwaukee
ADDRESS	2220 North Terrace Avenue, Milwaukee
PHONE	414/271-3656
FAX	414/271-3986
WEBSITE	www.cavtmuseums.org
DIRECTIONS	While the gardens face Lincoln Memorial Drive, the entrance is on Terrace Avenue, two blocks south of the North Point Water Tower at the end of East North Avenue.
ADMISSION	$5 for adults; $3 for seniors, military, and students with IDs. Free for museum members and children 12 and under.
HOURS	1 p.m. to 5 p.m. Wednesdays through Sundays.
AMENITIES	Small parking lot. Toilets and water inside the building.

 ## West of the Lake

MANITOWOC

ONCE THE PRIVATE ESTATE of the late Ruth and John West, the West of the Lake Gardens are designed to mimic English formal gardens. Located on a six-acre estate, these formal gardens were once Ruth West's pride and joy.

In 1934, the Wests purchased the land and Ruth, along with Bill Mueller, a local German farmer, began to hand spade the acreage, taking nine years to complete the task. Seventy Colorado spruce trees were planted to form the windbreaks running along the north and west portions of the property. With the arrival of the first of many seed catalogs, Ruth ordered two hundred tulip bulbs and began the process of converting a plot previously filled with thistles and quack grass into a series of beautiful formal gardens.

Colored stone paths lead visitors to the furthest north set of plantings, the Japanese Garden. Intricate patterns of stone, clipped evergreens, and bonsai displays contrast with the bright colors of the remaining gardens. The nearby greenhouse carries on the Zen theme with its displays of cacti and other succulents.

From the Japanese Garden, it's just a few hundred yards to the Sunken Garden. Seven round chairs with matching metal tables invite visitors to sit and admire the annuals that frame the pool. John, an engineer and chairman and president of The Manitowoc Company, used his engineering skills to create the water feature in this garden.

A kite-shaped reflecting pool with a one-of-a-kind fountain that John also designed centers the rose garden. Purple ageratum, begonias, and impatiens accent shrub and hybrid roses. Because pink and blue were Ruth's favorite colors, many of the plantings are chosen accordingly.

From the Rose Garden, follow the perennial beds that comprise the Main Gardens. In the center of the Red and White Garden, look for the statue of a little girl holding a small shell. The Path, which is now filled with ageratum, alyssum, yarrow, snapdragons, stella d'oro and daylilies, just to name a few selections, was where the first two hundred tulips were planted. The Mae West Garden, likely named because of the curvilinear shape, showcases monarda, astilbe, gerbera daisies, as well as delphinium and coral bells.

At the end of the Main Gardens is the Formal Garden that contains crushed marble in an intricate knot design supported by purple ageratums and red begonias. An Italian marble statue anchors the center. This garden is offset with pots of succulents set on pink rock. Clipped hedges border the north and the south, giving this garden a feeling of concealment. The final garden, called the Loop, eschews the formal setting of the Formal Garden for a more natural display of hostas, daylilies, and annuals.

There are no paths in the garden or weeds in the lawn. Meticulous is the word that comes to mind when you view the entire setting. Two full-time gardeners work year-round to grow all the annuals. Extra staff is added during the summer. The grass is manicured to within an inch of its life. Planting choices are left to the determination of the head gardener, but always reflect Ruth's taste.

The Sunken Garden at West of the Lake

Those first two hundred tulips that Ruth bought have multiplied into 17,000. Add another 26,000 hyacinth bulbs and numerous daffodils, and springtime is not to be missed. When the spring flowers first appear, the Garden hosts a Tulip Tea. Ruth started the tradition more than four decades ago to give the public a look at her handiwork and to raise money for charity. Future plans include adding fall color to keep the garden in bloom longer.

COUNTY	Manitowoc
ADDRESS	915 Memorial Drive, Manitowoc
PHONE	920/684-6110 or 920/684-8506
FAX	920/684-7381
EMAIL	westfdt@lsol.net
WEBSITE	www.westofthelake.org
DIRECTIONS	From I-43, take exit 152. Turn east onto U.S. Highway 10, which becomes Waldo Boulevard. Take Waldo Boulevard to Lake Michigan. Turn north onto Memorial Drive. At the first stoplight, you'll see the sign for the gardens.
ADMISSION	Free
HOURS	10 a.m. to 5 p.m. daily.
AMENITIES	Parking lot. Toilets and water available.

 Wind Point Lighthouse Friends' Commemorative Garden

RACINE

LAKE MICHIGAN is a famous backdrop for many of the state's public gardens. But the Friends' Commemorative Garden found on the grounds of the Wind Point Lighthouse wins the award for being the one closest to the lake.

Despite its 1880 birth date, Wind Point is the oldest and tallest lighthouse still in operation on Lake Michigan. While there are plantings outside of the lighthouse keeper's home, including a water feature and an old ship's anchor, the commemorative garden, which was installed in 2002, is located between the lighthouse and the Fog Horn Building Museum. A series of garden beds both border and interject themselves into a commemorative red stone paver patio with benches. The pavers include one for Astronaut Laurel Clark who lost her life in the Challenger accident. Two stone benches anchor each end. Signage and a reclaimed ship's winch complete the hardscapes.

This perennial garden features a variety of selections from yucca to spirea, hostas to monarda, sedums to shrub roses. The vivid colors of the potentilla, lilies, and rudbeckia must compete with the lake's ever-changing landscape. Still, the placement seems inspired as the two forces of nature subtly anchor and define the shoreline.

COUNTY	Racine
ADDRESS	Lighthouse Drive, Village of Wind Point
PHONE	262/639-3524
DIRECTIONS	Located off of State Highway 32 between Three and Four Mile roads. Both Three and Four Mile roads end in Lighthouse Drive.
ADMISSION	Free
HOURS	6 a.m. to 11 p.m. daily.
AMENITIES	Parking lot. Toilets.

 # *Wolfenbuttel Park*

KENOSHA

PLACED ALONGSIDE LAKE MICHIGAN, Kenosha's Wolfenbuttel Park is home to a set of formal gardens that, admittedly, compete for attention with the view of the Kenosha harbor. While the waterfront is stunning, the gardens more than hold your attention.

Dedicated in 1972, this 29.9-acre park is named for a German sister city. It features eleven flowerbeds plus one large circular bed. The city grows annuals from starter plants, with plant selections and designs changing annually. The beds at Wolfenbuttel are but a small portion of the one hundred eighteen flowerbeds scattered around the city.

While the annuals provide an intense burst of seasonal color, it's the eye-catching wooden pergola that anchors the flowers to the site. Stone pillars

A glimpse of the large pergola at Wolfenbuttel Park

support the wooden slats on this very large, semi-circle pergola. A semi-circle of trees and shrubs around the pergola's exterior mimics the geometry of the structure.

White concrete sidewalks form a traditional formal design with axes and the large center bed as the focal point. With Lake Michigan to the east and the pergola to the west, the beds are defined. An expanse of grass offers a soothing transformation between the water and the flowers.

Just a short distance to the north of the pergola is a circular bed that's dedicated as a Youth Memorial. A tree anchors the bed that's filled with memorial pavers, an inner ring of annuals, and an outer ring of red shrub roses. Three black metal benches complete the hardscape.

COUNTY	Kenosha
ADDRESS	5901 Third Avenue, Kenosha
PHONE	262/653-4080
EMAIL	parks@kenosha.org
DIRECTIONS	The park is located at the junction of 59th Street and Third Avenue. From I-94, exit 340 (Kenosha/Burlington) onto 120th Avenue. Go half a mile and turn left on Burlington Road (State Highway 142 East). Highway 142 East turns into Burlington Road (County Road S East). Turn right onto Sheridan Road (State Highway 32) and go one mile. Turn left on 58th Street for several blocks and then right on Third Avenue.
ADMISSION	Free
HOURS	Seasonal. Daily, dawn to dusk.
AMENITIES	Parking lot. Toilets and water in the park.

 ## Charles A. Wustum Museum of Fine Arts

RACINE

ALFRED BOERNER, the genius behind Milwaukee's famed Boerner Botanical Gardens, also put his stamp on Racine, designing the landscape for the Charles A. Wustum Museum of Fine Arts. Consisting of thirteen acres of park and a one-acre formal garden, Boerner's design for the Wustum Museum includes color, structure, whimsy, and formality. The formal garden, located on the south side of the 1856 Italianate-style farmhouse, offers a striking contrast to the contemporary art inside and Cherry Barr Jerry's Italian tile mosaic of St. Francis of Assisi on the home's exterior south wall.

Slightly to the north of the front entrance is a fountain and pool featuring Milton Hebald's sculpture, *The Great Fortune*. The white of the house offsets the dark green of the trees and clipped shrubs. The fountain and pool are ringed with bunches of intensely colored annuals. The sky blue from the pool's interior contributes to the colorful statement.

On the museum's south side, red brick pavers lead to a small white gazebo with a cedar shake roof. Two rows of benches border the walkway to the structure and annuals ring the foundation. Looking out from the gazebo, a cement pond with its aerating fountain, koi, and aquatic plants acts as a focal point, drawing the eye into the distance. Borders of daylilies and hostas hug the walkway leading from the museum to the eastern corner of the formal garden, whose four corners are decorated with annuals.

Clipped hedges, which begin near the walkway entrance to the gazebo border the garden's western corner. Curvy mixed beds of petunias, dusty miller, salvias, and sedums extend around the perimeter separating the grassy expanse of lawn from the red brick walkway on one side. The focal point is a half-size aluminum cast of an original sculpture by Anna Hyatt Huntington called *The Fighting Stallions*, which portrays two horses locked in combat. Peonies, lilacs, crab apple trees, large evergreens, and other mature trees are all part of the landscape. Also on the grounds is a cast bronze birdbath by Gerhard Kroll.

The formal Wustum Gardens

COUNTY	Racine
ADDRESS	2519 Northwestern Avenue, Racine
PHONE	262/ 636-9177
WEBSITE	www.ramart.org
DIRECTIONS	From I-94, exit State Highway 20 East. Turn north on State Highway 31. Turn south on State Highway 38. Northwestern Avenue is also Highway 38. The museum is located on the west side of the highway.
ADMISSION	Free
HOURS	10 a.m. to 5 p.m. Tuesday through Saturday and noon to 5 p.m. Sunday.
AMENITIES	Parking lot. Toilets and water inside the museum.

APPENDIX 1 : *Arboretums*

Al's Auto Body and Arboretum, W6866 North Walworth Road, Walworth, 262/275-2800, questions@alsautobodyandarboretum.com, alsautobodyandarboretum.com
The arboretum features hostas situated among mature oak, hickory, and walnut trees.

Arbor View Gardens, E10540 County Road C, Clintonville, 715/823-2763, arborvw@frontiernet.net
Several gardens are included among 1,000 varieties of woody plants.

Boerner Botanical Gardens, 9400 Boerner Drive, Hales Corners, 414/525-5600, boernerbotanicalgardens.org This 1,000-acre arboretum contains one of the nation's largest ornamental crab tree collections.

Alice Moody Chapin Arboretum, 2001 Alford Park Drive, Kenosha, 262/551-8500, whoare@carthage.edu, carthage.edu The campus of Carthage College is an arboretum.

Joseph J. Chopp Arboretum, University of Wisconsin-Whitewater, 262/472-1194

Cofrin Arboretum, 2420 Nicolet Drive, Green Bay, 920/465-2277, uwgb.edu/biodiversity/arboretum
A courtyard in the Mary Ann Cofrin Hall serves as a gateway to a 270-acre arboretum that encircles the UW-Green Bay campus.

Gottfried Arboretum UW Fond du Lac Campus, 400 Campus Drive, Fond du Lac, 920/923-7645, Ext. 4, erikajen@sbcglobal.net, fdl.uwc.edu/arboretum
A three-acre arboretum with 176 native trees and shrubs is found on the two-year campus.

Harmony Arboretum, Highway 64 and E, Marinette, 715/732-7510, uwex.edu/ces/cty/marinette
This 460-acre county farm contains hardwood forest, walking trails, a restored prairie, and demonstration gardens.

Havenwoods State Forest, 6141 North Hopkins Street, Milwaukee, 414/527-0232, 414/527-0761 (fax), judy.klippel@wisconsin.gov
This urban arboretum is part of a 237-acre open green space in Milwaukee.

Hawthorn Hollow Nature Sanctuary and Arboretum, 880 Green Bay Road, Kenosha, 262/552-8196, hawthornhollow@wi.rr.com, www.hawthornhollow.org
This 12-acre arboretum features a variety of trees, shrubs, and a lilac collection.

Howard Arboretum, Spring Green Park, 3640 Spring Green Road, Howard, 920/434-4640, Ext. 1316, cclark@villageofhoward.com, www.villageofhoward.com
This demonstration arboretum showcases 124 species for homeowners who are considering adding trees to their property.

Kohler Arboretum, Kohler Gardener, 765 Woodlake Road, Suite A, Kohler, 920/458-5570, BotanicalGardens@kohler.com, DestinationKohler.com
This twenty-acre arboretum features more than 150 varieties of shade and ornamental trees.

Paul Lange and Ora Rice Arboretum, Terrace Street at Lake Comus, 123 South Second Street, Delavan, 262/728-5585
The Lange portion encompasses 24.6 acres while the 6.1-acre Rice portion serves as the northerly expansion of the Lange arboretum, which was named after the father of Arbor Day in Wisconsin.

Ledge View Nature Center, W2348 Short Road, Chilton, 920/849-7094, ledgeview@co.calumet.wi.us
The center contains an arboretum with 55 species of trees and 25 species of shrubs.

Lee Park Arboretum, 9206 County Highway W Clinton, 608/757-5451, 608/757-5470 (fax)
The 40-acre park contains an eight-acre arboretum.

Listeman Arboretum, entrances on U.S. Highway 10 and West Second Street, Neillsville, clark-cty-wi.org/Listeman.htm
Fifty acres of woodlands are found along the Black River with groomed trails, benches, and spring wildflowers.

Mary C. Nelson Arboretum, Eighth Avenue between Drexel and Mackinac Avenues, South Milwaukee, 414/762-4844 Created by the Woman's Club of South Milwaukee, this arboretum features more than 67 trees comprising 45 species on 2.5 acres.

Maywood Environmental Park, 3615 Mueller Road, Sheboygan, 920/459-3906, 920/459-4089 (fax), maywood@ci.sheboygan.wi.us, gomaywood.org This 120-acre environmental park includes habitats of prairie, maple and evergreen forests, wetlands and wildlife ponds.

Orchard Lawn, 234 Madison Street, Mineral Point, 608/987-2884, mphistory@mhtc.net, mineralpoint.com/living_history/orchard_lawn.html
The grounds of this historic home contain a 38-tree arboretum featuring Wisconsin's first catalpa tree.

Paine Art Center and Arboretum, 1410 Algoma Boulevard, Oshkosh, 920/235-6903, thepaine.org A 15-acre arboretum can be found on the grounds of this historic home.

Platteville Community Arboretum, Located at 275 Highway 151, Platteville; 608/342-1689, 608/342-1088 (fax), pca@plattevillearboretum.org, plattevillearboretum.org
A linear arboretum runs from the University to Mound View Park along the Rountree Branch stream and trail.

Richland Center City Arboretum, Highway 14, Richland Center, 608/647-8108
Some 200 trees and shrubs representing 65 varieties are planted along the bike trail located behind the city's utility buildings.

Rotary Gardens Arboretum, 1455 Palmer Drive, Janesville, 608/752-3885, 608/752-3853, rotarygardens.com The arboretum contains 60 varieties of trees and shrubs and connects the gardens with the Triangle Prairie.

University of Wisconsin-Madison Arboretum, 1207 Seminole Highway, Madison, 608/263-7888, 608/262-5209 (fax), info@uwarboretum.org, uwarboretum.org
This 1,260 acre arboretum features prairies, oak savanna, oak woods, a pine stand, spruce and fir plantings, mixed hardwood forest and wetlands.

University of Wisconsin-Marinette Arboretum and Greenhouse, Marinette, 715/735-4326, wjohnson@uwc.edu
Thirty-six woody plant species and subspecies are found in this arboretum.

University of Wisconsin–Richland, 1200 Highway 14 West, Richland Center, 608/647-6186, richland.uwc.edu A 135-acre arboretum begins with the Edie Symons Arboretum Pathway.

University of Wisconsin-Marshfield/Wood County Arboretum, 2000 West Fifth Street, Marshfield, 715/389-6530, Marshfield.uwc.edu/LEARNABOUT/uwmwc/arboretum.asp
This 140-acre natural forest is a remnant of the vegetation that once covered central Wisconsin.

APPENDIX 2: *Butterfly Gardens*

American Family Insurance corporate headquarters, 6000 American Parkway, Madison, 608/249-2111

Aurora Health Center, 855 North Westhaven Drive, Oshkosh, 920/303-8700, aurorahealthcare.org/facilities/display.asp?ID=0041

Beaver Creek Reserve, Fall Creek, 715/877-2212, beavercreekreserve.org

Cave of the Mounds, 2975 Cave of the Mounds Road, Blue Mounds, 608/437-3038 caveofthemounds.com

Community Memorial Hospital, W180 N8085 Town Hall Road, Menomonee Falls, 262/252-5302, communitymemorial.com

Eble Farm Garden, 19400 W. Blue Mound Road, Brookfield

Free S.P.I.R.I.T. Equine Center, W3950 Highway 23 East, Fond du Lac, 920/924-9920, info@freespiritriders.org, freespiritriders.org

The Garden Door, 4312 State Highway 42 North, Sturgeon Bay, 920/743-5406, 920/743-1080 (fax)

Gardens of the Fox Cities, 1313 E. Witzke Boulevard, Appleton, gardensfoxcities.org

Gateway Technical College, 3520 30th Avenue, Kenosha, 252/564-2200, gtc.edu

Great River Road Learning Center Gardens, Freedom Park, Prescott, 715/262-0104

Green Bay Botanical Garden, 2600 Larsen Road, Green Bay, 920/490-9457 or 877/355-GBBG, gbbg.org

Hawthorn Hollow, 880 Green Bay Road, Kenosha, 262/552-8196, hawthornhollow@wi.rr.com, hawthornhollow.org

Hellestad Memorial Butterfly Garden, Gordon Bubolz Nature Preserve, 4815 N. Lynndale Drive, Appleton, 920/731-6041, bubolz@dataex.com, athenet.net/~bubolz/

Hixon Forest Nature Center and Butterfly Garden, 2702 Quarry Road, La Crosse, 608/784-0303, 608/784-0322, hixonforest@centurytel.net

Kohler Gardener, 765 Woodlake Road, Suite A, Kohler, 920/458-5570, BotanicalGardens@kohler.com, DestinationKohler.org

Lake Park, 3133 E. Newberry Blvd., Milwaukee

Lakeside Park, West Scott Street, Fond du Lac, 920/929-2950

Lapham Peak State Park, W329 N846 Highway C, Delafield, 262/646-3025

Ledge View Nature Center, W2348 Short Road, Chilton, 920/849-7094, ledgeview@co.calumet.wi.us

Lenfestey Family Courtyard Gardens, Cofrin Center for Biodiversity, University of Wisconsin Green Bay, 920/465-5032, hower@uwgb.edu, uwgb.edu

Lincoln Park Zoo, 1215 N. 8th St., Manitowoc, 920/684-9933

Ron Mann Butterfly Garden, Urban Ecology Center, 1500 E. Park Place, Milwaukee, urbanecologycenter.org

Meadowbrook Elementary School, 3130 Rolling Ridge Drive, Waukesha, 262/970-2010

Milwaukee County Zoo, 10001 W. Blue Mound Road, Milwaukee, 414/771-5500 or 414/771-3040, milwaukeezoo.org

Monk Botanical Garden, Wausau, 715/261-6284, pwhitake@uwc.edu, uwmc.uwc.edu/monkgard

Mosquito Hill Nature Center, N3880 Rogers Road, New London, 920/779-6433, co.outagamie.wi.us/Parks/MH_home.htm

Navarino Nature Center, W5646 Lindsten Road, Shiocton, 715/758-6999, nnc1@tds.net, navarino.org

Olbrich Botanical Gardens, 3330 Atwood Ave., Madison, 608/246-4550, olbrich.org

Old World Wisconsin, S103 W37890 State Highway 67, Eagle, 262/594-6300, 262/594-6342, www@whs.wisc.edu, http://oww@wisconsinhistory.org

Puelicher Butterfly Wing, Milwaukee Public Museum, 800 W. Wells St., Milwaukee, 414/278-2700, mpm.edu/exhibitions/permanent/puelicher.php

Southeastern Wisconsin Master Gardeners' Model Backyard, Department of Natural Resources Enclosure, Wisconsin State Fair Park, 8100 West Greenfield Avenue, West Allis

Trempeleau Elementary Community and School Gardens, 24231 Fourth St., Trempeleau, 608/534-6394

Vesper Park and Sports Facility, Vesper

West Bend School District: All of the schools in the district have butterfly gardens

Wisconsin Rapids Municipal Zoo, 1911 Gaynor Ave., Wisconsin Rapids, 715/421-8240, wisrapids.com/index/zoo.html

Woodland Dunes Nature Center, 3000 Hawthorne Ave., Two Rivers, 920/793-4007, woodlanddunes.com

APPENDIX 3: *Garden Clubs*

This is just a sample of the garden clubs in the state. Local contacts of these specialty clubs are listed on the Web sites. To locate a local garden club, contact the Wisconsin Federation of Garden Clubs, an area botanical garden, or your local Master Gardener group.

Badger State Dahlia Society, dahlias.net/adscontacts.htm

Bay Area Bonsai Society, http://mababonsai.org/pages/Wisconsin.html

Bay Area Daylily (BAD) Buds, c/o Phil Korth, 920/833-2804, pkorth@netnet.net

Botanical Club of Wisconsin, Wisconsin's Native Plant Society, http://wisplants.uwsp.edu/BCW/contact.html

Chippewa Valley Rose Society, northcentralrose.org/localsocieties.html

Coulee Region Orchid Guild, couleeorchids.com

Daylily Society of Southeastern Wisconsin, c/o Harold Steen, daylilywi234@sbcglobal.net, dssew.org

Fox Valley Bonsai Society, http://mababonsai.org/pages/Wisconsin.html

Gateway Rose Society, Kenosha, northcentralrose.org/localsocieties.html

Green and Gold Hosta Society of Northeast Wisconsin, c/o Mary Miller, 920/499-6641, whipgardens@juno.com

Green Bay Area African Violet Society, c/o Pat Robinson, 1641 Bruce Lane, Green Bay, 920/499-3877

Invasive Plants Association of Wisconsin, PO Box 5274, Madison, 53705, info@IPAW.org, ipaw.org

Madison Aquarium Gardeners Club, c/o John Glaeser, jglaeser@wisc.edu, http://aquariumgardeners.com/org/index.html

Madison Area Iris Society, aisregion8.org

Madison Herb Society, P.O. Box 8733, Madison, 53708, info@madisonherbsociety.org, madisonherbsociety.org

Madison Rose Society, www.Madrose.org

Milwaukee Bonsai Society, P.O. Box 198, Brookfield, 53008, mbsweb@hotmail.com, milwaukeebonsai.org

Milwaukee Rose Society, milwaukeerose.org

NEW Rose Society, Green Bay, www.geocities.com/new_rs/ or northcentralrose.org/localsocieties.html

North American Water Garden Society, Madison Chapter, 608/873-9343, madison.com/communities/nawgsmadisonwi

Northeastern Wisconsin Orchid Society, www.newisos.org

Northeast Wisconsin Unit of the Herb Society of America, c/o Jackie Johnson, 920/246-7377, scentedgardens@msn.com

Northwest Wisconsin Hosta Society, NWHS@midwesthostasociety.org, midwesthostasociety.org/society contacts.html

Orchid Grower's Guild, P.O. Box 5432, Madison 53705, orchidguild.org

Pond and Water Garden Club, c/o Lynn Share, 262/784-3636, vlshare@wi.rr.com, geocities.com/pondandwatergardenclub

The Prairie Enthusiasts, theprairieenthusiasts.org/chapter/chapter.htm

Sierra Club, .sierraclub.org/wi

Southeast Wisconsin Hosta Society, SEWHS@midwesthostasociety.org, sewisconsinhosta.org

Southern Wisconsin Butterfly Association, naba.org/chapters/nabawba/index.html

Waukesha Rose Society, Waukesha, northcentralrose.org/localsocieties.html

Wet Thumbs Pond and Water Garden Club, c/o Diana Murphy, 920/926-9767, wetthumbs@sbcglobal.net

Wild Ones, Native Plants, Natural Landscapes, for-wild.org/chapters.html

Wisconsin Cactus and Succulent Club, wicactusclub@yahoo.com, wicactusclub.org

Wisconsin Dahlia Society, dahlias.net/adscontacts.htm

Wisconsin Daylily Society, wisdaylilysoc.org

Wisconsin Garden Club Federation, c/o Carol Catlin, crcat@hughes.net, wisconsingardenclub.org

Wisconsin Gourd Society, wisconsingourdsociety.org

Wisconsin Hardy Plant Society, whps05@yahoo.com, madison.com/communities/wisconsinhardyplantsociety/

Wisconsin Hosta Society, WHS@midwesthostasociety.org, sewisconsinhosta.org

Wisconsin-Illinois Chapter of the North American Rock Garden Society, nargs.org/meet/chapters.html

Wisconsin Iris Society, aisregion8.org

Wisconsin Mycological Society, wisconsinmycologicalsociety.org

Wisconsin Orchid Society, questions@wisconsinorchidsociety.com, wisconsinorchidsociety.com

Wisconsin Regional Lily Society, wrls.org

Wisconsin Unit of the Herb Society of America, http://herbsocietywi.com

Wisconsin Water Gardeners, nawgs.com/findchapter/details.php?id=161

Wisconsin Wetlands Association, 222 S. Hamilton Street, #1, Madison, 608/250-9971, wisconsinwetlands.org

Wisconsin State Chapter of African Violet Clubs, c/o Alice Peterson, 608/833-5552, peters56@tds.net

APPENDIX 4: *Garden Art*

Andercraft Woods, Division of Whispering Creek, 620 E. Church St., Mishicot, 920/755-4289, andercraft@verizon.net

L. Barnard Woodworking, Inc., 534 S. 29th St., Manitowoc, 920/684-7026

Paul Bobrowitz, Jr., Metal Sculpture, N93 W29174 Woodchuck Way, Colgate, 262/538-1495, pbjart@execpc.com, execpc.com/~pbjart

Cate's Secret Garden, W2744 Highway QQ, Waupaca, 715/258-2594

Carved Stone Creations, 2101 Progress Way, Kaukauna, 920/759-1920, 920/759-2020, info@carvedstonecreations.com carvedstonecreations.com

Cedar Ridge Crafts, 460 Norton Ave., Oshkosh, 920/235-4381

Diggins, N3176 Highway 42, Kewaunee, 920/388-4849, 920/388-4859 (fax)

Dragonfly Studio, 46400 Blue Moon Road, Drummond, 715/798-3848, info@sarabalbin.com, sarabalbin.com

Emporium I, 70 W. Montello St., Montello, 608/297-7438

Dr. Evermor, Highway 12, North Freedom, 608/643-8009

Susan Falkman, Mequon, susan@susanfalkman.com, susanfalkman.com

Flowforms America, W2890 County Road E, East Troy, 877/642-2810, flowformsamerica.com

The Flying Pig Gallery and Greenspace, N6975 Highway 42, Algoma, 920/487-9902, theflyingpig.biz

Garden Art by Kathy Houghton, 5712 Running Deer Trail, McFarland, 608/838-3544

Garden Star, 6300 120th Ave., Kenosha, 262/857-3600

Greenway Homescapes, N3401 Greenway Road, Campbellsport, 920/602-1908

Heart to Heart, 119 Persnickety Place, Kiel, 920/894-2735

Heavy Critters, 3528 Nekimi, Oshkosh, 920/235-2864, 920/231-7655 (fax), heavy@athenet.net, heavycritters.com

Iron Images, 4022 Finger Road, Green Bay, 920/371-2276

Irony at Joeann Genetti Perennials and Herbs, W1331 Harding Road, Rubicon, 920/474-4769

Lenz Concrete Creations, 1211 U.S. Highway 8, Amery, 715/268-9712, 715/268-8712 (fax), lenzconcretecreations.com

Jurustic Park, M222 Sugarbush Lane, Marshfield 715/387-1653, clyde@jurustic.com, jurustic.com

MB Metalworks, 312 N. Third St., Madison, 608/255-6382, mike@mbmetalworks.com, mbmetalworks.com

Ellis Nelson, 124 W. Catherine St., Muscoda, 608/739-3067

Niemi Sculpture Gallery, 13300 116th St., Kenosha, bruceniemi.com

Nita's Garden Gate, 8081 Highway 57, Bailey's Harbor, 920/839-9090 or 839-5600, nitasgardendoorcounty.com

Picture It Perfect, 1347 Brown Deer Ave., Arkdale, 608/564-7663

Pots R Us, N4895 State Highway 42, Kewaunee, 920/388-2224

Riana's Studio and Sculpture Garden, N7652 650th St., Beldenville, 715/273-5959, concretemosaicsculpture.com

The Root Cellar at Tisch Mills Farm Center, N104 Mill Lane, Tisch Mills, 920/776-1299

Rustic Garden Metal Works, W5270 Pine Road, Withee, 715/897-3477

Smith Brothers Landing, W9557 State Highway 35, Pepin, 715/442-2248, smbrland@hbci.com, pepinsmith.com

Stone Gryphon Studios, S15900 Townline Road, Fairchild, 715/334-1575, sgryphon@triwest.net, stonegryphon.com

Stone Silo Concrete Lawn Ornaments, N6047 State Road 26, Rosendale, 920/872-2718

Swanstone Gardens, 4696 Swan Road, Green Bay, 920/866-9367, David@swanstonegardens.com, swanstonegardens.com

T&T Lawn Ornaments, 3409 Church St., Stevens Point, 715/254-0030, ntepp@charter.net

Willow Woods, 3900 Norway Court, Pulaski, 920/822-8496

Woodlot Gallery, 5215 Evergreen Drive, Sheboygan, 920/458-4798, woodlot@woodlotgallery.com, woodlotgallery.com (by appointment only).

APPENDIX 5: *Healing Gardens*

Agnesian Health Care, 430 E. Division St., Fond du Lac, 920/929-2300, agnesian.com

Aurora Medical Center of Manitowoc, 5000 Memorial Drive, Two Rivers, 920/794-5000, aurora.org

Aurora Medical Center, 855 N. Westhaven Drive, Oshkosh, 920/456-6000, aurora.org

Baldwin Hospital (planting bed), 730 10th Ave., Baldwin, 715/684-3311, baldwinhospital.com

Beaver Dam Care Center, 410 Roedl Court, Beaver Dam, 920/887-7171

Beloit Memorial Hospital, 1969 W. Hart Road, Beloit, 608/364-5011, beloitmemorialhospital.org

Bethesda Lutheran Home and Services, 600 Hoffman Drive, Watertown, 800/369-4636, blhs.org

Burnett Medical Center, 257 W. St. George Ave., Grantsburg, 715/463-5353, burnettmedicalcenter.com

Christian Community Home, 1320 Wisconsin St., Hudson, 715/386-9303, cchhudson.org

Columbia-St. Mary's Ozaukee Campus, 13111 N. Port Washington Road, Mequon, 262/243-7300, columbia-stmarys.org

Columbus Community Hospital, 1515 Park Ave., Columbus, 920/623-2200, cch-inc.com

Community Memorial Hospital, N180 N8085 Town Hall Road, Menomonee Falls, 262/251-1000, communitymemorial.com

Edgewater Haven, 1351 Wisconsin River Drive, Port Edwards, 715/885-8300, edgewaterhaven.com

Flambeau Hospital, 98 Sherry Ave., Park Falls, 715/762-2484, ministryhealth.org

Franciscan Skemp Healthcare, 700 West Avenue South, La Crosse, 608/785-0940, franciscanskemp.org

Grant Regional Medical Center, 507 S. Monroe, Lancaster, 608/723-2143, grantregional.com

Hess Memorial Hospital, 1050 Division St., Mauston, 608/847-6161, milebluff.com

Holy Family Memorial, 2300 Western Ave., Manitowoc, 920/320-2011, hfmhealth.org

Hospice Alliance Meditation Garden, 10220 Prairie Ridge Blvd., Pleasant Prairie, 262/652-4400, hospicealliance.net

Hudson Hospital, 405 Stageline Road, Hudson, 715/531-6000, hudsonhospital.com

LeRoyer Memorial Walkway at Langlade Medical Center, 112 E. Fifth Ave., Antigo, 715/623-2331, langladememorial.org

Marshfield Clinic's Wisconsin Rapids Center, 220 24th St., South, Wisconsin Rapids, 715/424-8600

Memorial Health Center, 135 S. Gibson St., Medford, 715/748-8100, memhc.com

Memorial Medical Center, 1615 Maple Lane, Ashland, 715/685-5500, ashlandmmc.com

Mercy Medical Center, 500 S. Oakwood Road, Oshkosh, 920/223-2000, affinityhealth.org

Oconomowoc Memorial Hospital, 791 Summit Ave., Oconomowoc, 262/569-9400, oconomowocmemorial.org

Our Lady of Victory Hospital, 1120 Pine St., Stanley, 715/644-5571, ministryhealth.org

Rusk County Memorial Hospital and Nursing Home, 900 College Ave., Ladysmith, 715/532-5561

Sacred Heart Hospital, 900 W. Clairemont Ave., Eau Claire, 715/839-4121, sacredhearthospital-ec.org

St. Clare's Hospital, 707 14th St., Baraboo, 608/356-1449, stclare.org

St. Clare's Hospital, 3400 Ministry Parkway, Weston, 715/393-3000, ministryhealth.org

St. Elizabeth Hospital, 1506 South Oneida St., Appleton, 920/738-2000, affinityhealth.org

St. Joseph's Regional Medical Center, 5000 W. Chambers St., Milwaukee, 414/447-2000, covhealth.org

St. Mary's Hospital, 1726 Shawano Ave., Green Bay, 920/498-4200, stmgb.org

St. Mary's Hospital, 707 S. Mills St., Madison, 608/251-6100, stmarysmadison.com

Sacred Heart St. Mary's Hospital, 2251 North Shore Drive, Rhinelander, 715/361-2000, ministryhealth.org

St. Nicholas, 3100 Superior Ave., Sheboygan, 920/459-8300, stnicholashospital.org

Sauk Prairie Memorial Hospital, 80 First St., Prairie du Sac, 608/643-3311, spmh.org

Seasons of Life Garden at Dr. Kate Hospice, 8951 Woodruff Road, Woodruff, 715/356-8805

Southwest Health Center, 1400 East Side Road, Platteville, 608/348-2331, southwesthealth.org

Upland Hills Health Nursing and Rehab Center, 800 Compassion Way, Dodgeville, 608/930-8000, uplandhillshealth.org/rehab

Vernon Memorial Hospital, 507 S. Main St., Viroqua, 608/637-2101, vmh.org

Villa Loretto Nursing Home, N8114 Calvary St., Mount Calvary, 920/753-3100

Western Village, 1640 Shawano Ave., Green Bay, 920/499-1577

APPENDIX 6: *Master Gardeners*

Adams County Master Gardeners, Adams County Extension Office, 569 North Cedar Street, Suite 3, Adams, 608/339-4237

Barron County Master Gardeners, Barron County Extension Office, 330 East LaSalle Avenue, Room 2206, Barron, 715/537-6250

Bluff County Master Gardeners, La Crosse County Extension Offices, Administrative Center, 400 4th Street, La Crosse, 608/785-9593, bluffcountrymg@yahoo.com

Calumet County Master Gardeners, Calumet County Extension Office, Courthouse, 206 Court Street, Chilton, 920/849-1450

Chippewa Valley Master Gardeners, Chippewa County Extension Office, 711 North Bridge Street, Room, 13, Chippewa Falls, 715/726-7950; 715/726-7958

Clark County Master Gardeners, Clark County Extension Office, Courthouse, 517 Court Street, Neillsville, 715/743-5121

Columbia County Master Gardeners, Columbia County Extension Office, 120 West Conant Street, PO Box 567, Portage, 608/742-9682, uwex.edu/ces/cty/columbia/ag/MasterGardener.html

Coulee Region Master Gardeners has disbanded. Contact the Trempeleau County Extension at the Courthouse in Whitehall, 715/538-2311

Dodge County Master Gardeners, Dodge County Extension Office, Room 108, County Administration Building, 127 East Oak Street, Juneau, 920/386-3790

Door County Master Gardeners, Door County Extension Office, County Government Center, 421 Nebraska Street, Sturgeon Bay, 920/746-2260

Eau Claire Area Master Gardeners, Eau Claire County Extension Office, 227 First Street West, Altoona, 715/839-4712, eauclairemastergardeners.com

Fond du Lac County Master Gardeners, Fond du Lac County Extension Office, Room 227, Administration/Extension Building, 400 Campus Drive, Fond du Lac, 920/929-3173

Glacial Master Gardeners, Florence Natural Resource Center, HC1, Box 82A, Florence, 715/528-4480

Grant County Master Gardeners, Grant County Extension Office, 916 East Elm Street, Fairgrounds, Box 31, Lancaster, 608/723-2125, http://grantcomg.org

Iowa County Master Gardeners, Iowa County Extension Office, 222 North Iowa Street, Suite 1, Dodgeville, 53533; 608/935-0391, uwex.edu/ces/cty/iowa/hort/IowaCountyMasterGardenersPage.html

Juneau County Master Gardeners, Juneau County Extension Office, 211 Hickory Street, Mauston, 608/847-9329, 608/847-9332 (fax), uwex.edu/ces/cty/juneau/hort/index.html

Lafayette County Master Gardeners, Lafayette County Extension Office, Ag Center, 627 Washington Street, Darlington, 608/776-4820

Lake Superior Master Gardeners, Douglas County Extension Office, Courthouse, 1313 Belknap Street, Superior, 715/395-1363, 715/395-1399 (fax)

Madison Area Master Gardeners Association, PO Box 259318, Madison, 53725, 608/224-3700, www.madison.com/communities/mamga/

Manitowoc County Master Gardeners, Manitowoc County Extension Office, County Offices Building, 4319 Expo Drive, Manitowoc, 920/683-4167, uwex.edu/ces/cty/manitowoc/hort/index.html

Master Gardeners of the North, Oneida County Extension Office, 3375 Airport Road, #10, Rhinelander, 715/365-2750, somojim@yahoo.com, mgsofthenorth.bravehost.com

North Central Wisconsin Master Gardeners, 212 River Drive, Suite 3, Wausau, 715/261-1231, ncwi.mg@ces.uwex.edu

North Country Master Gardeners, Spooner Agricultural Research Station, W6646 Highway 70, Spooner, 715/635-3506

Northeast Wisconsin Master Gardeners, Brown County Extension Office, 1150 Bellevue Street, Green Bay, 920/391-4610, co.brown.wi.us/uw_extension/Horticulture/index.htm

Northern Lights Master Gardeners, Marinette County Extension Office, Courthouse, 1926 Hall Avenue, Marinette, 715/732-7510, linda.warren@ces.uwex.edu, uwex.edu/ces/cty/marinette/hort/mastergardener.html

Northwoods Master Gardeners, Forest County Extension Office, Courthouse, 200 East Madison, Crandon, 715/478-2212

Outagamie County Master Gardeners, Outagamie County Extension Office, 3365 West Brewster, Appleton, 920/832-5121, outagamiecountymastergardeners.org

Ozaukee County Master Gardeners, Ozaukee County Extension Office, 121 West Main Street, Box 994, Port Washington, 262/238-8288 or 262/284-8288, daniel.oneil@ces.uwex.edu, co.ozaukee.wi.us/MasterGardener/Index.htm

Polk County Master Gardeners, Polk County Extension Office, 100 Polk County Plaza, Suite 210, Balsam Lake, 715/485-8600

Portage County Master Gardeners, Portage County Extension Office, Courthouse Annex Building, 1462 Strongs Avenue, Stevens Point, 715/346-1316

Racine/Kenosha Master Gardeners, Racine County Extension Office, 14200 Washington Avenue, Sturtevant, 262/886-8460 or Kenosha County Extension Office, 19600 75th Street, Box 550, Bristol, 262/857-1945, uwex.edu/ces/cty/racine/hort/mg or uwex.edu/ces/cty/kenosha

Rock Prairie Master Gardeners, Rock County Extension Office/Rotary Gardens, 1455 Palmer Drive, Janesville, 608/757-5696, kennedy@co.rock.wi.us, uwex.edu/ces/cty/rock/hort/index.html

Rusk County Master Gardeners is no longer active in the Wisconsin Master Gardeners Association. Contact: Rusk County UW-Extension, 311 East Miner Avenue, Suite S140, Ladysmith, 715/532-2154, 715/532-2279

Sauk County Master Gardeners, Sauk County Extension Office, West Square Administration Building, 505 Broadway, Baraboo, 608/355-3250, 608/355-3550 (fax), phyllis.both@ces.uwex.edu

Sheboygan County Master Gardeners, Sheboygan County Extension Office, 650 Forest Avenue, Sheboygan Falls, 920/467-5740, uwex.edu/ces/cty/sheboygan/hort/mg.html

South Central Master Gardeners Association, Green County Extension Office, N3150B Highway 81, Monroe, 608/328-9440, kristi.leonard@ces.uwex.edu, uwex.edu/ces/cty/green/hort/mg.html

Southeast Wisconsin Master Gardeners, Milwaukee County Extension Office, Roosevelt Education Center, 932 South 60th Street, West Allis, 414/290-2412 or Waukesha County Extension Office, 1320 Pewaukee Road, Room G22, Waukesha, 262/548-7770, kathy.reese@ces.uwex.edu, (Milwaukee), ann.wied@ces.uwex.edu, (Waukesha), milwaukee.uwex/edu/mg/index.cfm

Shar-a-Gardeners, Waushara County Master Gardeners, Waushara County Extension Office, Courthouse, 209 South St. Marie Street, Wautoma, 920/787-0416

St. Croix Valley Master Gardener Association, Pierce County Extension Office, 412 West Kinne Street, Ellsworth, 715/273-6781, stcroixvlymga@pressenter.com

Taylor County Master Gardeners, Taylor County Extension Office, Room 103 County-USDA Service Center, 925 Donald Street, Medford, 715/748-3327

Thyme Shares Master Gardeners and Friends, Marquette County Extension Office, Box 338, 480 Underwood Avenue, Montello, 608/297-9153

Walworth County Master Gardeners. Walworth County Extension Office, W3929 County Highway NN, Elkhorn, 262/741-3178

Waupaca County Master Gardeners, Waupaca County Extension Office, Courthouse, 811 Harding Street, Waupaca, 715/258-6230

Winnebago County Master Gardeners, Winnebago County Extension Office, 625 East County Road Y, Suite 600, Oshkosh, 920/232-1971, winnebagomastergardeners.org

Wood County Master Gardeners, Wood County Extension Office, Courthouse, 400 Market Street, Wisconsin Rapids, 715/421-8440

Additional and current contact information for individual master gardeners' groups can be found on the University of Wisconsin Horticulture Web site at: www.hort.wisc.edu/mastergardener/

APPENDIX 7: *Labyrinths*

Jayne Bachman Linger Longer Labyrinth, Hudson Hospital, 405 Stageline Road, Hudson, 715/531-6000, 715/531-6571 (fax) hudsonhospital.org 7-circuit, decomposed granite, concrete pavers and garden spaces, Medieval Circle of Peace (classical) design

Cedar Valley Retreat Center, 5349 County Road D, West Bend, 262/629-9202, 262/629-9962 (fax) cvcinfo@cedarcommunity.org 11-circuit, grass, Chartres replica

Christ the Servant Lutheran Church, 2016 Center Road, Waukesha, 262/542-7100, office@christtheservant.org, christtheservant.org 11-circuit, grass, Chartres replica

East Immanuel Lutheran Church, 207 120th Street, Amery, 715/268-2143, contact@EastImmanuel-Lutheran.org, eastimmanuel-lutheran.org 11-circuit, fieldstone/pea gravel, Chartres replica

Faith Lutheran Church, 120 Faith Drive, (Business Highway 151 and State Highway 73) Columbus, 920/623-3610, faith@faithcolumbuswi.org, faithcolumbuswi.org 11-circuit, brick/paver, Chartres replica

First Congregational United Church of Christ, 724 East South River Street, Appleton, 920/733-7393, 920/733-7022 (fax), congo@athenet.net, firstcongoappleton.org 11-circuit, concrete/paint, Chartres replica

First Presbyterian Church, 200 South Lincoln Avenue, Marshfield, 715/384-2484, bewert@tznet.com, fpcmarshfield.org 11-circuit, brick/paver, Chartres replica

Franciscan Skemp Healthcare – Center for Advanced Medicine and Surgery, 800 West Avenue South, La Crosse, 608/785-0940, franciscanskemp.org 11-circuit, brick/paver, Chartres replica

Holy Family Memorial Hospital, 2300 Western Avenue, Manitowoc, 920/686-3487, hfmhealth.org 7-circuit, brick/paver, Classical

Holy Trinity Lutheran Church, 605 Madison Street, Marshall, 608/655-3978, randers96@charter.net 11-circuit, grass, Chartres replica

LeRoyer Memorial Walk, Langlade Memorial Hospital, 112 East Fifth Avenue, Antigo, 715/623-2331, langladememorial.org 11-circuit, stone/gravel, Chartres replica

Lifelight University, HC73 Box 537A, Cable, 715/794-2638, schirah@cheqnet.net, http://lifelightuniversity.org/Labyrinth.html 11-circuit, stone/grass, Chartres replica

Luther Point Bible Camp, 11525 Luther Point Road, Grantsburg, 715/689-2347, info@lutherpoint.org, lutherpoint.org (call ahead for availability) 7-circuit, rocks/grass, Circle of Peace (classical)

Madison Christian Community, 7118 Old Sauk Road, Madison, 608/836-1455, office@madisonchristiancommunity.org, madisonchristiancommunity.org 11-circuit, grass, Chartres replica

Monte Alverno Retreat Center, 1000 North Ballard Road, Appleton, 920/733-8526, montealverno.org or capuchinfranciscans.org (call ahead for availability) 11-circuit, grass, Chartres replica

Norbertine Center for Spirituality, St. Norbert Abbey, 1016 North Broadway, DePere, 920/337-4315, norbertinecenter@yahoo.com, norbcenter.org 11-circuit, grass, Chartres replica

Phoenix Park, where the Chippewa and Eau Claire Rivers converge, Eau Claire, 715/833-0567 7-circuit, bricks/pavers, Classical style

Racine Dominicans, 5635 Erie Street, Racine, 262/639-4100, Ext. 276, rdweb@rootcom.net, racinedominicans.org 7-circuit, grass, Cretan style—also a labyrinth garden

Radiant Path, 20225 82nd Street, Bristol, 262/857-8601, radiant-path.org (call ahead for availability) 7-circuit, rock/gravel; Medieval (modified)

Regner Park, 800 North Main Street, West Bend, 262/338-6903, Info@westbendlabyrinth.com, www.westbendlabyrinth.com 7-circuit, grass/flowers/stones, Cretan

Sacred Grove, Webster, 715/886-7798, dragonfly_@centurytel.net, sacredgrove.us 11-circuit, rocks/sawdust, Chartres replica—also a meditation garden

Mary Ellen and Bill Schmelzer, T4546 Little Trappe Road, Wausau, 715/539-3851, wbschme@dwave.net (private, call ahead for availability) 11-circuit, grass/wildflowers, Chartres replica

Servite Center for Life, 1000 College Avenue West, Ladysmith, 715/532-9611, servitecenter.org 11-circuit, grass, Chartres replica—also a healing garden

Sinsinawa Mound, County Road Z, Sinsinawa, 608/748-4411, Ext. 800, centerprog@aol.com, sinsinawa.org/MoundCenter/Labyrinth.html 11-circuit, brick/gravel, Chartres replica

St. Anthony Retreat Center, 300 East 4th Street, Marathon, 715/443-2236, 715/443-2235 (fax), info@sarcenter.com, sarcenter.com 11-circuit, grass, Chartres replica

St. Christopher's Episcopal Church, 7845 North River Road, River Hills, 414/ 352-0380, 414/352-0381 (fax), stchris@execpc.com, stchristopherswi.org 7-circuit, stones/grass, Classical

St. Clare's Hospital, 707 Fourteenth Street, Baraboo, 608/356-9520, stclare.com 7-circuit, brick/pavers, Classical (Tree of Life pattern)—part of garden

St. Joseph's Catholic Church, 1619 Washington Avenue, Grafton, 262/375-6500 7-circuit, stella d'oro lilies/grass, Classical

St. Joseph Retreat, 3035 O'Brien Road, Baileys Harbor, 920/839-2391, stjosephretreat@juno.com, stjosephretreat.org (call ahead for availability) 11-circuit, grass, Chartres replica

St. John in the Wilderness Episcopal Church, 13 South Church Street, Elkhorn, 262/723-4229, wilderness@idcnet.com 11-circuit, colored gravel, a variation on a Chartres replica

St. John Neumann Parish, 2400 West State Highway 59, Waukesha, 262/549-0223, sjnwauk.org 11-circuit, grass/plants, Chartres replica

Tippecanoe Presbyterian Church: Living Waters Contemplative Life Center, 125 West Saveland Avenue, Milwaukee, 414/481-4680, tippechurch@milwpc.com, tippechurch.org 5-circuit, rock/stone, Classical/Baltic—serenity garden

Utech's Rainbow Dairy Goat Farm, 3880 Rainbow Drive, Merrill, 715/536-7271, rainbowberryfarm@hotmail.com (private, call ahead for availability) 7-circuit, stone/grass, Classical

Wild Iris Shores Bed and Breakfast, 2741 11th Street, Cumberland, 715/822-8594, 11-circuit, native grasses, Chartres replica

APPENDIX 8: *Specialty Display Gardens*

Many of these gardens are in private yards. It is essential that you call or e-mail ahead before visiting them.

Wisconsin Display Gardens of the American Hemerocallis (Daylily) Society

Angkor Gardens, Byron Annis, N2207 Pammel Pass West, La Crosse, 608/788-1812, bannis@centurytel.net

Blodgett Gardens, Linda and Eugene Blodgett, 1008 East Broadway, Waukesha, 262/547-5099, eulibl@juno.com (open after July 4)

Fitchward Gardens, John E. Sheehan, 5656 Barbara Drive, Madison, 608/274-4921, johnsheehan@charter.net

The Pearcy Garden, Jane and Hiram Pearcy, 407 Lincoln Street, Verona, 608/845-9249, pearcyj@mailbag.com

Potter Daylily Collection, Rotary Gardens, 1455 Palmer Drive, Janesville, 608/752-3885, rotarygardens.org

REH Landscape Garden, Roger E. Heffron, 3828 13th Avenue, Kenosha, 262/914-8699, rogheff@yahoo.com

Solaris Farms, Nathaniel Bremer, 7510 Pine Sva Road, Reedsville, 920/754-4335, solaris@lakefield.net, solarisfarms.com

Windswept Gardens, Rob Newlin and Karen Watson-Newlin, 7699 Almar Drive, Verona, 608/827-6180, kwatsonnewlin@tds.net

Wisconsin Display Gardens of the American Hosta Society

Boerner Botanical Gardens, 9400 Boerner Drive, Hales Corners, 414/525-5601, boernerbotanicalgardens.org

Foxfire Botanical Gardens, M220 Sugarbush Lane, Marshfield, 715/387-3050, foxfire@tznet.com, foxfiregardens.com

Garden Companions, 1809 Waunona Way, Madison, 608/221-2792, tcr112@aol.com

Hosta Hollow, Rotary Gardens, 1455 Palmer Drive, Janesville, 608/752-3885, rotarygardens.org

Johnson Hosta Gardens, 13685 Watertown Plank Road, Elm Grove, 262/786-1758, irwinjohnson@wi.rr.com

Oberstadt Landscapes and Nursery, N352 Highway W, Fremont, 920/667-4757, info@oberstadt.com, oberstadt.com

Olbrich Botanical Gardens, 3330 Atwood Avenue, Madison, 608/246-4550, olbrich.org

Witt's Hosta Garden, W2585 Rim Rock Road, Eau Claire, 715/834-0447, wittrm@uwec.edu

Woodland Gardens, W7689 Trellis Road, Crivitz, 715/854-7687, cathylin@century-tel.net (open only during annual plant sale; call or e-mail for dates)

Winter Greenhouse, W7041 Olmstead Road, Winter, 715/266-4963, mail@wintergreenhouse.com, wintergreenhouse.com

All-America Rose Selections Display Gardens

Boerner Botanical Gardens, 9400 Boerner Drive, Hales Corners, 414/525-5601, boernerbotanicalgardens.org

Olbrich Botanical Gardens, 3330 Atwood Avenue, Madison, 608/246-4550, olbrich.org

Bibliography

Alden, Sharyn. *Historical Wisconsin Getaways: Touring the Badger State's Past.* Madison: Trails Books. 2001.

American Horticultural Society. *Plants for Every Season: 1,000 Recommended Plants for Color All Year Round.* New York: DK Publishing. 2002.

American Horticultural Society. *Plants for Places: 1,000 Tried and Tested Plants for Every Site, Soil and Usage.* New York: DK Publishing. 2001.

Austin, Sandra. *Color in Garden Design.* Newtown, Conn.: The Taunton Press. 1998.

Beard, Henry and McKie, Roy. *Gardening: A Gardener's Dictionary.* New York: Workman Publishing Company. 1982

Bennett, Paul. *The Garden Lover's Guide to the Midwest.* Princeton, N.J.: Princeton Architectural Press. 2000.

Bradley, Fern Marshall. *The Experts Book of Garden Hints: Over 1,500 Organic Tips and Techniques from 250 of America's Best Gardeners.* Emmaus, Penn.: Rodale Press. 1993.

Brookes, John. *Well-Designed Garden: The Classic Garden-Design Sourcebook.* New York: DK Publishing. 2007.

Cunningham, Anne S. *Crystal Palaces: Garden Conservatories of the United States.* New York: Princeton Architectural Press. 2000.

Cybart, Sharon and Minnich, Jerry. Editors. *Olbrich Botanical Gardens: Growing More Beautiful.* Black Earth, Wis.: Prairie Oak Press. 2002.

Drower, George. *Gardeners, Gurus and Grubs: The Stories of Garden Inventors and Innovations.* Gloucestershire: Sutton Publishing. 2001.

Earl, Betty. *In Search of Great Plants: The Insider's Guide to the Best Plants in the Midwest.* Nashville: Cool Springs Press. 2004

Eck, Joe. *Elements of Garden Design.* New York: North Point Press. 2005.

Ellis, Barbara. *Shady Retreats: 20 Plans for Colorful, Private Spaces in your Backyard.* North Adams, Mass.: Storey Books. 2003.

Engebretson, Don and Williamson, Don. *Best Garden Plants for Minnesota and Wisconsin.* Auburn, Wash.: Lone Pine Publishing. 2006.

Fell, Derek. *Encyclopedia of Garden Design and Structure: Ideas and Inspiration for Your Garden.* Buffalo: Firefly Books Ltd. 2005.

Grounds, Roger. *The Plantfinders Guide to Ornamental Grasses.* Portland: Timber Press. 2003.

Gurda, John. *Silent City: A History of Forest Home Cemetery.* Milwaukee: Forest Home Cemetery. 2000.

Hattatt, Lance. *The Water Garden.* Bristol, England: Parragon. 1999.

Hanson, Krista Finstad. *Wisconsin's Historic Houses and Living History Museums: A Visitor's Guide.* Madison, Wis. Prairie Oak Press. 2000.

Herwig, Modeste. *Colorful Gardens,* New York City: Sterling Publishing Company. 1996.

Kingsbury, Noel. *Gardens by Design: Expert Advice from the World's Leading Garden Designers.* Portland: Timber Press, 2005.

Kingsbury, Noel and Oudolf, Piet. *Planting Design: Gardens in Time and Space.* Portland: Timber Press. 2005.

Klein, Carol. *Plant Personalities: Choosing and Growing Plants by Character.* Portland: Timber Press. 2005.

McClements, John K. and Fitzgerrell, Scott. *Sunset Landscaping Illustrated: Complete Guide to Ideas, Planning and How-to-Do-It.* Menlo Park: Lane Publishing Company, 1984.

McHoy, Peter. *Gardening in Small Spaces: A Comprehensive Practical Guide to Designing, Planning, and Planting a Garden in the Smallest of Spaces.* London: Hermes House. 2003.

McHoy, Peter. *The Complete Garden Planning Book: The Definitive Guide to Designing and Planting a Beautiful Garden.* London: Hermes House. 2003.

McKinley, Michael. *Step-By-Step Landscaping.* Des Moines, Iowa. Meredith Corporation. 2007.

Middleton, Pat. *Discover! America's Great River Road: Vol. 1, St. Paul, Minnesota to Dubuque, Iowa, The Upper Mississippi.* Stoddard, Wis. Heritage Press. 2000.

Minnich, Jerry. *The Wisconsin Almanac.* Madison, Wis. North Country Press. 1989.

Minnich, Jerry. *The Wisconsin Garden Guide.* Minocqua, Wis. Heartland Press. 1989

Myers, Melinda. *The Garden Book for Wisconsin.* Nashville: Thomas Nelson Press. 2005.

Niles, Susan A. *Dickeyville Grotto: The Vision of Father Mathias Wernerus.* Jackson, Miss. University Press of Mississippi. 1997.

Perry, Frances, Editor. *Simon & Schuster's Guide to Plants and Flowers.* New York: Simon & Schuster. 1974.

Rajer, Anton. *Museums, Zoos, and Botanical Gardens of Wisconsin: A Comprehensive Guidebook.* Madison, Wis. Fine Arts Publishing in cooperation with University of Wisconsin Press. 2006

Sachtjen, Marlyn Dicken. *Marlyn's Garden: Seasoned Advice for Achieving Spectacular Results in the Midwest.* Chicago: Chicago Review Press. 1994.

Scoble, Gretchen and Field, Ann. *The Meaning of Flowers: Myth, Language and Lore.* San Francisco: Chronicle Books. 1998.

Severa, Joan. *Creating a Perennial Garden in the Midwest.* Madison, Wis.: Trails Books. 1999.

Smith, J. Robert and Smith, Beatrice S. *The Prairie Garden: 70 Native Plants You Can Grow in Town or Country.* The University of Wisconsin Press. 1980.

Tekiela, Stan. *Trees of Wisconsin.* Cambridge, Minn.: Adventure Publications. 2002.

Tekiela, Stan. *Wildflowers of Wisconsin.* Cambridge, Minn.: Adventure Publications. 2000.

Thorpe, Patricia. *The American Weekend Garden.* New York: Random House. 1988.

Index